Covenant,
Community,
and the Spirit

Covenant, Community, and the Spirit

A Trinitarian Theology *of* Church

Robert Sherman

B)
Baker Academic
a division of Baker Publishing Group
Grand Rapids, Michigan

Published by Baker Academic
a division of Baker Publishing Group
P.O. Box 6287, Grand Rapids, MI 49516-6287
www.bakeracademic.com

Printed in the United States of America

Library of Congress Cataloging-in-Publication Data

Sherman, Robert (Robert J.)
    Covenant, community, and the spirit : a trinitarian theology of church / Robert Sherman.
        pages cm
    Includes bibliographical references and index.
    ISBN 978-0-8010-4974-3 (pbk.)
    1. Church. 2. Holy Spirit. 3. Trinity. I. Title.
BV600.3.S485 2015
262.001—dc23   2015014069

In keeping with biblical principles of creation stewardship, Baker Publishing Group advocates the responsible use of our natural resources. As a member of the Green Press Initiative, our company uses recycled paper when possible. The text paper of this book is composed in part of post-consumer waste.

15   16   17   18   19   20   21   7   6   5   4   3   2   1

This book is dedicated to the members of All Souls Congregational Church, Bangor, Maine, and to the ministers who have guided us with such Spirit-filled faithfulness, wisdom, and grace over many years: the Reverend Dr. James L. Haddix, Pastor and Teacher, and the Reverend Renee U. Garrett, Minister of Christian Nurture

Contents

Acknowledgments

This book has had a rather long gestation. In focusing on the Spirit's trinitarian role in relation to the Church, it was conceived as a complement to my earlier work, *King, Priest, and Prophet*, which emphasized the role of the Son in a trinitarian theology of the atonement. As with that previous book, I developed the basic arguments and did the bulk of my writing while a scholar-in-residence at the Center of Theological Inquiry in Princeton, New Jersey, in the spring term of 2009. That institution is an invaluable resource for the Church and for serious theological reflection in this challenging era. I want to extend a word of sincere thanks and appreciation to my colleagues for their thoughtful listening, suggestions, critiques, and encouragement. And I offer a special word of gratitude to the center's director, Dr. William Storrar, for his hospitality and support.

Of course, my stay at CTI was enabled by a sabbatical leave made possible by the president and trustees of Bangor Theological Seminary. To them, and to my faculty colleagues who helped hone my proposal and then bore my share of our common workload while I was absent, I say, "Thank you!"

As my sabbatical drew to a close, work remained to be done. But the demands of teaching and institutional challenges at BTS kept me from completing it. This delay did, however, allow me to present the main themes and particular content of the book to several more classes of students. I want to especially thank two who participated in a senior seminar, "What Does It Mean to Be the Church in This Time and Place?," Molly MacAuslan and Elizabeth White-Randall, for their thoughtful comments and encouragement. I also want to extend my appreciation as well to the members of our local pastor-theologian group. An offshoot of the Center of Theological Inquiry's national program, this ecumenical gathering of ministers, professors, and students has met regularly since 2004 under the able leadership of Dr. James Haddix. While certainly grateful for the various insights each offered when we directly discussed the contents of this book, I am even more thankful for their general graciousness and collegiality regardless of the topic. Together, they have modeled how the Church should engage in theological and pastoral reflection.

I also want to offer my sincere thanks and gratitude to my wife of thirty years, the Reverend Dr. Carol J. Sherman. She has supported and encouraged me in ways too numerous to count. She is a woman of enduring faith, strong conviction, practical wisdom, deep spirituality, and boundless patience, good humor, and hopefulness.

Bangor Theological Seminary completed its last classes and celebrated its final commencement in June 2013, just shy of its two-hundredth anniversary. Founded while James Madison was president, the seminary educated generations of ministers who served northern New England and beyond: during the Civil War, the westward expansion of the United States, the heyday of nineteenth-century overseas missions, the Great War, the "Roaring Twenties," the Great Depression, World War II, the boom years of the postwar era, the tumult of the sixties, the ups and downs of more recent decades, the September 11 attacks and their aftermath, up to the present day. For such an institution—having endured so many challenges through nearly two centuries and maintained an influence far exceeding its small size—to finally close its doors is, indeed, poignant. But the closure of BTS is also thought provoking. Times do change, yet the Church will always need pastors and teachers to serve as shepherds and to think about what it means to faithfully *be* the Church in differing times and places. Clearly, we are in a time of transition. What the Church will become, how we will understand and structure our common life, and where that life will lead us are not entirely clear at present. So my final word of acknowledgment and appreciation goes out to all those theologians, pastors, and thoughtful Christians everywhere who, open to the Spirit's prompting, are seeking to discern the new paths to which the Lord is calling us.

Introduction

God summons the Church to proclaim in Christ through the power of the Spirit a transcendent life of exhilarating grace and love, to embody a world of forgiveness and reconciliation, and to offer a foretaste of reality so glorious and compelling that most people would find it inconceivable. The Church that God calls us to become is—of course!—a community that befits God's own triune communion and majesty. And yet that Church is so much more than most people would even dare to imagine, let alone yearn for. Instead, it is all too common—even among faithful Christians—to be dissatisfied with the Church. But does our dissatisfaction arise because we ask too *much* of the Church or because we expect too *little* of it—and of God's restoring and transforming power? Might it be that we no longer really know how to be the Church because we have lost the vision God has for us? Have we become too caught up in ourselves, our individual wants, needs, and desires—and perhaps especially our own disappointments?

In the North American context, individual Christians speak quite unself-consciously of "church shopping." Church leaders respond with strategies for "marketing the Church," which include developing demographic niches, advertising slogans, and programmatic innovations. In a consumer society, this is hardly surprising. Additionally, individual congregations and denominations are increasingly polarized along political, moral, generational, racial, socioeconomic, educational, and other demographic lines. All these factors bespeak a cultural captivity and theological impoverishment regarding what the Church can and should be according to God's redemptive purposes and cosmic perspective.

Alternately, the "established" churches in Western European countries may have a status that in theory is the antithesis of American denominational fragmentation—and yet their churches are often empty on Sunday mornings, and popular culture finds them irrelevant, if not something to be mocked or resisted. My sense is that we need our ecclesiological imaginations reclaimed and reignited by a more biblical, theological, and pastoral vision of the Church: the community of nurture, accountability, and mission grounded in Christ and given life and a final purpose (*telos*) by the Holy Spirit. And I am convinced that many Christians hunger for more depth and substance in their common life and work and yearn to embrace such a Spirit-filled vision and reality.

My concern grows out of my classroom work as a professor training future ministers and my ongoing involvement in the life and mission of my local church. Teaching both seminarians and laypeople in my congregation, I have learned that many contemporary Christians in "mainline" or old-line denominations recognize the centrality of Christ but have only a vague sense of the Holy Spirit's presence and work. They also tend to take the Church for granted without having any real sense of why it is theologically necessary. Many would perhaps acknowledge Spirit and Church as helpful to the individual Christian's faithful living, while also assuming that such living is mostly a self-help effort. This repeats the ancient semi-Pelagian stance—although they would hardly know to label it as such! But most would be hard-pressed to describe the Spirit's various roles in the divine economy of salvation, let alone acknowledge the Spirit's particular work in empowering and undergirding the being and mission of the Church. Fewer still would likely recognize the Church as the divinely appointed community of nurture and accountability through which the Spirit typically empowers their life of Christian discipleship. What I write in the following pages seeks to address this situation.

A Trinitarian, Spirit-Focused Approach

My approach will be trinitarian in structure, grounded in a theological reading (rather than, say, a merely historical one) of the Bible as the Church's authoritative scriptures, guided by some key affirmations of the Christian, especially Reformed, tradition and attuned to the practical concerns of contemporary pastors and Christians. While I intend it to be scholarly and theologically rigorous, this book is not aimed at other theologians or academics. Its target audience is instead the students I teach, local pastors such as those in my community, and thoughtful and curious laypeople like those in my home congregation. Americans lead complex, multifaceted, and challenging lives. They know the value of education because their diverse professional lives require sophistication, skill, and expertise. Why should they be satisfied with only the theological concepts and resources they might have acquired as thirteen-year-old confirmation students? Shouldn't adult Christians have an adult theological sophistication?

Some might say that focusing on the Holy Spirit's activity within the Church presents a too-constricted understanding of the Spirit's work. As portrayed in the biblical witness, the role and work of the Spirit clearly encompass more than just ecclesiology. From the very beginning, God's Spirit has been involved with creation, granting life to the animate and providentially governing the inanimate. Likewise, the Spirit has been the power inspiring prophets, priests, and kings to do the Lord's bidding. Indeed, some echo John 3:8 to suggest that the Spirit is bound in no way: "the Spirit blows where it wills." Yet just as the Son, the eternal Logos, has a part to play in creation, so too did he have a particular role, taking on human flesh to become the crucified and resurrected Messiah, Jesus of Nazareth. And it is this latter, more particular role that gives true insight into—even defines—the former, more general role. In a similar manner, I will focus in this book on the Spirit's particular work in establishing the Church, sustaining it in its witness and manifold mission, and bringing it to consummation. And this particular life-giving and perfecting work is the key for understanding the Spirit's more general movements in creation and history. It also indicates that just as redemption is a work of the Triune God, yet recognized to be the special divine work of the Son, so too is the Church a work of the Triune God, even while it may also be recognized as the special divine work of the Holy Spirit, who makes available the benefits of the Son and aligns the Church with the larger purposes of the Father.[1]

So in one respect, I am narrowing my focus on the Spirit. But I do so to counteract the unfortunate tendency of many to place Spirit and Church in tension, if not actually in conflict with each other. (Need I repeat the clichéd rationalization for avoiding Church participation: "I'm spiritual but have no use for 'organized religion'"?) Scripture and tradition each recognize that the Spirit works not just in individuals in an isolated, charismatic way but within communities and even institutional proceedings and structures (e.g., Acts 15:28). I will allude to some of the broader works of the Spirit in this project but will consider these fully only when I address creation, providence, and eschatology in the first (but yet to be written) volume of my planned theological trilogy.

---

1. As one flag to highlight this special work of the Spirit, I have chosen to capitalize "Church" throughout this book rather than use the more common, lowercase "church."

Outline of the Book

I will begin with two introductory chapters. The first will set the stage of our creation by God as social beings, our collective fall from this original blessing, and God's covenantal plan for our final restoration and fulfillment. The second chapter will offer a "pneumatology," that is, a theological consideration of the Holy Spirit's place and role in the Trinity and the divine "economy of salvation," which is God's plan to redeem and reorient a fallen creation to his originally intended end. The heart of the book will then address the nature and purpose of the Church, fleshed out under the rubrics "The Body of Christ," "The People of God," and "The Temple of the Holy Spirit." Employing these rubrics to understand the Church is, of course, not original to my work. And neither are they the only images the Bible uses to elicit an understanding of the Church in its various aspects. Paul Minear's classic work *Images of the Church in the New Testament* discerned dozens of distinct metaphors, images, and descriptions of the Church. Most of these images were minor, and clearly more evocative than normative; yet others were more developed and have come to constitute how the Christian tradition understands the nature and role of the Church. My focus on these three rubrics hardly exhausts all the ways the Church could be conceived. It is instead meant to highlight the need for trinitarian balance in understandings of the Church: various ecclesial images and models need to complement one another. I will certainly consider several other biblical images or themes under each of these larger rubrics.

For example, in considering the Church as the body of Christ (chap. 3), I describe how this image provides the basis for thinking of the Church as God's gift of complementarity and structure for the community of faith. I will consider how individual Christians are incorporated into Christ's story and into the broader biblical narrative as their new "family history." One way this image of bodily union has been developed in the tradition is by means of the Church as the "bride of Christ," built on Scripture passages referring to husband and wife leaving their old lives behind to become one body. Another way this image has been developed is through more extended, multigenerational family imagery, particularly as that is related to an understanding of faith being transmitted and nurtured. Thus, the constitutive role of worship, preaching, and the sacraments of baptism and the Lord's Supper will be examined. One concern will be to defend infant baptism, relating it to the following chapter's discussion of covenant. Among other points, I will develop the parallel between circumcision and infant baptism that the Reformed tradition has emphasized, the former being a typological foreshadowing of the more inclusive latter practice. I will also develop the connection between baptism and communion, including an explanation of the view of "open communion" as a meal for baptized Christians. This chapter will include an examination of the institutional structure of the Church as a charismatic gift—but as a gift that then also necessarily entails certain responsibilities, as members of the Church (individually and communally) are nurtured and transformed. It will also address the relation between baptism and confirmation in terms of the Reformed rubrics of the covenant of grace and the covenant of works, the latter being the human response and pledge grounded in and oriented by the free gift of the former.

In examining the Church as the people of God (chap. 4), I will be concerned particularly to understand the Church within the broader sweep of the Father's gracious covenantal purposes. In an explicit sense, this began with the covenant God established with Abraham and Sarah. Yet its origins extend back to creation itself and God's eternal decree, while its culmination reaches out to the end of the age. I will describe how Jesus's preaching on the "kingdom of God" stands in continuity with Old Testament understandings of Israel as a "holy nation" and "royal priesthood," even as it transforms and fulfills those understandings. This chapter will also continue consideration of the biblical image of Israel as God's bride, particularly as that is paralleled with the New Testament image of the Church as Christ's bride. It will consider as well the perennial issue of how the Church should relate to "the world," that is, how it is called to be "in the world but not of the world." Another practical and pastoral goal in this chapter will be to give Christians a sense of the Church's rootedness in and continuity with the faith of Israel. God's covenant with the Church does not make God's covenant with Israel "obsolete," so there is no basis for Christian supersessionism. As Paul asserts regarding the election of the Jews: "For the gifts and the call of God are irrevocable" (Rom. 11:29 RSV).

Finally, as I examine the Church as the temple of the Holy Spirit (chap. 5), one of my main goals is to address Christian holiness as a mark of our calling and fulfillment. Chapter 5 will therefore address how Christians should understand the "fruit of the Spirit" (Gal. 5:22), "gifts of the Spirit" (1 Cor. 2:14), and the process of "discerning" and "testing" the spirits (1 Cor. 12:10; 1 John 4:1). Throughout I will again employ the underlying theme of the covenant, and develop the continuity between the Jewish understanding of Pentecost (the festival celebrating the giving of the law at Sinai) and the Christian understanding of Pentecost (when the Spirit was poured out in fulfillment of Jer. 31:31–34). In this discussion I will seek to reestablish the basis of Christian discipline and accountability by employing the classical notion of the "power of the keys" and the Reformed notion of "the third use of the law."

A Future with the Church

A number of influential voices have said that the American Church now finds itself in a post-Christian age. This may be an overstatement for some parts of the country, but certainly for other parts and segments of the nation it seems quite accurate. While the United States has never had a legally established church, it has long had a "cultural establishment." Those days appear to be fading. A corollary issue confronting the Church is the reality that for many faithful Christians, it is also a postdenominational age. On a practical level, the ecumenical movement seeking to overcome denominational differences has truly succeeded among the laity! New-member Sundays are often made up of individuals who have attended churches of various denominations over the years. Denominational loyalty remains most prevalent among the clergy and those working in denominational offices at a regional and national level. It seems clear that we are in a period of transition: we know where we've come from but are not yet clear where we are going.

That said, I believe that Christianity can survive a postdenominational age, but it cannot survive a postecclesial age. As theologian Robert Jenson has quipped, "To be sure, we are permitted to believe that the gates of hell will not finally prevail against the universal church, but there is no such guarantee for the Presbyterians or the Baptists."[2] Denominations may prove to have been an appropriate response in a particular time and place—a providential expedient, if you will—but they are not necessarily essential. The Church, however, in some corporate or institutional form, *is* essential. I am concerned primarily with recovering and renewing biblical and theological themes, categories, and structures to help faithful Christians recognize and reclaim this essence, so that they may more clearly know and embrace God's gracious call to join his holy assembly (*ekklēsia*), the Church.

Easter 2014

2. Robert W. Jenson, *Canon and Creed*, Interpretation: Resources for the Use of Scripture in the Church (Louisville: Westminster John Knox, 2010), 3.

1

The Story Begins

Communion: Human Being Is Social Being

> Then the LORD God said, "It is not good that the *adam* should be alone; I will make him a helper as his partner." (Gen. 2:18)

We yearn for community because we were meant for community: it is built into our very nature as human beings. Created in the image of the Triune God, we are made to be in relation to God, to one another, and to God's good creation. Our very existence is a gift from God, who, although self-sufficient in the eternal, loving communion of Father, Son, and Holy Spirit, extends that communion by creating that which is not God. This is one of Christianity's basic affirmations: the fact that anything exists at all stems from God, who has freely and graciously chosen to create a cosmos and to be in continuing relation with it. We truly *exist*. And we exist *distinct* from God, with our own being and ability to act. Creation is not merely an extension of God, an emanation from the divine being that has no true individuality. Neither is creation a kind of divine cloning that is at root an expression of divine egotism or even narcissism. Creation is truly different and unique, the result of divine graciousness that does not fear or begrudge or compete with the existence of beings other than God. To the contrary, God delights in having brought into existence a reality other than himself—and is even gracious enough to grant an analogous power to the creatures of that reality rather than make them depend always and only immediately upon him.

1

While God remains the fundamental and final source of all that is, we have also been made to depend upon one another. In any given moment, we depend upon one another through society and our interconnections with the natural world. And God has made these forms of interdependence to extend over time. The fact that any one of us exists derives from God's granting living creatures the power to exercise their own agency, including the capacity for procreation. As individuals, we do not make ourselves, and in an immediate sense neither does God make us. Rather, God exercises that power through the mediation of our parents, and we in turn become the means by which God brings about the next generation.

And while God has made us and desires to remain in continuing relation with creation, we humans have also been made in such a way that that relation is not automatic. God has embedded us in a fecund and malleable creation and in a relatively open-ended time. The future expands before us, and we cannot see over its horizon. We have been given freedom and power to choose from among multiple paths. Indeed, God grants and sustains us in the power even to turn away from him and his purposes for us. To be sure, given such a creation, with such agency and embedding, it should come as no surprise that Christianity also affirms that just as our origin is truly *understood* only in relation to God, so too is our end truly *realized* only through embracing in particular ways the divine and diverse creaturely connections that give us our lives. This contrasts with the modern Western emphasis on individualism. As Barry Harvey states it: "In place of the universal man posited by Descartes's *cogito, ergo sum*, therefore, the church proposes a radically different starting point for all thought and action: *Deus amat, ergo sumus*. From this ecclesial standpoint we learn that the purpose of our very being is to love as God loves."[1] At the heart of our being stands not the egocentric "I think, therefore I am," but the theocentric "God loves, therefore we are." Our truest fulfill-ment, both as individuals and in community, comes when we recognize and align ourselves with that depth and breadth of fellowship with one another and with God that God has intended for us from the very beginning.

Indeed, the Church has recognized this was God's intention even before "the beginning," in that this divine desire for communion was what motivated and structured God's very creation of the cosmos. This is the point to which the doctrine of election speaks: God's determination from before time to be *with* and *for* the humanity he would create. Described in technical intratrini-tarian terms, it was the Father's will that creation be structured and oriented

1. Barry Harvey, *Another City: An Ecclesiological Primer for a Post-Christian World*, Chris-tian Mission and Modern Culture (Harrisburg, PA: Trinity Press International, 1999), 161.

in this manner, which he accomplished through his "two hands" of Son and Spirit, the former being the *Logos*, the organizing principle, and the latter the *Pneuma*, the animating power of the one divine work of creation. In one strand of the Reformed theological tradition, this is understood as the *pactum salutis* ("counsel of peace"), the covenantal "work plan" established among the persons of the Trinity before creation itself.[2] Recall Jesus's saying from Luke 14:28–30 (RSV): "For which of you, desiring to build a tower, does not first sit down and count the cost, whether he has enough to complete it? Otherwise, when he has laid a foundation, and is not able to finish, all who see it begin to mock him, saying, 'This man began to build, and was not able to finish.'" These words take on a whole new meaning and depth when we consider the cost God would gladly accept to enable his purpose to reach its fulfillment.

The Communal Nature of Human Nature

So while each of us is a discrete person, with his or her own innate and individual dignity and worth, we are also irreducibly social beings, in our origins, our ongoing existence, and our end. This will be a fundamental assumption of this book, grounded in the scriptural narratives that have formed Christian theology for millennia. The first of those narratives is the creation accounts in Genesis, and the last is a vision of a heavenly city at the end of Revelation. But it is also an assumption that a mere cursory reflection shows to be self-evident, even without appealing to explicitly religious presuppositions. Just consider: each of us is placed within a particular historical and cultural ecology, upon which we depend for our individual lives and to which we contribute for good or for ill. Our physical existence derives from a long chain of progenitors. Our psychological, linguistic, and spiritual existence is nurtured by family, friends, teachers, indeed, a whole cultural matrix rooted in the past and extending into the future. Our fears and concerns, our hopes and aspirations, are always fostered by and exercised within a particular communal context—itself typically a mix of subordinate and varied social networks—that we simultaneously receive and further. We did not give birth to ourselves, nor did we raise ourselves. Each and every one of us has a mother and a father, two sets of grandparents, four sets of great-grandparents, and so on back into the recesses of time. We are the offspring of complex, and by us largely unknown, webs of relationship. And none of us would have survived our infancy unless we had been raised by others: mothers, fathers,

2. See, for example, Herman Bavinck, *Reformed Dogmatics*, ed. John Bolt, trans. John Vriend (Grand Rapids: Baker Academic, 2006), 3:194, 212–16, and Michael S. Horton, *Covenant and Salvation: Union with Christ* (Louisville: Westminster John Knox, 2007), 130–34.

grandparents, aunts, uncles, brothers, sisters, neighbors, friends. Those not raised in communities of caring—perhaps neglected in impersonal institutions, caught up in dysfunctional families or dangerous neighborhoods—typically suffer psychological and spiritual damage, which sometimes also manifests itself in a physical failure to thrive.

Even as we each increase degrees of self-sufficiency moving into adulthood, we remain more dependent than not upon the choices and labors of others. None of us do all of the following: grow our own food; make our own clothes; educate ourselves; manufacture our own tools; build our own houses; establish our own employment; care for ourselves medically; construct our own roads, bridges, or social infrastructure; provide for our own safety and security . . . This list could continue indefinitely—and so far includes only tangible aspects of our common life. It is just as true to say that none of us invent our own language, create our own worldviews, develop our own values, or are the sole author of any of the various elements of our intellectual, emotional, or spiritual landscapes. We may modify them as we grow older—or even reject them—but such changes always have the character of fine-tuning or resisting something already given. With only brief reflection, we recognize how our lives are inextricably intertwined with and depend upon those around us and those who have come before us.

And in the same way, those who will come after us depend utterly upon us. It is an inescapable biological fact that we are always only one generation away from extinction. And it is not just a matter of the sheer fact of existence. Continued existence is, of course, the necessary presupposition for anything else, but surely mere survival is not our only concern. Indeed, it is probably not our driving concern. For good or for ill, we must ask ourselves: what is the function or goal of human life? Human beings can survive just about anything other than the loss of meaning or purpose. What drives us? What will we bequeath to latter generations? Will we do our best to leave things better than we found them for our children? Or will we assume, either consciously or unconsciously, that the posterity about which previous generations were concerned somehow culminates and ends with us?

The *New York Times Magazine* once featured an article examining the writing of Jodi Picoult, a novelist who specializes in what the magazine described as the new "children in peril" genre.[3] After opening with a summary list of the relentlessly gruesome variations in which Ms. Picoult has developed this genre ("terrible things happen to children of middle-class parentage:

3. Ginia Bellafante, "Jodi Picoult and the Anxious Parent," *New York Times Magazine*, June 17, 2009, 36.

they become terminally ill, or are maimed, gunned down, killed in accidents, molested, abducted, bullied, traumatized, stirred to violence"), the article concludes with these words—words that are all the more chilling because the article's author seems oblivious to their logical implication: "In so many of her books children seem like more work than most ordinary people can handle. If Picoult's fiction means to say anything, it is that parenting undoes us perhaps more than it fulfills, and it makes a thousand little promises it can never keep."[4] If this is so, then the obvious response becomes: "So then why bother?" The fact that birthrates in many Western European nations have fallen below replacement levels suggests that for some, having children is indeed too much of a bother. Will we succumb to such generational hopelessness—or is it narcissism mixed with nihilism? Or will we transcend it? If the former, what explains such myopia and selfishness? If the latter, what are the ideas, habits, and structures that will enable us to think beyond ourselves?

Complemental Origins

The obvious answer to this last question is to look where God has placed us and what he has given us. We are social creatures, dependent upon God, upon the fecundity and predictability of the natural world, and upon the intricate interrelations of human society. This is how we were made, and, more to the point of this theological exercise, this is how we are *supposed* to be. The majestic cadences of the Bible's opening account of the world's creation describe the rich and varied natural context in which humanity is given life. That context abounds with a variety of inanimate and animate beings. Thus will the wild profusion of creaturely life expand and grow, with the creatures connected to one another in being ("according to their kind") and through time ("be fruitful and multiply"). And the Bible's opening account also makes clear how humanity at its most fundamental is not singular but plural: "male and female he created them" (Gen. 1:27). That is, we are "social" from the start—and not just with one another, in splendid species isolation. Rather, God establishes our humanity in relation to the rest of the earth and in so doing charges us with a vocation, to be responsible stewards in exercising dominion over that earth (1:28), to till and keep the earthly garden (2:15). We alone among God's creatures have been entrusted with a moral responsibility in our relationships, rather than being left to merely natural interactions. And in this we are also an image of the Triune God: we are given freedom to choose, just as God himself freely chose to create the cosmos in the first place.

4. Ibid., 37.

In light of all this, it is worth noting that according to the biblical accounts of God's good creation, the first thing mentioned as "not good" was
"that the human should be alone" (Gen. 2:18 NRSV modified). Having already established in Genesis 1:27 that humanity comprises female and male
together, this second story functions as a negative way of saying the same
thing: it is not good to construe human beings in isolation. This is said of
the *adam*, the generic "human" made from the *adamah*, or "humus"—or, in
another way of translating the Hebrew play on words, the "earthling" made
from the "earth." At this point, the word is not so much a proper name as
it is a generic description or label—and God recognizes that this creature
needs a partner. First, he creates various animals to see if they can fill this
role, but that is unsuccessful (2:19–20). So God causes the human to fall
into a deep sleep and takes a rib from which to form a true partner. When
the *adam* awakes and encounters this other, he calls her "woman [*ishah*],
for out of man [*ish*] this one was taken" (2:23). In effect, the story implies,
it is only after this divine surgery that the sexual dimorphism of humanity
appears, as that is reflected in the changed Hebrew terminology: the single
adam becomes woman and man. In other words, this story reaffirms the
message of Genesis 1:27 that humanity's full being is fundamentally social,
as originally and most basically represented in the complementary nature
of male and female.

Of course, men and women have much in common, sometimes to the
extent that individual women and men will have more in common with one
another than they do with other members of their own sex. This may be due
to nature or to nurture, or some combination thereof. If I need a transfusion,
I obviously would prefer to receive it from a woman who matches my blood
type rather than from a man who does not! Alternately, it is easy to imagine
how a man and a woman from one time and place could have far more in
common than either would with a member of his or her own sex from a
different culture from a different era speaking a different language. And yet
fundamental differences between men and women remain, both biologically
and cross-culturally, which common experience confirms and ideologically
driven agendas to the contrary cannot finally negate. True, those differences
can be construed in ways that are in practice dysfunctional and inhumane
(on which more below, when we discuss human sinfulness). And yet those
differences are also an instance and sign that humanity is far more than the
sum of its parts. When living as God intended, men and women bring the
best out in one another: strengthening here, moderating there, balancing and
completing one another's beings in ways that cannot be accomplished by
either in isolation. Together, women and men create something more than

just themselves. The most obvious example is offspring, but such creativity and fruitfulness also extends far beyond the merely biological.

Something mentioned above helps confirm this point. It is self-evident that all human history, all human achievement, all human creativity has as an unavoidable prior condition the continuing procreativity of men and women. If there were no male or no female, humanity would disappear in one generation. The human chain would break and God's project would end. This is one of the reasons that the Bible so often spends time recounting various genealogies. It is not just that we are linked with those around us, but we are linked with those before us. Indeed, it is precisely these past links that join us with those around us even when other factors might work against our recognizing these connections. For example, some creation stories found in other cultures portray differing tribes or classes or groups as having divergent, even antagonistic, origins. The biblical accounts, by contrast, make clear that all humanity stems from one original pair. In other words, we are all related to one another; we are all one human family. Intriguingly, one branch of modern evolutionary theory converges with this view when it describes the human family tree as stemming from "mitochondrial Eve," located on the African continent.[5]

More significant, this recognition of common ancestry also produces certain moral imperatives. There used to be a common phrase—not heard much nowadays due to its dated terminology—employed to evoke empathy for others: "the brotherhood of man." The rhetorical force of the phrase was that we have an obligation to the well-being of others because we are one family; we share a common humanity. Conversely, if we lose this sense of a common humanity, what might be the moral implications? It is common in times of warfare for one side to denigrate the other, and one typical way of doing so is to imply or explicitly develop the idea that the enemy is "less than human" or "subhuman." This danger still exists. But other, newer threats to our sense of our common humanity are emerging. For example, what dangers might arise with the advance of certain medical technologies such as in vitro fertilization and cloning? If particular individuals are the product of human manufacture rather than procreation, do they run the risk of being construed as somehow less human? Fiction is already raising the specter of human clones produced for spare body parts. Could this possibly be considered ethical? The reaffirmation of our common humanity, of our embeddedness in a long

5. There is as yet no scientific consensus on this theory—and, it should be noted, the biblical accounts do not stand or fall on how these scientific arguments conclude. See Michael Brown's article "Mitochondrial Eve" on the Molecular History Research Center's website, http://www.mhrc.net/mitochondrialEve.htm.

line of progenitors, may be one way of resisting such new technologies and affirming the God-given sacredness of personhood.

Of course, to recognize humanity as male and female together is not to say that persons in isolation, whether male or female, are somehow less than human. Nor is it to say that all individuals must produce offspring in order to be truly human. It is rather to make the point (too easily overlooked in our modern, individualistic Western society) that no single person— whether male *or* female—can fully define humanity, because an accurate definition must always presuppose our irreducibly social nature. On this matter, the feminist critiques of older anthropologies are spot-on: if the human is defined solely on the basis of males, that definition will be not only incomplete but pernicious. The unique characteristics and tendencies more typically associated with females will not be included in what is "normatively" human and will thereby come to be dismissed as inconsequential or as an aberration. This is wrong descriptively and morally. It is an insight revealed earlier by Scripture, in the way the biblical creation stories both describe a fact about humanity's constitutively male and female character and also assert our complementary equality. In so doing, these stories also provide a parable for all the other ways in which our existence as humans is irreducibly and undeniably social.

The Social Embedded in Time

As my observations have already implied, the social character of our lives is not an abstract or timeless reality. It cannot be captured in a snapshot that freezes us in some random moment. Rather, our lives are dynamic: the character of our social relations changes from day to day, from year to year, from decade to decade. Our human ecosystems are not just social and cultural but historical. Human life has an arc, both individual and corporate, and its full meaning is realized only over time. Each person lives in a particular time and place, with particular parents, particular connections, and particular possibilities laid before him or her. As an infant, each of us has these particularities impressed upon him or her with no real say in the matter. Each of us, for good or ill, is largely a passive recipient and utterly dependent upon those around us. As we mature and attain adulthood, that passivity is gradually augmented by a certain independence and our own individual activity. And yet our thoughts and actions never fully transcend our initial upbringing: they always reflect, whether through continuation or reaction, how, when, and where we were raised. And even when they edge into the creative and new, they are also always bounded by a particular cultural context. And as we age, with weakened bodies and minds, we often return to a dependence on others not unlike that of our childhoods.

Has it been a good life? A hard life? A squandered life? A noble life? Who can finally say until one's life has reached its end in death? And even then, a thorough and true evaluation of a person's life may have to wait a generation or two. Considered in isolation, a given individual's life might appear to amount to little. But what if that person's contribution lies dormant until a later time, when suddenly it is recognized as the key element of some new wonder? Or what if that person has instilled in his or her child, student, or neighbor certain gifts that enable that child, now grown, to cure a deadly disease, to build a business, to invent new technologies, to stand up against an injustice, to create an inspiring piece of art, or to make some other contribution to the common good?

Generations have a similar arc, as do peoples, cultures, and nations. They frequently have a kind of collective personality. To those fluent in the current parlance of American popular culture, the label "Greatest Generation" refers to a particular age group and conjures certain very specific character traits. Similarly, we know who the "Baby Boomers" are, and the label elicits a different set of character traits. "Generation X," the "Millennials," and "Gen Z" are three additional sets. To be sure, generational stereotypes easily tend to caricature; yet even with the risk of oversimplification, real distinctions do remain. And as it happens, the distinctive personalities of these generations are often determined precisely through their interactions with, and reactions to, one another, and less by the particularities of their own historical eras. One generation vows to avoid the preoccupations or excesses of another and falls into the vices at the opposite extreme. And then, in spite of it all, how frequently does it happen that at some point, a member of a "younger" generation will be struck by the realization that "I've become my mother" or "I've turned into my father." This is when the arc becomes clear in a personal way—and the more perceptive among us recognize ourselves as recapitulating patterns greater than we are and more deeply embedded than our own choices and personal predilections. Particular differences do remain, contexts do differ, and we must remain attuned to them. Yet with a broader perspective, we also discern deeper commonalities and recognize that our variations are often simply variations on a theme. Immersed in the day-to-day, we need time and distance to come to know the bigger picture.

The biblical story recognizes this common experience, even as it portrays humanity in all its variation as fitting under a larger narrative arc. At their most basic, the Christian scriptures outline the whole human arc as beginning in a garden (Gen. 1–2) and culminating in a new heaven and a new earth, centered in a city (Rev. 21–22). This biblical story is fundamentally concerned not with giving us the "facts" of human life but with describing the *meaning* of human life. The scientific disciplines might provide us with the details of the former, but they are not equipped to provide us with the latter. That requires a different, although complementary, discipline. The sciences explain natural processes, but they cannot explain humanity's— indeed, creation's—*purpose*. The sciences may tell us how a human body "works," but they cannot tell us the grounds for a person's innate human dignity. These must be found in a different kind of story. The trajectory of where we are from and where we are going is precisely the kind of "metanarrative" that the Bible provides.

Let me give an overview. First of all, the beginning of the biblical trajectory suggests that God's intention for humanity as a whole is not to remain in a "natural" or static state. The earth exists as a dynamic, thriving place, full of potential and energy. This is part of the reason for the biblical injunction to "be fruitful and multiply" (which, it should be noted, God gives to animals before giving it to humans; cf. Gen. 1:22, 28). On this basis, then, we have also been given a purpose, a telos or goal. Presupposing the instruction to be fruitful and multiply, humans are to follow a path in which *culture* emerges: not over against nature, but finally in harmony with the natural. This is signaled by the presence of the tree of life and the river in both the garden of Eden and the new Jerusalem (compare Gen. 2:9–10 with Rev. 22:1–2, 14, 19). Tragically, as the early chapters of Genesis make clear, this trajectory is disrupted by Adam and Eve's sin, "the fall," which estranges humanity from God and the natural order. Yet before I consider that fall more fully, it is worth noting that the course of human development is still traced in passages that hint how culture appears not merely as a result of human sinfulness but rather as an aspect of God's original intention for humanity—even if that culture can itself become the victim and vehicle of human sin. Consider Genesis 4:17–22, which contains the first of Scripture's many genealogical lists, while also describing the origins of the first city, the first appearance of certain trades (livestock herders, musicians, and toolmakers), and, apparently, communal worship ("At that time people began to invoke the name of the LORD" [v. 26]). The ties of family, neighbors, commerce, the arts, and religion have grown up and become intertwined, all reinforcing and expanding upon the divine observation that "it is not good that the human should be alone" (2:18 NRSV modified). Even in a narrative that presupposes that a fundamental disorder has infected human existence, it remains clear that human fellowship or communion (*koinōnia*) is God's original, continuing, and final intention for us, grounded in his eternal election.

The Fallenness of Human Community

> They heard the sound of the LORD God walking in the garden at the time of the evening breeze, and the man and his wife hid themselves from the presence of the LORD God among the trees of the garden. But the LORD God called to the man, and said to him, "Where are you?" He said, "I heard the sound of you in the garden, and I was afraid, because I was naked; and I hid myself." He said, "Who told you that you were naked? Have you eaten from the tree of which I commanded you not to eat?" The man said, "The woman whom you gave to be with me, she gave me fruit from the tree, and I ate." Then the LORD God said to the woman, "What is this that you have done?" The woman said, "The serpent tricked me, and I ate." (Gen. 3:8–13)

Pain and suffering exist. Only the naïve, oblivious, willfully ignorant, hermetically sheltered, or mentally incapacitated could not recognize this fact. Pain and suffering afflict individuals as well as communities. Physical agony and mental and spiritual anguish respect neither time nor place, neither social status nor ethnicity, not sex, nationality, nor any human distinctive. Indeed, they afflict not just humans but animals as well. To be sure, less biologically developed creatures may not have the nervous system necessary to experience psychological anguish, but it is hard to deny that something like it can afflict mammals, particularly primates. Pain and suffering are a seemingly unavoidable and universal characteristic of actual creaturely existence. But are they an *essential* aspect of that existence? And to raise the existential stakes further: are they *evil*? Even more, does existence have to be this way—that is, was it in some sense *intended* to be this way? If we answer yes, pain and suffering belong irreducibly to the very definition of existence—if that's just the way things are, then our response should be obvious. We must simply learn to live with it. If, however, we answer no, it was not meant to be this way, that something has gone wrong, then this will elicit a far different response. Pain and suffering cannot remain a mere fact of life. Rather, they become something to be relieved and overcome; indeed, they may even be an offense, something that must be strenuously condemned, resisted, and defeated, if possible—in a word, something evil.

Consider your own experience. When did you first utter the complaint "That's not fair!"? Probably as a child, in response to something done by a parent or a sibling, a friend or one of the "big kids." Somebody did something to you—or left you out of something—and it hurt you or hurt your feelings. Something happened and you knew it wasn't just an accident; it was a personal affront. You were offended, and you said so. You likely uttered the complaint not because of something happening to someone else or some abstract inequality or injustice but in response to something happening to you directly, and your complaint was likely immediate. Now consider the implication of the words: you didn't just resign yourself to the situation by accepting that the person was bigger or had outsmarted you or got to operate by different rules. You didn't just acquiesce to the outcome by saying, "These things happen." You did recognize that something *had*, in fact, occurred, that this was now the way things *were*. But you refused to acknowledge that that was how things *should* have been. In other words, even at a young age you did not resign yourself to the worldview that "might makes right" or that blind fate rules or that those who were more clever or were insiders got to play the system to their benefit over against yours. You already had a deeply ingrained intuition that the bald fact that things are the way they are does not automatically mean that that is the way they ought to be.

Of course a full analysis like this presumably did not go through your head the first time you cried, "That's not fair!" But evoking the memory of this feeling indicates that even as a child, you sensed that individuals or circumstances could throw life out of balance, that things could go askew in ways that were not just unfortunate but wrong. A bad thing happened because someone intended to frustrate or hurt you—and that was just not right. You had an immediate sense that a certain event or a given reality represented a moral derailment in the world, and you felt a justified sense of moral indignation that it should be corrected and that someone should be held accountable for fixing it and (perhaps the same someone) should be punished for having caused it—although again, you probably did not phrase it precisely this way!

Cultivating Moral Discernment

To be sure, childhood perceptions should not be the last word in determining our mature perspectives on the world. After all, cries of "that's not fair" may well be self-serving. Still, on thoughtful reflection we will recognize that not everything we experience as bad is necessarily evil in a moral sense. Accidents do happen, as the result of unforeseen and unforeseeable circumstances beyond anyone's control, so there's not always someone who must be blamed. On other occasions, events may be morally ambiguous, and determining whether certain actions are morally right or wrong depends upon the specific details, context, and purpose. Certainly one could say that intentionally inflicting pain upon another person is wrong—unless, for example, one is giving that person a medical injection as an inoculation against a life-threatening disease. Having a needle stuck in one's body does hurt, but it is a pain worth inflicting and bearing for a greater benefit. Inflicting pain was not the intention but rather an unavoidable consequence of what is, in itself, a moral act. Indeed, to withhold such an inoculation, and thus the inevitable short-term pain, from someone threatened with that particular disease would itself be an *immoral* act, because long-term suffering and death might otherwise occur. Yet clearly, if one simply approached a stranger on the street and stabbed him with a needle, one would be doing something immoral—and shouldn't be surprised if an assault charge followed. On yet other occasions, bad things befall us which, given our druthers, we would prefer to avoid. But once we have endured them, we may come to realize that they have benefited us in ways we had not anticipated. A disease or disaster strikes that wreaks havoc in our lives, but it calls forth a personal strength or family closeness that we otherwise never would have found. We have all heard cases where people reflect upon such tragedies with the words "I wouldn't wish it on someone else, or want to go through it again, but it's actually the best thing that ever happened for me."

So not everything bad is evil in a moral sense. In certain cases, moral language simply does not apply. If you were to fall off a cliff, you might immediately think to yourself, "Uh, oh. This is really bad." But in the few moments before impact, you probably would not hold gravity or the rocks below morally culpable for the injury or death that awaited you when you hit bottom. To blame gravity or the rocks would be to make a category mistake: they simply are what they are, having no choice or agency in the matter. However, if you were pushed, you would certainly have a justified sense of moral outrage—at least for a moment or two—toward the person who shoved you over the edge. You would blame the person who pushed you because he or she did have moral agency. The individual could choose to act, or not act, in one way or another, and could have been presumed to have some basic sense of right and wrong. So discernment is needed. Some acts may in fact be morally neutral, but other acts may be labeled quite appropriately, even necessarily, praiseworthy or blameworthy. The praise or blame may be qualified in certain cases: if a particular outcome is not what the person intended, if others also acted, if the act was done in a way that is usually innocent even if this time it caused harm, and similar mitigating circumstances. Still, the element of freedom and choice remains a presupposition of morality, as does some basic sense of right and wrong, both of which society expects of individuals once they reach a certain age. To be sure, in our everyday experience we recognize how a series of good or bad choices may develop into a habit, a kind of second nature or "default mode," such that in a specific instance the person acts not so much as the result of conscious choice but out of this pattern of previous behavior. Nevertheless, it is still that individual who is acting or not acting in a particular set of ways, so that he or she remains ultimately responsible.

The Social Embeddedness of Evil

So why can't we all just make better choices and get along? Why is there such animosity, hatred, envy, greed, dissembling, and suspicion in the world? Why is there such violence on the part of some? Why such apathy—or secret support—on the part of others? Couldn't we just start a grassroots movement, beginning on an individual level, in which each person pledges to be kinder, more generous, more patient—simply put, to be more virtuous—while at the same time pledging to avoid such vices as lying, greed, violence, and the like? If individuals just worked to be more moral, wouldn't all the evil in the world eventually just disappear? In theory, of course. But experience teaches that this seemingly simple solution is unlikely to work because it relies on a simplistic notion of where evil is "located." Clearly, individuals can be evil. Individuals can indeed engage in acts that bring suffering and misery not just to other individuals but to whole groups of persons. They can commit evil deeds the repercussions of which extend far beyond the immediate aftermath of the act itself, such that the overall consequences grow far out of proportion to the original incident, however horrendous.

This is why it does not suffice to locate immorality and evil solely in individuals. The repercussions of individual acts embed themselves in a broader context, so that the acts and their context then combine and interact in unexpected ways and, as a result, become the context in which further individual acts are done. (Christianity's take on which ultimately comes first—the individual or the context—is a philosophical and theological issue I will address in a moment.) The upshot is that the morally wrong, the evil, becomes systemic. That is, evil is a matter no longer merely of particular misdeeds but also of broader structures and patterns of being, of received cultures and thought worlds. Past acts shape the ways individuals and societies perceive reality; that perception then becomes the basis upon which individuals, groups, and whole societies engage in further actions—or refrain from acting. A reality established in part by previous actions (or inactions) and their entrenched effects thereby influences or even determines future courses of acting or not acting. In a very real sense, no *one* is to blame because to some degree all are complicit. The context is, after all, the product of a collective, and the context itself seems morally misaligned. And yet we recognize that while this is the way the world is, it is not the way the world should be. Somehow, the demands of moral accountability remain. In some way, we sense that not just individuals but the world itself need to be put right.

Sin

This sense that the world is, in some deep-seated manner, *dis*oriented (which, of course, presumes it properly has a prior and more fundamental orientation) is precisely what the Christian doctrine of original sin describes. Up to this point I have presented matters in terms of good and evil, described in moral terms. But now what does it mean to introduce the notion of "sin" into the conversation? How does that help and, presumably, change the nature of the discussion? The first and most important thing to say is that sin is primarily a *theological* concept, and only *secondarily* an ethical or moral one. That is, by invoking the term "sin," theologians are stating that the world's fundamental orientation—and therefore its current disorientation—is in relation to *God*. Christian faith does not assume that the world exists in a kind of neutral space, that it is merely "natural." Rather, Christianity affirms that the world is created by God, who intends for it to exist in a particular kind of continuing relation to him and a particular kind of interrelation with itself. In fact, God created human beings in a particular way so that they could be oriented to God and their fellow creatures in particular ways. These are the "design specifications" given us in our creation, and the realization of our truest selves happens when we live into them: we were made to be in loving relation with God and our neighbors. This is what truly defines us as human beings. However, when these design specifications of that creation and its relations are disrupted, when humans seek to define themselves by themselves (whether through a self-aggrandizing pride, through a self-negating abasement, or in some other manner), in isolation from their proper relation to, and true fulfillment in, God, they fall into a state of sin. On the basis of this fundamentally *theological* understanding, the notion of sin may then be said to have a derivatively ethical meaning. In that sense, sin describes both a state of being and ways of acting.

SIN AND SINS

One way to illustrate this point is to repeat a commonly used distinction, namely, the contrast between "sin" and "sins." "Sin" is the fundamental orientation away from God and the persistent inclination to disobey God; "sins," which are the *fruit* of sin, are the wrongs one does in relation to the neighbor. In other words, they are the negative image of, or antithesis to, the two tables of the Decalogue and the Great Commandment, both of which present our duties to God and neighbor in a definite order. That is, the first commandments of the Ten Commandments have to do with one's proper relation to God, and the ones that follow, with proper relations among humans (Exod. 20:1–17; Deut.

5:6–21). The same is true with Jesus's response to the question, "Teacher, which commandment in the law is the greatest?" He answered, "'You shall love the Lord your God with all your heart, and with all your soul, and with all your mind.' This is the greatest and first commandment. And a second is like it: 'You shall love your neighbor as yourself.' On these two commandments hang all the law and the prophets."[6] This scriptural order is the basis for the succinct quip sometimes attributed to Saint Augustine: "Love God, and do what you will." The point is that if one's love is rightly ordered first toward God, then one's love of neighbor will be a rightly ordered natural by-product. Conversely, in the case of sin there is a definite "disorder." Once the proper relation to God is disrupted, inappropriate relations with our neighbors are bound to follow.

THE PERSISTENCE OF SIN

So, original sin speaks to the sense that underlying various immoral or evil acts is a fundamental disordering or corruption of our being, with "being" understood in systemic and collective, as well as individual, terms. It is not just individuals who are "fallen" but the context in which they exist. And this context includes the historical: original sin speaks to the temporal dimension of our existence. In other words, original sin is in some sense hereditary. But that raises the question, how is it inherited? Now it is true that in centuries past, Christian theologians appealed to the science of their day in seeking to explain how sin was passed down from our first progenitors. One biblical text seemed suggestive: "Wash me thoroughly from my iniquity, and cleanse me from my sin! For I know my transgressions, and my sin is ever before me. Against thee, thee only, have I sinned, and done that which is evil in thy sight, so that thou art justified in thy sentence and blameless in thy judgment. Behold, I was brought forth in iniquity, and in sin did my mother conceive me" (Ps. 51:2–5 RSV). To some premodern ways of thinking, this made it sound as if original sin were inherited biologically. Yet other descriptions were more nuanced, making distinctions to demonstrate that the use of biological categories is to be taken not literally but metaphorically.[7]

Certainly, as we have come to refine our scientific understanding of the world, more strictly biological explanations have simply become implausible.

---

6. Matt. 22:36–40//Mark 12:28–31. Cf. Luke 10:25–28.

7. Consider, e.g., Saint Anselm's description, written in the eleventh century, which recognizes scriptural references to sin being passed down at conception or in the male "seed" as being true, but not literal. In other words, they describe an inherited human reality, but the apparently biological terms are figures of speech, not descriptions of the actual process. See Anselm of Canterbury, "Why God Became Man," in *A Scholastic Miscellany: Anselm to Ockham*, ed. and trans. Eugene R. Fairweather, Library of Christian Classics (Louisville: Westminster John Knox, 1956), 10:192–93.

Especially in light of modern understandings of evolution and genetics, we know that, biologically speaking, acquired characteristics are not inheritable. For example, if a person loses a limb to amputation, that individual's future offspring will not be born minus that limb. If a person gains wisdom through long study and hard work, that individual's future offspring will not as a result be born more intelligent. By analogy, our ancestors' morality or immorality is not something we inherit by way of our genes. Yet the notion of inheritance is not completely misplaced, because the sensed reality of a world gone askew remains. It is not just that evil too often occurs, but that it seems inevitable, as somehow given. Life's deck seems stacked; we know we're not the ones responsible for stacking it; yet there doesn't seem to be anything we can finally do about it—it's just always been that way. It is this perception, this intuition—namely, that we inherit a world that is fundamentally disordered in ways that are morally deplorable—to which the Christian doctrine of original sin speaks. Some might consider the doctrine outdated, especially if its essential insight is understood to be inseparable from a biological explanation.

Sin's Persistence as a Cultural Inheritance

The doctrine, however, does not stand or fall with this particular approach; with a different tack, it still has explanatory power and insight. For example, while it may not be fruitful to view original sin as a biological condition, it can be enlightening to recognize the reality to which the doctrine points as a *cultural* condition, because acquired *cultural* characteristics *are* inheritable. In this sense, the doctrine describes not a biological defect but an existential inevitability grounded in our social and historical existence.[8] In other words, no matter how hard we try, no matter the success of efforts to counter it here, the disorder and corruption always reemerge, often in a different manner and frequently worse than before. The doctrine of original sin simply recognizes in a clearheaded manner that sin is a recurring and universal aspect of the human condition, both on an individual and psychological level and, more insidiously and pervasively, on a social and historical level. One need not affirm a literal Adam and Eve eating a literal fruit in a literal garden to recognize how this story speaks to a real and verifiable truth about human existence: that individual acts of sin and evil tend to grow and take on a life of their own.

8. The mid-twentieth-century theologian and ethicist Reinhold Niebuhr wrote often on various aspects of systemic sin, a theme perhaps captured most tellingly in the title of his classic work *Moral Man and Immoral Society: A Study in Ethics and Politics* (New York: Scribner's Sons, 1932). A more contemporary but also powerful treatment may be found in the work by Alistair McFadyen, *Bound to Sin: Abuse, Holocaust and the Christian Doctrine of Sin*, Cambridge Studies in Christian Doctrine (Cambridge: Cambridge University Press, 2000).

In fact, one can argue that the Christian notion of original sin allows for a fuller and more adaptable explanation of reality and our lived experience than some other common views. Consider, for example, its contrast with a still-influential perspective from the seventeenth- and eighteenth-century Enlightenment, which described the individual as being born with a tabula rasa (a "blank" or "clean slate"). This notion holds that each person, in effect, engages life with the same existential option possessed by Adam and Eve. That is, each individual has volitional autonomy, able in each moment to freely choose between the good and the bad, with no prior "bent" or bias. In addition, it assumes that our natural and social context is rather uncomplicatedly open and amenable to human industry and management. This approach is admirable for its clarity and its encouragement of individual moral responsibility, and it has been fruitful in many ways.

Yet especially in light of the twentieth century's totalitarian movements and massive horrors of war and genocide, it also seems unrealistically optimistic and inadequate for the task of explaining the complexity and intransigence of the human condition. In this regard, the Christian doctrine is simply better equipped to explain the paradox and tragedy of our lives. It acknowledges that sin can manipulate our institutions, laws, cultural mores, and "group identities," whether family, ethnic group, national history, or the like. Another key claim is that sin affects our attitudes and moral choices in ways of which we might not even be aware. Thus, for example, when the theologian and ethicist Reinhold Niebuhr acknowledges—with distinct Christian qualifications—the insights of psychology to describe how our subconscious can influence, even determine our actions,[9] this is more in keeping with the views of original sin than the Enlightenment views just described. Original sin is like a virus: its parasitic existence depends upon a host, and while it may be very simple in itself, its power and persistence are due to its ability to adapt. It is a constantly moving target made even worse by its capacity to masquerade as the desirable and good.

Different cultures, different generations, different eras each have their distinct personalities and characteristics, for good and for ill. For example, one characteristic of contemporary Western culture seems to be its overwhelming desire for uniqueness—perhaps an inevitable desire, given the repetitive sameness of a mass, even global, economy and the omnipresence of mass media. In our particular time and place, we are obsessed with the new and different: anything that will help us stand out from the crowd, to gain celebrity. Thus, an

---

9. Note the various references Niebuhr makes to Freud's claims in his Gifford Lectures, published as *The Nature and Destiny of Man: A Christian Interpretation* (New York: Scribner's Sons, 1941), 34, 36, 42–44, 52–53, 121.

ancient vice—vainglory—appears in brand-name, designer clothes.[10] And this obsession displays a remarkable egalitarianism. Whether low-brow, middle-brow, or high-brow, whether in our professional lives or our personal lives, whether in public life and entertainment or private lives and consumption patterns, we just can't seem to get enough of the latest thing. Yet if we were honest with ourselves, we would recognize that there simply isn't enough of the new and different to satisfy our seemingly insatiable appetite for it. This is not to say that the new and different doesn't happen; it's just that it doesn't typically happen at the relentless pace and quantity that our desires demand. Even the briefest reflection on the actual flow of our lives will show this to be true. Think of cyberspace: how much of what goes out on tweets or personal blogs is really new and different? Think of cable news cycles and popular entertainment: they entice you into thinking they have some new insight or perspective, but you quickly realize how repetitive they are.

In my own professional environment of the academic world, the ideal insists that dissertations, articles, and books be original, new, and cutting-edge. The reality is that even the best scholars typically only engage variations on a theme, perhaps adding a minor adjustment here or a minor new insight there. Yet the pressure to be new and different is so great that it often only produces its own self-caricature. If the latest fashion is to be "X," then the way to be original is to assert "anti-X"—or to combine various and wildly disparate elements and assert that far from being an arbitrary or wildly contradictory combination, they are in fact deeply intertwined in ways that no one but the author has had the brilliance to notice before. After a while, one cannot help but think that the sage of Ecclesiastes had the more accurate take on things: it is vanity to think there is anything new under the sun (see Eccles. 1). This is not so much a universal and all-encompassing claim that nothing new *ever* happens as it is an unmasking of the delusion and arrogance that the old no longer applies because we have moved on to the new. "That was then, this is now" is not so much a descriptive statement of conditions as it is a declaration not to be constrained by what has gone before. Underlying rules, eternal principles, natural laws are not recognized as such but are said to be outdated and no longer applicable.

"Original Sin" Reflects Real Life—and Points to Our Hope

Another word needs to be added, especially for those who may tend to react against the whole notion of "original sin" as somehow outdated or

10. For a very accessible and insightful treatment of the vices-and-virtues tradition, see Rebecca Konyndyk DeYoung, *Glittering Vices: A New Look at the Seven Deadly Sins and Their Remedies* (Grand Rapids: Brazos, 2009).

off-putting. While popular treatments of original sin often identify the particular sin involved in caricatured ways (usually having something to do with lust), the Christian tradition has actually explained it in a number of ways over the centuries. The Western Christian tradition, influenced as heavily as it is by Augustine, has often spoken of sin as humanity's willful disobedience to God. Here the emphasis has been on human guilt, with humanity sometimes characterized as a "mass of perdition" (*massa perditionis*) that deserves nothing better than damnation. We might not like it, but given the carnage of the twentieth century, we should probably concede the description is not without justice. Willful human evil is certainly a reality.

The Eastern Orthodox tradition does not ignore this way of thinking, but from its early centuries, it also developed another viewpoint. One example stems from the second-century theologian Irenaeus. He spoke of Adam and Eve's original sin as less a matter of willful rebellion and more a kind of youthful indiscretion that nevertheless had very unfortunate consequences. In this strand of his thinking, the emphasis is less on their guilt than on their need for increased maturity, for growing into faithfulness.[11] And, of course, other theologians have pointed out that Adam and Eve are as much the victims of sin as the perpetrators, in that most of the blame should fall on the serpent who tempted them.[12] While the original Genesis account does not itself make the connection, later tradition of course understood the serpent to be Satan, now subjecting humanity to the bondage of sin and death.[13]

In other words, there are various approaches in the tradition—and the tradition continues to allow for variation. I gave my own general definition above with these words: when humans seek to define themselves by themselves (whether through a self-aggrandizing pride, through a self-negating abasement, or in some other manner), in isolation from their proper relation to, and true fulfillment in, God, they fall into a state of sin. This diverse understanding of the nature of humanity's fall corresponds to the Christian tradition's multifaceted understanding of the nature of Jesus Christ's saving work,[14] but that is not the reason for noting that fact here. The point is rather to acknowledge that Christian theology has long recognized the insidious

11. See Irenaeus of Lyons, *On the Apostolic Preaching*, trans. John Behr (Crestwood, NY: St. Vladimir's Seminary Press, 1997), 47, and John Hick, *Evil and the God of Love* (New York: Macmillan, 1966), 217–21.

12. After all, once God realizes what has happened, he first curses the serpent. See Gen. 3:13–15.

13. See, for example, the classic study by Gustaf Aulén, *Christus Victor* (New York: Macmillan, 1969), 20–28.

14. I address this diversity and seek to provide an overarching unity for it in my work *King, Priest, and Prophet: A Trinitarian Theology of Atonement* (New York: T&T Clark, 2004).

complexity of human sinfulness and its continuing ability to mutate into new and different forms. It knows that if one misunderstands or underestimates one's enemy, one is bound to fail.

One final dilemma, which also often goes against our grain, is the apparent absurdity that we're "free" only to sin yet are nevertheless responsible for that sin. This is indeed tragic. But it is also a necessary assertion if we are to be respected seriously as moral agents—as moral adults, rather than as mere children who don't know better. Or, more insidiously in our day and age, as victims of a kind of disease or mental disorder that needs therapy rather than accountability. After all, to resolve the dilemma by saying that either we are not free or that we are not responsible would leave us with fatalistic determinism or moral anarchy. And, of course, according to the biblical witness and Christian faith, God does not surrender us to this fallen state but instead initiates a way for the world finally to be redeemed from the power and consequences of sin and evil in the world. The extent, complexity, and durability of evil allow no simple or simplistic solutions. When such solutions are attempted, they often merely compound the problem, either directly or through the law of unintended consequences. Any enduring solution will have to be more deeply rooted and pervasive; complex and able to adapt; cultural and historical in a way mirroring the sin itself; and durable to the point of being eternal.

Salvation Will Be Social *and* Individual: Establishing Covenant, Setting the Pattern

> Now the LORD said to Abram, "Go from your country and your kindred and your father's house to the land that I will show you. I will make of you a great nation, and I will bless you, and make your name great, so that you will be a blessing. I will bless those who bless you, and the one who curses you I will curse; and in you all the families of the earth shall be blessed." (Gen. 12:1–3)

So the biblical story—and if we are not completely oblivious, our own experience—throws us into a quandary. We know our own yearning for connection: for families that are whole, for communities that are vibrant and thriving, for nations that are at peace and productive, for a planet that is healthy. We have the theological affirmation that *koinōnia*, or "fellowship," is God's intention for us originally, now, and in the fullness of time. Recall the discussion above (pp. 1–3): it was the Father's desire to be in special relation with the human beings he would fashion, so he covenanted with the Son and the Spirit to order and animate precisely such a creation. The winsome image of God walking in the garden in the cool of the day to be with the man and the woman he has made evokes the intimacy he intended—and yet by then, heart-breakingly, that intimacy had already been broken and lost (Gen. 3:1–13). And that loss reverberates and grows down the ages: we know how broken we now are, and how intractable that brokenness is. Alienation and animosity across cultural, ethnic, racial, class, and political lines thrive. We are distanced from the natural world in our urban settings or are overwhelmed by the natural world through tsunamis, earthquakes, or pandemics. Believers of various faiths clash with one another—and they are all repudiated by secularists and increasingly dogmatic atheists. And overall, the human capacity for self-destruction and environmental devastation grows at a seemingly uncontrollable rate. In such a situation, even those individuals or groups who by any objective standard possess substantial power and influence can feel helpless.

> Mere anarchy is loosed upon the world,
> The blood-dimmed tide is loosed, and everywhere
> The ceremony of innocence is drowned;
> The best lack all conviction, while the worst
> Are full of passionate intensity.[15]

What can one person do when whole demographics feel disenfranchised? Who hasn't at times been overcome by a sense that the best course of action would be to wipe the slate clean and start over?

Genesis: Book of Beginnings

The biblical book of Genesis is the Bible's book of beginnings. This may seem so obvious as to be not worth mentioning, given the opening verse: "In the beginning God created the heavens and the earth." It's clearly meant to be the start of the story, an ancient equivalent to our "Once upon a time . . ." One has to start somewhere, and such words are the literary device that serves this function. True, opening words like these are actually rather arbitrary, but typically we go along with them—because otherwise, how would we ever get into the story? How can one get farther back than the beginning? The anecdote is told of Martin Luther, who, when asked what God was doing before creation, responded, "Cutting sticks to beat people who ask such silly questions." The image of a too-smart-for-his-own-good student trying to divert his teacher from the lesson does come to mind. But we should not let Luther's reply prevent us from recognizing what we have already noted: that God had a purpose in creating, namely, deep communion between God, humans, and

15. From William Butler Yeats, "The Second Coming," 1920.

the whole created order. And it seems safe to assume further—God is indeed God, after all—that he would not let human waywardness and sin derail that purpose in the long run. In fact, the Father, who made creation through his Word and Spirit, will now redeem, reconcile, and re-create that fallen world through his Word and Spirit. In this unfolding story, the "order of creation" has now been joined by the "order of salvation" (*ordo salutis*).[16]

In other words, the Bible's "book of beginnings" describes not just the beginning of the created order; it also describes the beginnings of God's unfolding plan of salvation. The former description—from the account of the first six days followed by a day of rest, to the story of Adam and Eve and their fall from grace—occupies only the first three of fifty chapters. But if one considers the whole of the book, from its first chapter to its last, as the book of beginnings, one can more clearly recognize how the book as a whole sets the stage and establishes the covenantal patterns for everything that follows in the subsequent thirty-eight books of the Old Testament[17] and the twenty-seven books of the New Testament. Genesis is the book of beginnings for the Bible because it establishes who the characters are, describes their behavior (which is simultaneously concrete and typological), and sets the foundation for the major and minor themes that will thread through the remainder of Holy Scripture. Genesis is not a treatise of abstract philosophy or theology; it is a story describing God's creation of the world and God's continuing interactions with that world, especially with humans. It is not mythology (presenting time-less, ideal truths) but saga (which takes the shifting particularities of history and its actors seriously and understands them as "going somewhere").[18] It sets certain parameters, ruling certain deeds or paths as "in," while excluding

16. There is debate within the Reformed tradition as to whether God established this "order of salvation" *before* the fall, indeed, before creation itself ("supralapsarianism") or in some sense *after*, and in response to, the fall ("infralapsarianism"). The impetus for the debate is concern for what each position seems to imply about God: those advocating the first view hold that the infralapsarian position suggests that God was "surprised" by the fall and had to improvise a response (seemingly undermining divine omniscience). Those advocating the second view hold that the supralapsarian position can be taken as saying the fall was somehow necessitated by this prior decree, hence implicating God in evil (seemingly undermining divine justice). For a helpful summary and some brief historical examples, see William Stacy Johnson and John H. Leith, eds., *Reformed Reader: A Sourcebook in Christian Theology*, vol. 1, *Classical Beginnings, 1519–1799* (Louisville: Westminster John Knox, 1993), 107–15. While I understand the logic and concerns of each camp, the position of this book does lean to the supralapsarian side—but understood along the lines of Karl Barth, who held that the true subject of the Father's eternal election, both condemnation and justification, was Jesus Christ.

17. The number is based on the common Protestant usage, which does not include the books of the Apocrypha included in Roman Catholic versions of the Bible.

18. See Karl Barth's insightful discussion of this distinction in his *Church Dogmatics* III/1, §41, "Creation and Covenant" (Edinburgh: T&T Clark, 1958), esp. 60–94.

others. And it establishes certain templates or interpretive patterns for under-standing, evaluating, and anticipating future deeds, characters, and outcomes. It also points to where God desires ultimately to bring us.

Noah and Babel

As I have already discussed, the opening chapters portray God's creation of heaven and earth and creation's forward movement in time in a recurring rhythm of seven days. These chapters describe how God, humanity, and the earth are meant to relate to one another, as well as the ways creatures dis-rupt that intended relation through the fall: our life together is broken. The communion in which and for which we were created has been disordered and corrupted. The serpent manipulates the divine commands in speaking to Eve. In consuming the forbidden fruit, Adam and Eve violate their com-munion with God and in the process turn upon one another and bring upon themselves an alienation from the earth itself. In the heritage of this broken trust and alienation springs the first murder as Cain kills his brother Abel. Simultaneously, the Bible describes God's just and merciful response to that disruption, and then portrays the emergence, for good and for ill, of human culture and politics. Within ten generations, however, the "LORD saw that the wickedness of humankind was great in the earth, and that every inclination of the thoughts of their hearts was only evil continually. And the LORD was sorry that he had made humankind on the earth, and it grieved him to his heart" (Gen. 6:5–6). On its own, humanity stumbles from bad to worse, such that the whole world becomes corrupt. So God decides to wipe the slate clean, with only Noah finding favor in his sight. God gives Noah the task of building the ark, which is to save him, his family, and male and female representatives of each of the animals from the coming deluge. Why a flood? It signals that God is taking things back almost as far as the original, precreation void, when darkness was upon the face of the deep and "the Spirit of God was moving over the face of the waters" (Gen. 1:2 RSV).

But note: God does not take things *all* the way back. Instead, he calls upon a segment of humanity to maintain continuity and to further the divine will, and makes his relationship with this remnant explicit through a covenant (Gen. 6:18). When the waters of the flood recede and he smells Noah's burnt offer-ing, God also vows to himself: "I will never again curse the ground because of humankind, for the inclination of the human heart is evil from youth; nor will I ever again destroy every living creature as I have done. As long as the earth endures, seedtime and harvest, cold and heat, summer and winter, day and night, shall not cease" (Gen. 8:21b–22). In other words, the stage of God's original creation project will be sustained: in spite of our sin, God still grants us a place and a time. God then blesses Noah and his three children, repeating to them his original commission to humanity ("Be fruitful and multiply, and fill the earth")[19] and clarifying the new ground rules, revised since Adam and Eve in light of the circumstances.[20] Next, God reiterates his covenantal vow and explicitly extends it to all living creatures "for all future generations." Finally, God places his war bow[21] in the sky as a reminder of his promise never again to let loose the waters of primordial chaos (Gen. 9:8–17).

So how does all this remain a matter of "beginnings," nine chapters into the book of Genesis and ten generations into the human history there described? It remains so by setting the stage and establishing the patterns of how God will interact with humanity for the remainder of the story. One may assume that God's purpose and intentions for creation have not changed, but given our finitude, recalcitrance, and sin, God has accommodated himself to humanity's present condition. In other words, God has already shown himself to be a God of righteousness *and* mercy. God is not simply an arbitrary hierarch of inflexible demands. Rather, God's power is in service to his justice, his compassion, and his original intentions, in such a way that he will even obligate himself to his creatures by entering into a covenant with them. God is indeed almighty, but according to this covenant with Noah, God has now taken certain options off the table in dealing with humanity, indeed, with the whole earth.

So what does humanity then do? (Note well: it is essential that Noah and his family be recognized not just as isolated figures, as specific individuals from "back then," but also as our ancestors, as members of our family whom we must properly acknowledge. In this way, Noah also serves as a representative figure, an "everyman" in whom we can also see ourselves.) Humanity falls back into its bad habits. The survivors of the flood do multiply, and the first peoples and nations emerge and go about their filling of the earth. And yet as if the sins of individuals and small groups were not enough, eventually the power and presumption of the human collective appears. One people builds a city and proposes to build a tower up to the very heavens. God scatters this people and confuses their languages, and is then portrayed taking a different tack in guiding creation to the goal he originally intended for it.

19. Gen. 9:1, which echoes Gen. 1:28.
20. That is, human food is no longer limited to plants, although the consumption of blood is restricted because it is understood as containing life itself. Moreover, the punishment for murder is specified, in light of Cain's murder of Abel.
21. We moderns should not sentimentalize the rainbow as a merely benign and beautiful natural occurrence: to ancient eyes it represented the multicolored bow carried by the king, or in this case, by God. Cf. Lam. 2:4; Hab. 3:9–11.

Abraham and Sarah

Rather than covenanting with humanity in general, a situation that might in the natural course of events seem to favor those peoples and nations that are politically powerful and important in human terms, God instead seeks out an obscure old man and his wife, a couple beyond childbearing years, to make for himself a new people: "And by you," God tells Abram, "all the families of the earth shall bless themselves" (Gen. 12:3 RSV). This is, of course, the covenant that God will establish with Abram and Sarai—later renamed Abraham and Sarah—calling them to leave their home in order to grant them a new land, and offspring, and a name that will endure down through the ages. It may seem curious that this covenantal blessing takes a meandering path and a fair amount of time to unfold. Yet this slow and circuitous unfolding is itself a divine lesson for Abraham and Sarah; it also foreshadows the character and pace of God's covenantal activity in the rest of Genesis—indeed, in the remainder of the biblical story. God begins with the smallest human unit, a male and a female. Abraham and Sarah are, of course, descended—through Noah and his family—from Adam and Eve. They continue the human lineage begun in the garden, even while also representing a recapitulation of the first couple and thereby serving as a new beginning. Unlike Adam and Eve, however, their offspring come not after the divine command to use the procreative powers given them at creation but as a result of the divine promise given in this new covenant. That promise will come to fruition, but as the unfolding story exemplifies, it will do so according to God's timetable and often unexpected actions. In the narrative itself, this often means that God's activity recedes from view, only to be recognized by the characters occasionally or in hindsight. I will speak to this point more fully below.

The passage just cited (Gen. 12:3) occurs when Abram is in the land of Haran, from which the Lord summons him to travel to the land of Canaan. He goes, taking with him Sarai and his nephew Lot and his wife. God again encounters Abram in Canaan, showing him the land his descendants will inherit (12:7). But a famine soon drives them all to seek refuge in Egypt. Eventually they return, and when Abram and Lot divide the land between them, God once more speaks to Abram regarding the land (13:14–18). Sometime thereafter, warfare erupts in the area, and Lot is taken captive. Abram assembles a small army, achieves victory, and secures Lot's release. Yet for all his worldly success, Abram still does not have an heir. God again comes to reassure him, showing him the night sky and promising that his descendants will be as numerous as the stars. Abram believes him, and the Lord "reckoned it to him as righteousness" (15:2–6). At this point God consummates or "cuts" a covenant with Abram (the "cutting" referring to the sacrificial animals cut in two, between which the smoking fire pot and flaming torch of God pass), formally sealing the promise of his descendants and the land (15:7–21). In the idiom of such covenantal practices, it was the weaker partner who passed between the sacrificial pieces, vowing that such would happen to him should the covenant be broken. Astonishingly, in this instance God takes this male-diction upon himself, even when it is not he but his human partners who will break the covenant. Christians, of course, recognize him as finally taking this curse upon himself centuries later in Jesus's crucifixion.[22]

Yet in the more limited time frame of Abram's perspective, the promised offspring still does not arrive. So Sarai determines that her husband should produce an heir through her servant girl Hagar. Hagar conceives, and, per-haps not surprisingly, relations between the two women sour. Hagar flees for her life and that of her unborn child, but an encounter with an angel of the Lord reassures her and sends her back, to give birth to Ishmael, whom Abram raises as his own.

Thirteen years later, God again appears to Abram, reaffirming his covenant, changing Abram's name to Abraham, and instituting the covenantal sign of circumcision. God also changes Sarai's name to Sarah and reiterates that she will bear Abraham a son. Abraham laughs at hearing this, given his and Sarah's age, while also expressing his concern for Ishmael. God reassures Abraham that he will care for Ishmael but that his covenant will be with the son Isaac, whom Sarah will bear in a year's time. When God departs, Abraham follows through on the command to circumcise all the males of his household (Gen. 17:1–27). The next time, when the Lord appears to Abraham at the oaks of Mamre, it is Sarah's turn to laugh at the thought that she might bear a child at her advanced age. The Lord overhears her laughter, which she is suddenly too embarrassed and fearful to admit. Yet his response, in the form of a rhe-torical question, lingers: "Is anything too hard for the LORD?" (18:1–15, esp. 18:14a, RSV). The answer, of course, is no.

However, the episode that immediately follows the encounter at Mamre makes it clear that in his acts, God wills to include his chosen ones. Heading toward Sodom, the Lord asks himself: "Shall I hide from Abraham what I am about to do, seeing that Abraham shall become a great and mighty na-tion, and all the nations of the earth shall bless themselves by him? No, for I have chosen him, that he may charge his children and his household after

---

22. See Sandra L. Richter, *The Epic of Eden: A Christian Entry into the Old Testament* (Downers Grove, IL: IVP Academic, 2008), 78–79, 159–62.

him to keep the way of the LORD by doing righteousness and justice; so that the LORD may bring to Abraham what he has promised him" (Gen. 18:17–19 RSV). Abraham immediately demonstrates his willingness to "keep the way of the LORD by doing righteousness and justice" when he implores God not to destroy the city, lest he also slay any righteous remnant there (18:23–33). One cannot help but think that God smiled at Abraham's audacious appeals for mercy, as he bargained with the Almighty to spare the wicked multitude for the sake of the righteous few. Of course, given the final destruction of both Sodom and Gomorrah, it became apparent that not even ten righteous persons remained in the two cities.

Finally, the Lord visits Sarah when he had said he would, and does as he had promised. She conceives and bears Abraham a son, whom he circumcises at the appointed time, as God has commanded (Gen. 21:1–4). Yet it does not take long for Sarah's resentment of Hagar to rekindle. She sees Ishmael as a threat to the inheritance due Isaac and wants the rival and her son both sent away. Abraham is displeased because he has fatherly concern for both lads, but God tells him to accede to Sarah's wishes, reassuring him that he will care for Hagar and Ishmael. Life then appears to settle into a routine for a man of Abraham's position and prosperity: matters of resolving property disputes, settling water rights, and establishing peaceful relations with neighboring tribes. However, it is precisely in the midst of such routine that God comes again:

> After these things God tested Abraham, and said to him, "Abraham!" And he said, "Here am I." He said, "Take your son, your only son Isaac, whom you love, and go to the land of Moriah, and offer him there as a burnt offering upon one of the mountains of which I shall tell you." So Abraham rose early in the morning, saddled his ass, and took two of his young men with him, and his son Isaac; and he cut the wood for the burnt offering, and arose and went to the place of which God had told him. On the third day Abraham lifted up his eyes and saw the place afar off. Then Abraham said to his young men, "Stay here with the ass; I and the lad will go yonder and worship, and come again to you." And Abraham took the wood of the burnt offering, and laid it on Isaac his son; and he took in his hand the fire and the knife. So they went both of them together. And Isaac said to his father Abraham, "My father!" And he said, "Here am I, my son." He said, "Behold, the fire and the wood; but where is the lamb for a burnt offering?" Abraham said, "God will provide himself the lamb for a burnt offering, my son." So they went both of them together.
>
> When they came to the place of which God had told him, Abraham built an altar there, and laid the wood in order, and bound Isaac his son, and laid him on the altar, upon the wood. Then Abraham put forth his hand, and took the knife to slay his son. But the angel of the LORD called to him from heaven,

and said, "Abraham, Abraham!" And he said, "Here am I." He said, "Do not lay your hand on the lad or do anything to him; for now I know that you fear God, seeing you have not withheld your son, your only son, from me." And Abraham lifted up his eyes and looked, and behold, behind him was a ram, caught in a thicket by his horns; and Abraham went and took the ram, and offered it up as a burnt offering instead of his son. So Abraham called the name of that place The LORD will provide; as it is said to this day, "On the mount of the LORD it shall be provided."

And the angel of the LORD called to Abraham a second time from heaven, and said, "By myself I have sworn, says the LORD, because you have done this, and have not withheld your son, your only son, I will indeed bless you, and I will multiply your descendants as the stars of heaven and as the sand which is on the seashore. And your descendants shall possess the gate of their enemies, and by your descendants shall all the nations of the earth bless themselves, because you have obeyed my voice." (Gen. 22:1–18 RSV)

The "binding of Isaac" story is one of the most famous passages in all of Scripture—and one of the most challenging. For millennia, Jewish and Christian thinkers have wrestled with its meaning and implications. For the purposes of this book, however, I want to focus on only two points. First, the passage obviously emphasizes Abraham's deep trust that "the LORD will provide." To understand the full importance of this affirmation, we must remember the context in which the whole saga began, namely, a fallen world, "wiped clean" for a new start following the flood. God is working out his redemptive purposes for creation and will make whatever provision is necessary so that those purposes are not derailed. The words "the LORD will provide" do not just speak of Abraham's faith in this specific episode but serve as an affirmation for all the faithful whatever the circumstance. That is why the narrator includes Abraham's naming of the place and the telling phrase "as it is said to this day."

The second point is, I believe, less obvious: while God clearly covenants with specific persons at specific times and specific places, working with and through them to fulfill his purposes, that work cannot be reduced to merely natural processes. Recall my earlier suggestion that God did not covenant with humanity "in general" because in the usual course of events that would tend to favor those who are powerful and important in human terms. In a similar manner, even when choosing this obscure, elderly couple, God did not so embed his purposes in the natural offspring of Abraham and Sarah that the success of those purposes stood or fell with the character—or even survival!—of that offspring. But just as Abraham had faith in God to give him and Sarah a son past their natural childbearing years, so too did Abraham have faith in God even when it seemed God would take that son away—and with the son, the hope that God himself had given Abraham regarding his descendants! Trusting in God, he regained his son, and countless blessings besides. In this, Abraham actually exemplified what Jesus later commanded: "But seek first his kingdom and his righteousness, and all these things shall be yours as well" (Matt. 6:33).

Scripture certainly makes clear that God desires our covenantal partnership, to serve his purposes and our spiritual transformation. But Scripture also makes clear that God will work out his purposes not only with us, but without us, and at times in spite of us. And this realization can actually be a source of reassurance (as well as a continuing prompt to align ourselves more fully with the divine will, as we discern it). Simply consider the unfolding saga of Abraham, Isaac, Jacob, and Jacob's twelve sons in the remaining chapters of Genesis. Summarizing a few highlights from that narrative should illustrate my point. One is that the whole cast of characters is portrayed in all their faithfulness and foibles. Twice, fearing for his life, Abraham had tried to pass Sarah off as his sister rather than wife, with unfortunate consequences (Gen. 12:10–20; 20:1–18; intriguingly, like father, like son: Isaac made the same false claim regarding Rebekah, nearly bringing about the same result in 26:6–11). We saw how Sarah schemed to produce an heir for Abraham through her maid Hagar, yet turned on her when Ishmael was born (16:3–6 and 21:8–13).

Isaac, Jacob, and His Sons

When Abraham and Sarah later seek a wife for Isaac, the search is guided not just by family connections but by the divine hand (Gen. 24:1–27). Rebekah, like Sarah, is at first barren. Yet following Isaac's prayer, she conceives—although the fruit of their union is contentious even before the twins Esau and Jacob are born (25:21–26). It does not help matters that parental favoritism further pits the two against each other (25:27–28). Jacob takes advantage of Esau in a weak moment, gaining the latter's birthright (25:29–34), while later on Rebekah schemes with Jacob to fool his father into giving him a blessing that Isaac thinks he is bestowing upon Esau (27:1–45). Esau is outraged and comforts himself by planning to kill Jacob, so Rebekah urges Jacob to flee to the ancestral home in Haran (27:41–45). On the way he has his dream of the heavenly ladder, and of the Lord's promise of land and offspring, to which he responds by making his corresponding vow (28:12–22).

Jacob comes to stay with his kinsman Laban and falls in love with his younger daughter, Rachel, whom he wants to marry. Laban sets his terms (seven years of labor), but on the day of the wedding he tricks Jacob into marrying his older daughter, Leah. When Jacob complains, Laban has him work another seven years to earn Rachel's hand in marriage (Gen. 29:9–30). Not surprisingly, a degree of rivalry develops between the two women, and eventually between their sons. At last the Lord tells Jacob to return to his father's home in Canaan (31:3). But he is understandably anxious about how he will be received, so he prays for God's deliverance while also sending ahead many gifts in hopes of appeasing Esau's anger. It is on this journey that Jacob encounters the mysterious man with whom he wrestles until daybreak, gaining a divine blessing and a new name: Israel (32:22–31). When he sees Esau approaching with a company of four hundred men, he fears the worst but is stunned when Esau receives him warmly, and the two weep for joy (33:1–4). Jacob eventually settles in Canaan, and the story shifts its focus to the next generation (37:1–2a).

The tale of Jacob's twelve sons then unfolds in all its engaging and telling detail. On the one hand, it is a masterpiece of storytelling, with entertaining plot twists, a colorful cast of characters, and an unexpected protagonist: the simultaneously naïve and arrogant younger son Joseph. But on the other, it is a story of spiritual pilgrimage and growth, as well as the subtleties of God's providential care. The dramatic tension is established at the very outset. Joseph is his father's favorite (exemplified by his receiving the "coat of many colors"), who has vivid dreams of lording it over his brothers. This does not sit well with most of those brothers, who conspire to kill him. Reuben, the eldest son, persuades the others not to murder him outright, and Joseph is instead sold into slavery and taken to Egypt, where he is bought by Potiphar, an officer of the pharaoh (Gen. 37:2–36).

Joseph in Egypt

Now the Lord is "with Joseph" and causes all that he does "to prosper in his hands" (Gen. 39:2–3), which leads Potiphar to make him overseer of his household. Yet this good fortune is soon undone by Potiphar's wife, who, her sexual advances having been rebuffed by Joseph, angrily denounces him as having made sexual advances on her. As a result, Potiphar throws him in prison (39:7–20). Yet the Lord shows steadfast love toward Joseph, giving him favor in the eyes of his jailer, who puts him in charge of caring for the other prisoners (39:21–23). Sometime later, Pharaoh's cupbearer and baker are jailed, and Joseph is charged with caring for them as well. One night each of them has a dream, and they are troubled that they cannot understand the dreams' respective meanings. Joseph asks each to recount his dream so that he might interpret them. He tells the cupbearer that his dream indicates that in three days' time he will be restored to his former position. Joseph asks only that when that happens, the cupbearer put in a good word for him with Pharaoh. This happy interpretation heartens the baker. But when Joseph explains the baker's dream, it is to say that in three days' time the baker will be executed. Each interpretation comes to pass as Joseph has said, yet the cupbearer forgets him (40:1–23).

Has God also forgotten Joseph? Has he forgotten the covenantal pledges he had made to his forebears? Or will he demonstrate his faithfulness in ways that his partners simply do not anticipate? Two years pass and Pharaoh himself has disturbing dreams, which none of the magicians or wise men of Egypt can interpret. Only at this point does Pharaoh's cupbearer remember the promise he made to Joseph. So Joseph is called into Pharaoh's presence, and Pharaoh asks him to interpret his dream. Joseph clarifies that it is not he but God who can disclose the meaning (Gen. 41:16) and, upon hearing the dreams, that it is God actually revealing to Pharaoh what he is about to do (41:25). Joseph then declares that the two dreams (one of seven fat cows being consumed by seven lean ones, and another of seven ears of grain being consumed by seven thin and blighted ones) are in fact the same: they portend the coming of seven years of plenty followed by seven years of famine. Joseph encourages Pharaoh to appoint someone "discerning and wise" to oversee storing up a portion of the bountiful harvests to prepare for the lean years to come—and Pharaoh gives this role to Joseph (41:33–45). This interaction is indeed telling. Joseph says only that Pharaoh should appoint "someone"; he does not promote himself. The self-important Joseph we met at the outset of the story has apparently been humbled by what he has endured. Yet then Pharaoh himself identifies Joseph as the one through whom the spirit of God has been working, thereby making him the one discerning and wise enough to undertake what needs to be done. When the seven years of plenty end, famine extends from Egypt throughout the region. Yet due to Joseph's diligent preparation, grain is available for sale to Egyptian and foreigner alike (41:56–57).

When Jacob learns that food is available, he sends ten of Joseph's brothers (holding back the youngest, Benjamin) to buy grain. They do not recognize Joseph when they appear before him, but he knows them and—perhaps not surprisingly—treats them harshly, accusing them of spying and imprisoning them for three days (Gen. 42:1–17). But Joseph relents, saying he will test them by holding one brother hostage, sending the rest back with food, and requiring them to return with Benjamin. The brothers agree to these terms, believing it is a penalty for what they did to Joseph—still not recognizing that he is the one before them and that he can understand everything they say. He gives them grain and, secretly returning their payment to their bags, sends them on their way (42:18–25). At their first stop, they are stunned and frightened to see the money, presumably because they worry that the Egyptians will think that they have somehow stolen it back.

Eventually that food runs out, and Jacob tells them to go to Egypt once more. The brothers reluctantly set out, bringing Benjamin with them, as well as presents, double the money, and a willingness to explain all that had happened in hopes of gaining mercy. Joseph still does not reveal himself, but he receives them with hospitality, inquiring after their father. When he sees his brother Benjamin, he hurries from the room, lest his ruse be known because he is overcome with emotion. Washing his face and returning, Joseph commands the feast to begin—and the brothers are amazed (Gen. 43:1–34). When the meal is complete, Joseph orders his steward to fill the brothers' sacks with grain and secretly to place his own silver cup in Benjamin's sack. He will test them one more time. When they are a short way off on their return journey, Joseph sends the steward to accuse them of theft and ingratitude. They protest their innocence, but to their horror, when the bags are opened, the cup is found in Benjamin's. They return to Joseph and fall to the ground before him. As a spokesman for them all, Judah confesses: "What shall we say to my lord? What shall we speak? Or how can we clear ourselves? God has found out the guilt of your servants; behold, we are my lord's slaves, both we and he also in whose hand the cup has been found" (44:16). Joseph insists that only Benjamin need stay, but Judah responds that that cannot be because it would break their father's heart. He then relates the details of the vow he made to Jacob and asks that he become a slave in place of Benjamin (44:18–34). At this, Joseph can no longer contain himself, and he reveals his identity to his brothers, saying:

> And now do not be distressed, or angry with yourselves, because you sold me here; for God sent me before you to preserve life. For the famine has been in the land these two years; and there are yet five years in which there will be neither plowing nor harvest. And God sent me before you to preserve for you a remnant on earth, and to keep alive for you many survivors. So it was not you who sent me here, but God; and he has made me a father to Pharaoh, and lord of all his house and ruler over all the land of Egypt. Make haste and go up to my father and say to him, "Thus says your son Joseph, God has made me lord of all Egypt; come down to me, do not tarry; you shall dwell in the land of Goshen, and you shall be near me, you and your children and your children's children, and your flocks, your herds, and all that you have; and there I will provide for you, for there are yet five years of famine to come; lest you and your household, and all that you have, come to poverty." (Gen. 45:5–11 RSV)

So the brothers return, laden with food and gifts, to tell Jacob the good news. Initially, their father does not believe them, but the gifts and the wagons for the return journey convince him (Gen. 45:21–28). Thus, Jacob, his sons, and their extended families all travel to Egypt, to the land of Goshen, where Jacob and Joseph are reunited and the families settle (46:28–30). Matters seem to have resolved themselves. Yet Joseph's brothers worry that he may still hold a grudge against them, and when Jacob finally dies, they are concerned he may now exact retribution. So they approach him, saying, "'Your father gave this command before he died, "Say to Joseph, Forgive, I pray you, the transgression of your brothers and their sin, because they did evil to you." And now, we pray you, forgive the transgression of the servants of the God of your father.' Joseph wept when they spoke to him. His brothers also came and fell down before him, and said, 'Behold, we are your servants'" (50:16–18 RSV). Joseph's response to his brothers, anticipated in the long citation from Genesis 45 just quoted, makes an astonishing theological claim: "Fear not, for am I in the place of God? As for you, you meant evil against me; but God meant it for good, to bring it about that many people should be kept alive, as they are today" (50:19–20 RSV).

God Will Be Faithful and Work Out His Purposes

These words are astonishing not just because they bring comfort to Joseph's brothers and bring this particular story to a close. They also summarize the pattern of God's providence throughout the whole book of Genesis and thereby establish that pattern as that of God's providential activity through-out the remainder of the Scriptures. God will not abandon individuals but remains steadfast—while also employing them to serve his larger purposes. And those larger purposes include his care for his covenantal family, work-ing through their actions and loyalties—and sometimes working in spite of those actions and loyalties. Consider the comments and general conclusion that John Calvin draws regarding Joseph's words:

> He skillfully distinguishes between the wicked counsels of men, and the admi-rable justice of God, by so ascribing the government of all things to God, as to preserve the divine administration free from contracting any stain from the vices of men. The selling of Joseph was a crime detestable for its cruelty and perfidy; yet he was not sold except by the decree of heaven. For neither did God merely remain at rest, and by conniving for a time, let loose the reins of human malice, in order that afterwards he might make use of this occasion; but, at his own will, he appointed the order of acting which he intended to be fixed and certain. Thus we may say with truth and propriety, that Joseph was sold by

the wicked consent of his brethren, and by the secret providence of God. Yet it was not a work common to both, in such a sense that God sanctioned anything connected with or relating to their wicked cupidity: because while they are contriving the destruction of their brother, God is effecting their deliverance from on high. Whence also we conclude, that there are various methods of governing the world. This truly must be generally agreed, that nothing is done without his will; because he both governs the counsels of men, and sways their wills and turns their efforts at his pleasure, and regulates all events: but if men undertake anything right and just, he so actuates and moves them inwardly by his Spirit, that whatever is good in them, may justly be said to be received from him: but if Satan and ungodly men rage, he acts by their hands in such an inexpressible manner, that the wickedness of the deed belongs to them, and the blame of it is imputed to them. For they are not induced to sin, as the faithful are to act aright, by the impulse of the Spirit, but they are the authors of their own evil, and follow Satan as their leader. Thus we see that the justice of God shines brightly in the midst of the darkness of our iniquity. . . . So that whatever poison Satan produces, God turns it into medicine for his elect.[23]

Recall how I described sin as a fundamental orientation away from God, an alienation that disorders or severs the communion with God that he originally intended for us. In that sense, sin alienates us not just from God but from one another, and therefore from our own truest and most authentic selves. Moreover, this sin consists not simply of those acts that we individually do; rather, it is an inherited existential condition, an unavoidable social reality. Nevertheless, when we act out of it, whether individually or collectively, we are responsible—for otherwise we could not take ourselves or others seriously as moral agents. Taken at face value, it seems like a tragic paradox, an absurd and unfair catch-22. Yet we are not left to our own devices in trying to escape the conundrum: if we trust that God does indeed still act even in the midst of human evil, if we open ourselves to the leading of God's Spirit, there is a way out. Joseph has matured, as have his brothers, and they have been reconciled and made aware of deeper currents bearing them along. His words to his brothers are spoken in hindsight, as he looks back over what has happened and acknowledges this greater perspective. But placed here in Scripture, among the last verses of the *first* book, they are also words of foresight and promise, anticipating events to come—not for Joseph and his brothers, but for those reading and hearing these words in their own time of sojourning.

And thus Genesis, as the book of "beginnings," may conclude: the stage has been set, the personality of the main characters described, the providential and

---

23. John Calvin, *Commentaries on the First Book of Moses Called Genesis*, trans. John King (Grand Rapids: Eerdmans, 1948), 487–88.

saving acts of God—along with the habitual waywardness of humanity—have been established, and the general trajectory of the whole story foreshadowed. Now the rest of the story may unfold. And in contrast to other origin stories or assumptions about human nature,[24] in the telling of this story the Bible offers a more humane and perceptive portrayal of our existence when it presents a story of generational connections, of personal and communal rhythms and continuities, and of certain recurring patterns and types. We are indeed aimed toward something new. But the new arrives in fits and starts, and it doesn't simply replace the old as much as it brings it along, building upon and transforming it. This is a story with twists and turns, with dead ends and new beginnings. Yet the fundamental premise has been established: whatever happens, God intends ultimately to bring it to the good. God will, in his own time and in his own way, shepherd his covenant people (and with them the whole of creation) to that final destination he has had in mind from the beginning.

24. See the discussion above regarding creation myths from other cultures claiming different origins for different tribes (p. 7) and the Enlightenment's notion of the tabula rasa (p. 18).

2

The Spirit's Covenantal Role in the Work of the Trinity

The "Two Hands of the Father"

Therefore I want you to understand that no one speaking by the Spirit of God ever says "Jesus be cursed!" and no one can say "Jesus is Lord" except by the Holy Spirit. (1 Cor. 12:3)

But when the fullness of time had come, God sent his Son, born of a woman, born under the law, in order to redeem those who were under the law, so that we might receive adoption as children. And because you are children, God has sent the Spirit of his Son into our hearts, crying, "Abba! Father!" So you are no longer a slave but a child, and if a child then also an heir, through God. (Gal. 4:4–7)

One of Christianity's greatest truths and comforts also stands as one of its greatest mysteries: that God is Father, Son, and Holy Spirit. This is the doctrine of the Trinity, the seemingly paradoxical affirmation that the one God is single in being but three in persons. Of course, it is not the doctrine itself that is comforting but the divine reality to which it points. Still, if many find the doctrine confusing, how can it serve its purpose? Good question! One that requires a thoughtful response, not a formulaic answer.

The Trinity: Personal, Communal, and Real

First, we need to recognize that the doctrine points to some*one* rather than some*thing*. In other words, the doctrine describes a reality that is fundamentally personal rather than something primarily impersonal, abstract, intellectual, or mathematical. This means understanding the Trinity is like becoming friends with someone: you learn some personal details when first introduced, but truly getting to know the person takes time. And even after years, you can still learn new things. So being introduced to God as the eternal Father, Son, and Holy Spirit will never produce immediate comprehension. Questions will remain. But that does not mean the Trinity is a puzzle to be solved or an enigma to be explained—and then laid aside. Rather, it is a mystery beckoning our continuing engagement, so that we may ever more deeply and richly enter into a living, personal relationship with God. Greater than the most profound human friendship, our friendship with and knowledge of God always offer more to learn and enjoy. Indeed, this is what we were made for. That's the point of the famous opening words of the Westminster Shorter Catechism: "What is the chief end of man? Man's chief end is to glorify God, and to enjoy him forever."[1]

The second step is to recognize that the doctrine points to the reality that God has come to us and continues to reach out to us in redeeming and renewing ways. Christians affirm that we were created in God's "image" and according to God's "likeness" (Gen. 1:26) for the purpose of being in communion with one another and entering into that very fellowship which is God himself. "God is love" (1 John 4:8, 16) in eternal, interpersonal relation, and he created us in order to share this relation. As I discussed in the preceding chapter, we often ignore, resist, or reject this divine intention and desire. Yet even when we turn away from God, God reaches out to us through the saving work of Christ and the empowering work of the Spirit so that we might relate to God as a loving Father. God's love is steadfast, always welcoming us home to be reconciled with him and with one another. The comfort and joy this brings are boundless. This is who God is, the one with whom we are made to be in communion.

This is, in a manner of speaking, the "payoff" implied in the fundamental affirmation of classic Christian faith that God is triune: one God existing in three persons (in the ancient Greek formulation, one *ousia* in three *hypostases*). God is fundamentally and irreducibly one and communal. To be sure, the fullness of what this means remains incomprehensible to human

---

1. Office of the General Assembly, Presbyterian Church (USA), *Book of Catechisms— Reference Edition* (Louisville: Geneva Press, 2001), 134.

thought, and yet Christians confess that God may be truly known as Father, Son, and Holy Spirit. God does not exist in the first or most basic sense in undifferentiated unity, and only subsequently as Father, Son, and Spirit. Rather, Father, Son, and Spirit are the way the one God exists at the deepest level. This affirmation is not abstract speculation or human projection but God's own personal self-revelation as Father, through Christ, in the power of the Holy Spirit. It is a divine self-disclosure that retains the divine ineffability yet is also fully trustworthy because God has quite literally given us his Word: the incarnate Son Jesus Christ, who confirms this knowledge in us through the Holy Spirit. In this regard, the theologian Karl Barth did Christian theology a great service in insisting that God's revelation of the Trinity is nothing other than the Trinity revealing itself, that the message is the medium.[2] Revelation is not just the conveying of information (although knowledge is indeed communicated); it is far more a personal self-disclosure and interpersonal encounter.

Furthermore, it is not just that Christians experience God in three distinct modes, while God in himself remains indistinct and singular. The threeness of the one God is not merely a matter of human perception but God's eternal interpersonal reality. The theological tradition describes this reality by distinguishing between the *immanent* Trinity (God in himself, God as such in the divine eternal reality) and the *economic* Trinity (God acting in, and interacting with, creation over time),[3] while also insisting they are at root the same Trinity. God in the eternal, divine inner being is triune, and it is that same Trinity which engages the world. True, in terms of our human experience, the economic Trinity comes first, as evidenced by the early Church's witness in Scripture. The one God of Israel, whom Jesus addressed as Father, was presupposed. But then the earliest disciples of Jesus came to recognize— imperfectly during his ministry, but more clearly after the resurrection—that he was not just a prophet but the Messiah, the anointed Son of God and

2. See Karl Barth, *Church Dogmatics* I/1, "The Doctrine of the Word of God" (Edinburgh: T&T Clark, 1975).

3. The term "economic Trinity" derives from the Greek term *oikonomia*, which referred to the administration or management of an estate or household. While nowadays many people might think the term has to do solely with monetary or financial matters, the original sense of the word was closer to that connoted by the "home economics" courses that used to be common in American high schools. In a theological sense, then, the "economic Trinity" refers to the Triune God's continuing involvement in, and providential "management" of, creaturely life and history. By extension, theologians also speak of the "economy of salvation," which refers to the particular ways in which God carries out the divine purpose of redemption. In neither instance is the focus of "economic/economy" on a technical consideration of money or finances (although God is, of course, concerned with our attitudes toward, and use of, money!); rather, the focus is on God's right ordering or managing of things regarding creation.

risen Lord. And after Jesus's ascension, the earliest disciples experienced the mighty Spirit whom Christ promised he would send to empower and lead them. This manifold encounter with the three-personed God eventually led the Church to develop its formal doctrine of the Trinity. Among other things, this included the affirmation that God's triune nature actually preceded the human experience of it, that it is in fact God's eternal and fundamental reality. Hence, *theo*-logically, the immanent Trinity actually comes first, before the economic Trinity. The relation may be formulated thus: the economic Trinity reveals the immanent Trinity, while the immanent Trinity is the basis for the economic Trinity.

The Doctrine of the Trinity Matters

Now why this concern for a theological topic that leaves so many heads spinning and confused? Aren't such intricate trinitarian ruminations best left to theological specialists? Many do assume that these truths have little or no obvious practical use—but such questions and assumptions could not be more wrong. In fact, trinitarian affirmations have everything to do with practical, everyday Christian faith and practice. I would go so far as to say that without a sense of this trinitarian framework and its practical necessity, Christians almost inevitably fall into idiosyncratic spiritual individualism or insipid, perhaps dangerous, moralism. In any case, they deprive themselves of most of the true riches offered by life in Christ through the power of the Spirit dedicated to the Father's eternal purposes. These riches are grounded in the fact that "the external works of the Trinity are undivided."[4] This ancient theological axiom simply means that when you get one, you get them all: every act of God in the world involves all three persons of the Trinity, and we shortchange our sense of God and involvement with God if we close ourselves off to this reality.

Let me offer a more specific example dealing with the Spirit and the Church. Christians across the theological spectrum recognize the centrality and uniqueness of Christ in God's reconciling relation to the world. To call oneself "Christian" does, after all, connote something different from and more specific than describing oneself as a "theist" or as "spiritual." But among Western Christians (Roman Catholics and Protestants) who regularly speak of God or the Father and Jesus or Christ or the Son, far too many neglect the centrality, uniqueness, and necessity of the Holy Spirit's role in bringing salvation to its

---

4. The phrase has become a common touchstone in trinitarian discussions and traces back to Athanasius (ca. 297–373). The Latin is *opera ad extra trinitatis indivisa sunt* ("First Letter to Serapion," AD 359).

fulfillment. Many observers note that the tremendous worldwide growth of Pentecostalism is a response to this sensed lack. Yet many Christians belonging to the historic mainline denominations, and even many evangelicals, still express unease with Pentecostalism's "recovery" of the Spirit. Their focus remains on Jesus and God. It is as if one is required—or desires—to leapfrog from Christ (whether as "my personal Lord and Savior" or as an inspiring "historical, social activist Jesus" or something in between) directly to God or what God has promised, based on one's own decision, initiative, and efforts. Too often, such approaches betray either an overly personalistic and ahistorical or a highly political and entirely this-worldly understanding of salvation, based on what could be called a "binitarian" understanding of God. Yet as I argued in the previous chapter, the scriptural witness makes it abundantly clear that salvation is a social, covenantal reality that unfolds in time toward a divine end, and that the God effecting this salvation is trinitarian. The Triune God does not save by plucking individuals up to heaven or by us establishing a particular social agenda or political regime following Jesus's example. Rather, salvation is the fruit of God's embedding persons in a community called and sanctified (which is to say, set apart) by the Holy Spirit to be a witness to God's own fulfillment of creation's ultimate goal in the work of Jesus Christ.

On this latter understanding, then, the Church becomes an instrument in the realization of God's purposes, in its own way as important as the events surrounding the life, death, and resurrection of Jesus. This is not because the Church possesses this instrumentality in itself but because *it is the Holy Spirit who wields the Church* as his instrument. In fact, one may say that the Holy Spirit is to Church what the Son is to atonement: both are divine agents undertaking a specific work on behalf of the Father's ultimate redemption of humanity, indeed, of the whole of creation. That is why the third and final article of the Nicene Creed contains what it does:

> We believe in the Holy Spirit, the Lord, the giver of life,
> Who proceeds from the Father and the Son,
> Who with the Father and the Son is worshiped and glorified,
> Who has spoken through the prophets.
> We believe in one holy catholic and apostolic Church.
> We acknowledge one baptism for the forgiveness of sins.
> We look for the resurrection of the dead,
> And the life of the world to come.[5]

---

5. Office of the General Assembly, *The Book of Confessions* (Louisville: Office of the General Assembly, 2002), 3.

The first lines confess belief regarding the *nature*, or ontology, of the Holy Spirit: the Spirit is divine, as being *of* God (i.e., from the Father and the Son) and therefore as *being* God, equally worthy of worship and praise. The article then confesses the *works* of the Spirit, which span from the past to the present to the future: the ancient prophets did not speak on their own; they were the mouthpiece of God's Word spoken through the inspiration of the Spirit. The Church is not a merely human institution, for it was created and is sustained as a work of the Holy Spirit. Baptism is not a merely human ritual or an attempt to manipulate God; rather, it is effected by the Holy Spirit, who thereby makes available the benefits of Christ to believers here and now. Finally, the resurrection of the dead and the new creation also belong to the work of the Holy Spirit because the Spirit is the one who perfects, who brings to final fulfillment and fruition that which the Son first made possible and the Father originally decreed.

The theological ordering of this third article echoes the scriptural witness to God's being and act by indicating that there is a priority among the persons and their work: the Father "sets the agenda" that the Son and the Spirit carry out. Furthermore, one may distinguish between the Son and the Spirit by saying that the Son provides the content and shape to the Father's agenda, while the Spirit is the power enacting it. This is what the New Testament means when it speaks of the Holy Spirit being sent by Jesus, or in Jesus's name,[6] and why the Western version of the Nicene Creed came to describe the Spirit as proceeding from the Father "and the Son" (the infamous *filioque* clause, which the Western Church unilaterally included, much to the dismay of Eastern Orthodox Christians).[7] So while the divine persons do different things, the divine work proceeds in absolute unity and perfect harmony: Father, Son, and Spirit are never at odds with one another, even as each has a distinct, complementary role to play. "The external works of the Trinity are undivided." This is the recurring template evident in the Gospels and epistles of the New Testament, and this template then becomes the lens by which the Church reads and understands the Old Testament as well—following the lead of the risen Lord himself. Consider the following passage from Luke's Gospel:

> Then he said to them, "These are my words that I spoke to you while I was still with you—that everything written about me in the law of Moses, the prophets,

6. See Luke 24:49; John 14:26; 15:26; Acts 1:8.

7. The *filioque* was first officially recognized by the Council of Toledo in 589. Its effect was to emphasize the divinity of the Son and stress the unity of the Son and the Spirit's work. Unfortunately, it was also one of the reasons for the final schism between Roman Catholicism and Eastern Orthodoxy in the twelfth century.

and the psalms must be fulfilled." Then he opened their minds to understand the scriptures, and he said to them, "Thus it is written, that the Messiah is to suffer and to rise from the dead on the third day, and that repentance and forgiveness of sins is to be proclaimed in his name to all nations, beginning from Jerusalem. You are witnesses of these things. And see, I am sending upon you what my Father promised; so stay here in the city until you have been clothed with power from on high."[8] (Luke 24:44–49)

The Holy Spirit, "who has spoken through the prophets," which is to say, inspired everything written in the Scriptures, is the one who provides the anticipation of Jesus's life, death, and resurrection. And the Holy Spirit is also the power that Jesus will send, to clothe the disciples from on high after Jesus has ascended.

Now in following this scriptural portrayal of the Triune God's complementary activity, I am also adopting the early Church tradition that describes the Son and the Spirit as the "two hands of the Father" in accomplishing the divine purposes. The phrase was coined by the second-century theologian Irenaeus of Lyons, and it evocatively depicts the particular, mutually reinforcing work of the Son and the Holy Spirit.[9] Regarding the Father's redemptive intentions, the external or "objective" work of atonement is accomplished by the Son,[10] while effecting the benefits of that work in believers down through the ages is the "subjective" or internal work of the Holy Spirit. The Holy Spirit, the Lord and giver of life, is the one who implants, grows, and perfects Christ's benefits in his followers. The Holy Spirit is (to use the classic philosophical term of Aristotle) the "efficient" cause of the Church: it is the Spirit who establishes the Church's living relation with its risen Lord; it is the Spirit who makes the Church the living body of Christ; it is the Spirit who writes the law on the hearts of this people, making them a living temple in whom God is present. And from a theological point of view, it is crucial that the two hands always be understood together, and as belonging to the Father: the Holy Spirit without the Son is too amorphous and generic; the Son without the Holy Spirit is either merely historical or only a universal human ideal. In this regard, the Son serves as the shape and substance of the Spirit's animating work (in Aristotelian terms, the "formal" and "material"

---

8. See also vv. 13–43 and especially v. 27.

9. See Irenaeus, *Against Heresies*, trans. A. Cleveland Coxe, *Ante-Nicene Fathers* (Grand Rapids: Eerdmans, 1973), 4.Preface.4 (1:463); 4.20.1 (1:487–88); 5.1.3 (1:527); 5.6.1 (1:531); 5.28.4 (1:557).

10. Although not without the Spirit! For a fuller treatment of the Son as the other hand of the Father, see my work *King, Priest, and Prophet: A Trinitarian Theology of Atonement* (New York: T&T Clark, 2004).

causes), thus fulfilling the Father's original intentions and goal (the "final" cause). Salvation is an accomplishment of the whole Trinity, so it inevitably has a trinitarian character.

Errors to Avoid concerning the Trinity

Having said all this, I need to be precise about some of the things I am *not* saying. First, to tie the Holy Spirit so intimately to the Church is not to say that the Holy Spirit's activity is restricted to the Church, any more than it is to say that the Son's activity is confined to atonement. Just as Christianity affirms that the Word has a role to play in the larger theater of creation's beginning, purpose, and consummation, so too does the Holy Spirit have a role to play in the larger theater of divine activity "outside" the Church. And neither am I saying that the Church has to do only, or predominantly, with the Holy Spirit, and not the Son and the Father. As creation is a triune event, as redemption is a triune event, as the eschatological consummation of all things is a triune event, so too is God's establishing, sustaining, and fulfilling the Church a triune event. The ancient maxim still holds true here: "The external works of the Trinity are undivided."

Second, to say that the Church is a "triune event" or trinitarian in character does not mean that it should somehow re-create the intratrinitarian relations of Father, Son, and Holy Spirit. Some theologians have suggested, for example, that because there is a perfect harmony and equality among the divine persons, the Church's institutional structure should mirror this by being nonhierarchical and egalitarian.[11] This position makes a number of theological assumptions that are, in fact, quite debatable in light of the theological tradition. To begin with, it makes certain assumptions about the inner divine reality. On the one hand, its picture of the Trinity as being nonhierarchical and egalitarian does not obviously correspond to the biblical portrayal of Father, Son, and Holy Spirit. As a matter of fact, Jesus's Gethsemane prayer epitomizes a posture evident throughout the Gospels, namely, that the Son is characterized by subordinating himself to the Father: "Not my will, but thine, be done" (Luke 22:42 KJV). Similarly, the Holy Spirit is also portrayed as being subordinate to the Father, and in a certain sense to the Son as well. On the other hand, this position also neglects those parts of the theological tradition that balance

11. For instance, certain liberationist and feminist theologians (e.g., Leonardo Boff, *Holy Trinity, Perfect Community* [Maryknoll, NY: Orbis, 2000]) and some evangelicals (e.g., Millard Erickson, *Making Sense of the Trinity: Three Crucial Questions* [Grand Rapids: Baker Academic, 2000], 90). For a useful discussion of some of the issues, see Miroslav Volf, *After Our Likeness: The Church as the Image of the Trinity* (Grand Rapids: Eerdmans, 1998), esp. 191–220.

our knowledge of God with the humbling affirmation of God's continuing ineffability. While we can truly know God in Christ through the Spirit, while we can gain a true sense of the divine character, this does not mean we can know everything there is to know about God. Divine revelation may enable us to say truthfully that God is Father, Son, and Holy Spirit. Nevertheless, we remain creatures unable to comprehend fully the inner nature of God, so some aspects of that nature remain unknown to us.

And even if the inner divine reality could be comprehended by us, it is still a leap to assume that God's triune relationality can and should then be "brought down to earth" in a rather straightforward fashion to act as a template for determining our social reality. Created in the "divine image and likeness" is taken to mean that the Church somehow mirrors the immanent Trinity. Yet such a move blurs the distinction between the divine and the human, between the Creator and his creatures. It seems to imply that the divine-human communion intended for the Church occurs on a shared ontological level, as if we were no longer creatures in fellowship with God but perhaps demigods. This suggests that the Church would, in some sense, *possess* a "divine nature" in itself. The continuing human character of the Church, particularly in its fallibility, would be obscured. A better approach, in my view, would be to understand the Church's nature as an instrument wielded by God and shaped and reshaped according to the divine will and purpose. The ancient Church father Gregory of Nyssa speaks to this latter approach when he discusses the formation of Christ in believers. Ronald Heine summarizes Gregory's logic in the following way:

> Humanity began, as Genesis 1:27 teaches, in the likeness of God. The goal of Christianity is to restore humanity to this original state. But how, Gregory wonders, can humanity strain forward and become like God. Scripture does not demand, he claims, that human nature become like the divine nature. What it demands instead is that human nature imitate the activities of God, which are the virtues.[12]

Alternately, this "bringing the Trinity down to earth" template could cause a problem in a completely opposite manner. Rather than "deifying" the nature of the Church, it could instead diminish the nature of God in such a way that our conception of God's triune relations is used to justify an all-too-human sociopolitical agenda. We would not, then, be raising ourselves up to become

12. Ronald E. Heine, *Reading the Old Testament with the Ancient Church: Exploring the Formation of Early Christian Thought* (Grand Rapids: Baker Academic, 2007), 189–90. Heine draws his conclusions from Gregory's *Treatise on the Inscriptions of the Psalms*.

demigods but rather bringing God down to our level, so that descriptions of an egalitarian Trinity would really be only a projection of and justification for our prior worldly commitments. Either approach domesticates the transcendent reality of God while deifying the human in ways that could, when applied to the conceptions of the Church, make it dangerously prone to abuse and resistant to correction.

The Holy Spirit, the Lord and Giver of Life to the Church

This should clarify that ecclesiology should not concern itself with abstracting certain trinitarian principles to serve as a timeless blueprint on which to model the Church. This would generalize and spiritualize our understanding of the Church in such a way that we would lose our own creaturely identity and concreteness. Instead, the trinitarian character of the Church means it keeps two touchstones constantly in mind, one universal and the other specific. On the one hand, in all times and places the Church must acknowledge its continuing and total dependence upon the Father, Son, and Holy Spirit's creating, reconciling, and perfecting work. The Church does not exist of itself or from itself, but only as that existence is granted it by God's grace. It derives its being not from the *being* of God but from the free and loving will of God *acting* in particular ways. In that sense, the Church is a "creature," a creation with its own independent being. And we must remain mindful that as with God's other creatures, the Church can be subject to human sinfulness: not just as a victim, but as a perpetrator.

On the other hand, the Church must be ever mindful of its particular covenantal calling within its particular providential location. It must take seriously the specifics of each time and place and discern how God calls it to respond, that it might live more fully into God's intentions for it as a witness and instrument of the divine work. This may mean that at certain times a given church's structure will be more egalitarian, while in other circumstances it may more appropriately be hierarchical. In some places, a "house church" organization may be the most faithful; in others, denominationalism and all that that entails. Whatever the circumstances, the Church must acknowledge its dependence on the particular and diverse activities of the divine persons in establishing it, sustaining it in its eschatological instrumentality, and bringing it to its eschatological fulfillment. Perhaps I can summarize the distinction thus: the Church is trinitarian in the way it allows the Holy Spirit to align its life with the covenantal and saving work of the *economic* Trinity. If the Church's actual life in some manner mirrors the inner life of the *immanent* Trinity, then it does so not so much as the presupposition of its earthly existence but as its goal.

This last observation leads me to return to an earlier statement and pose the question: If the Holy Spirit is to Church what the Son is to atonement, what does this mean more fully and precisely? Consider this parallel: just as it is improper to suppose that humans can save themselves apart from the work of the Son as Savior and Mediator, just so is it improper to suppose that humans can be the Church apart from the work of the Holy Spirit as the Lord and Giver of *new* life, the Advocate and Sustainer of the community of faith. One of the key affirmations of the Reformation was that human beings are justified solely on the basis of God's grace, received by faith. We do not earn our salvation; it is rather a free gift. It is based solely on what God has done for us, rather than any "work" we do on our own behalf—hence, the rejection of any "works righteousness." And this exclusion of any work on our part includes faith itself, which is not understood as a work—that is, as a matter of mental effort or willpower on our part, a human achievement. Rather, faith, too, is understood as a divine gift.[13] To receive this gift requires not an effort on our part but a letting go, an active surrender and trust that what God has done for us in Christ is sufficient for our salvation. The Reformers sought to remedy what could be considered a kind of religious narcissism: they shifted the focus away from a preoccupation with our own inner spiritual efforts and status to the glorious work that God in Christ through the power of the Holy Spirit has done for us. Having accepted this gift, we align ourselves with God's will and purpose for us, so that our subsequent acts are an expression not of our merit but of our gratitude.

The Holy Spirit's Twofold Work in the Church

It is this classic Reformation understanding of salvation—most typically used in descriptions of the individual's salvation—that I will employ in my discussion of the Church as a whole. That is, I will presuppose throughout this book that in relation to the Church the Holy Spirit engages in a twofold work. On the one hand, the Holy Spirit communicates and effects the benefits of Christ for the Church in each age and place, as eternally intended by the Father, both for the community as a whole and for its individual believers. On the other hand, the Holy Spirit also enables, strengthens, and perfects the grateful human response, both for the community as a whole and for its

13. See, e.g., the answer to question 21, "What is true faith?," in the Heidelberg Catechism (1563): "It is not only a certain knowledge by which I accept as true all that God has revealed to us in his Word, but also a wholehearted trust which the Holy Spirit creates in me through the gospel, that, not only to others, but to me also God has given the forgiveness of sins, everlasting righteousness and salvation, out of sheer grace solely for the sake of Christ's saving work."

individual believers. This latter point is likely the one more alien to our usual way of thinking, so it deserves repeating: our response is not to be understood as *our* work and accomplishment—something of which we can boast[14]—but as our openness and surrender to the power and leading of *the Holy Spirit working in us.* That is why the most fundamental act of the Christian, whether communally or individually, is worship: thanksgiving, adoration, and prayer. Indeed, the two classic postures of prayer may be understood as signs of such submission and openness. One is kneeling, with head bowed. The other is standing, with arms up and spread. Nowadays, this latter stance is more typically associated with evangelical or charismatic worship, but in fact it dates back to the first Christian centuries, as evidenced by paintings found in the catacombs. If we then tie this stance to the other common meaning associated with it, the theological point will be obvious and appropriate: it is a posture of surrender—in this case, surrender to the Spirit to live and work through us.

This trinitarian dynamic reaching out to redeem fallen humanity—and the particular twofold work of the Holy Spirit—is based upon many passages of Scripture. One succinct example may be found in Romans 8. Consider this excerpt:

> If the Spirit of him who raised Jesus from the dead dwells in you, he who raised Christ from the dead will give life to your mortal bodies also through his Spirit that dwells in you. So then, brothers and sisters, we are debtors, not to the flesh, to live according to the flesh—for if you live according to the flesh, you will die; but if by the Spirit you put to death the deeds of the body, you will live. For all who are led by the Spirit of God are children of God. For you did not receive a spirit of slavery to fall back into fear, but you have received a spirit of adoption. When we cry, "Abba! Father!" it is that very Spirit bearing witness with our spirit that we are children of God, and if children, then heirs, heirs of God and joint heirs with Christ—if, in fact, we suffer with him so that we may also be glorified with him. (Rom. 8:11–17)

Note how the Holy Spirit is active from both sides: the Spirit, sent by the Father, the one who raised Christ from the dead, is also the one who recapitulates that work in those who are followers of Jesus. Humans cannot accomplish this new life in Christ on their own; it is something for which they are wholly indebted to God, most immediately through the Spirit's agency. The initiative is and remains God's. Yet that divine agency is then mirrored on the human side, because it is that same Spirit who enables us to claim the benefit now available in Christ: to put to death our old ways of acting, to become children

---

14. See Paul's comments in Rom. 3:21–28; 1 Cor. 1:28–31; 4:7; Gal. 6:14; Eph. 2:8–9.

of God (albeit "adopted," rather than natural, as Christ was), to be allowed and enabled to call upon God just as Jesus did: "Abba! Father!"

This trinitarian dynamic emphasizing the Spirit's twofold agency is also evident in Paul's writings to the church at Corinth. In 1 Corinthians 12, Paul clarifies how this twofold work not only benefits the individual as such but is performed so that each member may be an instrument of the Spirit for the benefit of the community as a whole. I will discuss the implications of Paul's image of the Church as Christ's body more fully in chapter 3, but here I note how that body is itself the work of the Spirit.

> Therefore I want you to understand that no one speaking by the Spirit of God ever says "Let Jesus be cursed!" and no one can say "Jesus is Lord" except by the Holy Spirit.
>
> Now there are varieties of gifts, but the same Spirit; and there are varieties of services, but the same Lord; and there are varieties of activities, but it is the same God who activates all of them in everyone. To each is given the manifestation of the Spirit for the common good. To one is given through the Spirit the utterance of wisdom, and to another the utterance of knowledge according to the same Spirit, to another faith by the same Spirit, to another gifts of healing by the one Spirit, to another the working of miracles, to another prophecy, to another the discernment of spirits, to another various kinds of tongues, to another the interpretation of tongues. All these are activated by one and the same Spirit, who allots to each one individually just as the Spirit chooses.
>
> For just as the body is one and has many members, and all the members of the body, though many, are one body, so it is with Christ. For in the one Spirit we were all baptized into one body—Jews or Greeks, slaves or free—and we were all made to drink of one Spirit. (1 Cor. 12:3–13)

The impetus of the Spirit's work is to bring to fruition what Christ has accomplished in furthering the Father's redemptive purposes. And that fruition is not isolated in individuals but occurs among a people: "To each is given the manifestation of the Spirit for the common good." In fact, Paul uses the image of "first fruits" in several of his letters, using it to describe what Christ has done, link it with the benefits he has produced, and explain how the Spirit conveys those benefits to the Christian community.[15] And, of course, the image is all the richer because it draws on a very important Old Testament tradition: the choicest of the harvest's first fruits were reserved for God, as required by Israel's covenant obligations.[16] By offering first fruits, Israel acknowledged in ritual that all comes from God and pledged continuing

15. See Rom. 8:23; 11:16; 1 Cor. 15:20, 23; 2 Thess. 2:13.
16. E.g., Exod. 23:19; Neh. 10:35.

fidelity to God. Remarkably, divine grace now inverts this tradition: it is *God* who brings the first fruits of Christ's resurrection to the community, by means of the Spirit's activity. This epitomizes God's redemptive intentions and pledges his continuing fidelity in the full harvest to come.

Seen more broadly, this "first fruits" imagery evokes a whole season of God's working out the divine purposes. First there is untilled soil, then planting, then germination and growth, then fruition, and finally harvest. In other words, we again recognize that we are dealing with a story, one that has a trajectory or narrative arc that takes time to unfold. While the Bible abounds with organic metaphors and growth analogies, playing a far more central role in the biblical drama is the concept of "covenant."

The Covenant of Grace

> Now the LORD said to Abram, "Go from your country and your kindred and your father's house to the land that I will show you. I will make of you a great nation, and I will bless you, and make your name great, so that you will be a blessing. I will bless those who bless you, and the one who curses you I will curse; and in you all the families of the earth shall be blessed." (Gen. 12:1–3)

> And [the word of the LORD] brought him outside and said, "Look toward heaven, and number the stars, if you are able to number them." Then he said to him, "So shall your descendants be." And he believed the LORD; and he reckoned it to him as righteousness. (Gen. 15:5–6 RSV)

> When Abram was ninety-nine years old, the LORD appeared to Abram, and said to him, "I am God Almighty; walk before me, and be blameless. And I will make my covenant between me and you, and will make you exceedingly numerous." Then Abram fell on his face; and God said to him, "As for me, this is my covenant with you: You shall be the ancestor of a multitude of nations. No longer shall your name be Abram, but your name shall be Abraham; for I have made you the ancestor of a multitude of nations. I will make you exceedingly fruitful; and I will make nations of you, and kings shall come from you. I will establish my covenant between me and you, and your offspring after you throughout their generations, for an everlasting covenant, to be God to you and to your offspring after you." (Gen. 17:1–7)

> Now it is evident that no one is justified before God by the law; for "The one who is righteous will live by faith." But the law does not rest on faith; on the contrary, "Whoever does the works of the law will live by them." Christ redeemed us from the curse of the law by becoming a curse for us—for it is

written, "Cursed is everyone who hangs on a tree"—in order that in Christ Jesus the blessing of Abraham might come to the Gentiles, so that we might receive the promise of the Spirit through faith.

Brothers and sisters, I give an example from daily life: once a person's will has been ratified, no one adds to it or annuls it. Now the promises were made to Abraham and to his offspring; it does not say, "And to offsprings," as of many; but it says, "And to your offspring," that is, to one person, who is Christ. My point is this: the law, which came four hundred thirty years later, does not annul a covenant previously ratified by God, so as to nullify the promise. For if the inheritance comes from the law, it no longer comes from the promise; but God granted it to Abraham through the promise. (Gal. 3:11–18)

"In the beginning God created the heavens and the earth" (Gen. 1:1 RSV). With these words, the story of God's dealings with creation begins. The God of the Bible does not merely create the world and stand aloof. Neither does God lord over that creation as an arbitrary despot. Rather, the Lord God freely establishes ordered and binding relationships with creation: with individuals, with their descendants, and thus with whole peoples, as well as with the earth itself.

That God relates in this manner to humanity—indeed, with the whole earth—is a theme recurring throughout Scripture, and the nature of that relation is defined most explicitly by the biblical term "covenant" (*berit*). God makes covenants again and again through the scriptural narrative—indeed, the Reformed theological tradition emphasizes how the theme of covenant frames the entire biblical story.[17] The term first appears in God's dealings with Noah and his family (Gen. 6:18), then with every living creature following the flood (9:10–17). God then establishes "an everlasting covenant" with Abram and Sarai and their descendants throughout their generations (15:18–21 and 17:2–21), in the process changing their names to Abraham and Sarah, establishing the sign of circumcision, and promising them a land and that they will be ancestors of a multitude of nations. Later, it is on the basis of his covenant with Abraham, Isaac, and Jacob that God takes notice of the groaning of the Israelites under Pharaoh in Egypt (Exod. 2:24) and sets in motion those events by which he will call Moses to be his prophet and their liberator (6:1–8). After freeing the people from their bondage, God leads the people to Sinai, the mountain of the covenant, where God communicates to Moses the precise terms of the relation between God and his people (Exod. 19–31).

The remaining three books of the Pentateuch (Leviticus, Numbers, and Deuteronomy) all elaborate on this covenant in one fashion or another: giving

---

17. Recall my discussion of the *pactum salutis* and *ordo salutis* in chap. 1 (pp. 3, 23).

further details regarding its terms, describing the people's tendency toward violating the covenant and God's responses, and repeatedly admonishing them to remain faithful. These books also make clear that any power or status that the Israelites have is not their own but derives only from the covenant itself, as demonstrated in extraordinary fashion by the events associated with the ark of the covenant, wherein are contained the two tablets. Possessing the ark of the covenant is having God's might virtually present. In one instance, the priests use it to back up the waters of the Jordan River, allowing the people to cross this body of water in a manner recapitulating their passage through the Red Sea (Josh. 3:13–17). Generations after the people have settled in the land, God inaugurates yet another covenant, with David. This one is a dynastic promise that through one of David's descendants God will establish "the throne of his kingdom forever" (2 Sam. 7:12–16; 23:5; cf. Pss. 89:3–4; 132:11–12; Isa. 11:1–5; 55:1–7).

These various covenants established the pattern and the lens by which the people of Israel understood their relation with God. They came to recognize that misfortune befell them when they disobeyed the covenant and that restoration required repentance and return to covenant faithfulness (e.g., Neh. 8:1–9:38; cf. Pss. 78, 105, 106, 111). In particular, the prophetic books of the Old Testament presuppose and build upon the covenantal obligations laid down in the Torah. Hence, it is a serious misreading of the words of Israel's prophets to suppose that they are announcing some new and alternative revelation from God, or that their words derive from the prophets' own personal commitments or some generic or universal ideals. Quite the contrary, their words are based entirely on the covenant. When they speak words of reproach, against either Israel's seeking after other gods or its injustices against the poor and defenseless, it is because Israel has violated the terms of the covenant (e.g., Isa. 24:1–6; Jer. 11:1–13). When they speak words of consolation and encouragement, these arise from God's promise to remain faithful to the covenant (e.g., Isa. 42:5–6; 54:7–19; Ezek. 16:59–60). When Israel was renewed, it was by returning to the terms of the covenant (e.g., Isa. 56:1–8). Indeed, the framework of the covenant came to be understood as extending all the way back to the world's very creation (Jer. 33:20, 25) and projecting into the world's final restoration (e.g., Isa. 11:6–9; 55:13). Mingled with these future hopes was the promise that one day the covenant would be renewed in ways it had never yet realized: that all travail would cease, that creation would be renewed, that the holy city would be restored, that all would know God, that the Spirit would be poured out on all flesh (e.g., Isa. 54:1–10; 65:17–23; Jer. 31:31–34; Joel 2:28–29). And, of course, the first Christians recognized in the life, death, resurrection, and ascension of Jesus that God had indeed fulfilled the promises of the old covenants in a way that effectively established a new covenant.

Scholars note how the covenantal relations between God and humans described in Scripture—particularly in the Old Testament—echo those of ancient Near Eastern "suzerainty treaties."[18] They make the point that such treaties have certain characteristic elements. A key initial aspect is that they are made not between equals but between a sovereign and a vassal. In this regard, they are not like business contracts negotiated between persons of more or less equivalent social or political standing. There are such contract covenants described in Scripture, but they are brokered between two human beings (e.g., Gen. 21:27–32; 31:44–54; 1 Sam. 18:3). The covenants established between God and humans, by contrast, are always initiated by God, indeed, dictated by God. Yet this should not obscure the fact that in such covenants obligation goes both ways, that both parties are bound to act—or not act—in certain ways. To be sure, it is not humanity that binds God to act in these ways. Rather, it is God who places these obligations upon himself. One result of this is that there are instances in the Bible in which God acts according to the covenant obligations not because of anything that his human partners have done or could do—and frequently in spite of what they have done!—but solely in order to honor his own name, to maintain his own covenantal fidelity. In this sense, it is because he has "promised himself" to be and act in this way over against his creatures that God fulfills the covenant.

The nominalist theologians of the late medieval era spoke to this character when they drew a distinction between God's "absolute" and "ordained" power when discussing divine omnipotence. Yes, they reasoned, the almighty God could have created the cosmos in any way he desired. This they defined as God's absolute power. But, they reasoned further, having created it in this particular manner, God has also chosen in certain respects to limit that power in ways that accord with the being, structures, and dynamics of creation. That is, God freely chooses to relate to creation in certain self-binding ways, as well as to allow creation itself its own potentials, its own forms of agency. This free choice by God they termed God's ordained power. These distinctions were not meant to deny God's omnipotence and certainly not God's providential governance of creation. Rather, they sought to describe the divine power and acts—as well as creaturely agency—in more nuanced and precise ways. And in so doing, they also better reflected the complexity of the divine-human relations portrayed in the biblical stories. For while the divine-human covenants

18. For two easily accessible examples, see *The New Interpreter's Dictionary of the Bible* and *The Anchor Bible Dictionary*, s.v. "Covenant."

described in Scripture are not relations between *equals*, they are nevertheless still true *relations*: they entail two distinct participants, each with their own agency. God does not simply manipulate matters like a divine puppeteer. Rather, the fulfillment of the covenantal relation between God and humanity will finally require the personal involvement and choices of both parties. The final outcome of God's covenantal intentions is not in doubt, but it will require faithful shepherding on God's part to bring humanity to its final destination—many times in spite of our own, contrary human inclinations. Scripture's oft-used shepherd/sheep metaphor is apt in more ways than one!

Another aspect of God's covenant that is often overlooked is its transgenerational nature. True, referring to "the God of Abraham, Isaac, and Jacob" has become well known. But is the phrase heard simply as a traditional figure of speech, or docs it evoke a deep-seated sense of God's commitment to later generations based on a covenant made to an earlier generation? The latter is certainly more true to the biblical witness. Perhaps some analogies from everyday life will help explain matters. Imagine a young person applying for a local job. The prospective employer says, "I don't know your work habits and you don't have much experience, but I know your folks and they're good people, so I'll give you a chance and hire you." Or a more serious scenario: a young person is accused of some adolescent vandalism. The sheriff knows the evidence is ambiguous, so when the parents arrive, he says to the accused, "I've met with your mother and father. They seem like good people and they've vouched for you. So I'm giving you the benefit of the doubt and letting you go." Two mundane examples, perhaps, but they do offer a suggestion of the grace involved in God's covenants: God blesses later generations simply on the basis of promises made to earlier generations. Even more, God often displays forbearance toward a later generation, in spite of what it might deserve, precisely because of his pledge of faithfulness to an earlier generation. God may patiently endure the faithlessness of one generation because of the faithfulness of a prior generation—or even more astoundingly, solely on the basis of being faithful to his own promise to a prior generation. There are times when judgment must finally come, and its repercussions may be felt for several generations. But then God's loving-kindness returns, and its effects redound for a thousand generations (e.g., Exod. 34:6–7).

A Reformed Perspective

As I suggested earlier, the Reformed tradition is that branch of Protestant Christianity noted for its incorporation of this covenantal perspective into its theological reflections. The Reformed emphasis on God's "eternal decree" with regard to humanity and its ultimate destiny presupposes this covenantal approach. Creation was not some neutral event that God just happened to undertake, nor was God obliged to relate to what he had created as a result of the act of creation. Rather, Father, Son, and Holy Spirit freely and graciously covenanted among themselves to create a cosmos in order to be in a particular kind of relation with the creatures their work would produce. When humanity fell into sin, that relation was disrupted. But given the Triune God's prior decision and commitment, the Father would not abandon creation to the consequences of this fall. Rather, he would, through the redemptive work of the Son and the sanctifying work of the Spirit, reclaim creation for himself and bring it to the final fulfillment originally intended for it. This commitment is what makes covenant the unifying theme of the Bible.

Some of the earliest voices of the Reformed tradition described this as God's singular "covenant of grace," a covenant that spans both the Old and the New Testaments. As Calvin insisted, "The covenant made with all the patriarchs is so much like ours in substance and reality that the two are actually one and the same."[19] That is, the faithful of the Old Testament are saved by faith in God's grace in Christ just as are the faithful of the New Testament and of later generations. The differences between the Testaments have to do rather with the forms that that covenant took, which Calvin understood as a divine accommodation to different ages. Calvin suggested that the character of the Old Testament covenant of grace tended more toward earthly, rather than spiritual, benefits; it offered figures and types rather than the full disclosure; it was more external and ceremonial than internal; it tended to evoke a bondage rather than freeing of the conscience; and it was confined to one nation.[20] Similarly, the Scots Confession speaks of the "promise" of Christ given to Adam immediately after the fall, which it understands as the promise of Christ's eventual victory over the devil and hence humanity's redemption.[21]

Other Reformed voices, emerging late in the sixteenth century and becoming commonplace in the seventeenth century, came to see God's covenantal relations taking one of two forms: the "covenant of works" and the "covenant of grace." This approach understood God as having created Adam with an innate capacity to obey his commands ("of the tree of the knowledge of good and evil you shall not eat" [Gen. 2:17]) and thus maintain the proper divine-human relationship through a "covenant of works." But with the fall,

19. John Calvin, *Institutes of the Christian Religion*, ed. John T. McNeill, trans. Ford Lewis Battles, Library of Christian Classics 20 and 21 (Philadelphia: Westminster, 1960), 2.10.2, p. 429.

20. *Institutes*, 2.11.1–13, pp. 450–63.

21. The Scots Confession, chap. 4, as found in Office of the General Assembly, *Book of Confessions*, 12.

Adam and Eve lost this capacity, not only for themselves but for all their descendants. God responded by instituting a "covenant of grace," a promise that in Christ the requirements of the first covenant would be fulfilled and the benefits thereof made available to the elect. A classic expression of this approach may be found in the Westminster Confession of 1647:

> The first covenant made with man was a covenant of works, wherein life was promised to Adam, and in him to his posterity, upon condition of perfect and personal obedience.
>
> Man, by his Fall, having made himself incapable of life by that covenant, the Lord was pleased to make a second, commonly called the covenant of grace: wherein he freely offered unto sinners life and salvation by Jesus Christ, requiring of them faith in him, that they may be saved, and promising to give unto all those that are ordained unto life, his Holy Spirit, to make them willing and able to believe.[22]

This dual type of covenantal theology typically goes by the label "federal" theology (from the Latin *foedus*, for "covenant"). One of its characteristics is the way it emphasizes Christ as the new "federal" or representative "head" of humanity, replacing the old "head," Adam. Yet while it differs from the understanding presented by Calvin, there is one noteworthy similarity that might be lost on many modern-day Christians: neither simply equated the "covenant of works" exclusively with the Old Testament and the "covenant of grace" with the New Testament. Rather, both acknowledge that both types of covenant are evident in the Old and the New Testaments alike.

As this comparison between Calvin and the Westminster Confessions suggests, there is no one Reformed understanding of the covenant or of "federal" theology. In fact, there was considerable variety and development of this framework among many different theologians—far too many to summarize here. But that suits my purposes, which are not so much historical as constructive. That is, because there is no standard, orthodox way of employing the covenantal framework, or the dual framework of the "covenant of grace" and "covenant of works," I am free to draw on a variety of voices from the Reformed tradition. I then hope to further develop matters in a way not necessarily bound to those traditions, but only as they help me illuminate what I understand to be required by the scriptural witness. After all, what's normative in the Reformed tradition is not tradition as such but Scripture alone (*sola scriptura*)!

22. The Westminster Confession of Faith, chap. 7, §§2–3, as found in *Book of Confessions*, 128–29.

The Holy Spirit Effects Salvation

All this does suggest, however, that I need to define clearly how I will be using various terms and what connotations I intend for them to carry. I have already said quite a bit about the biblical basis and character of "covenant," including the fact that it is not necessarily between equals. Nevertheless, I do want to make very explicit one key point. On the face of it, a covenant is an agreement of mutual obligation, regardless of how asymmetrical: one party promises to do these things, the other party those things. If either party fails to keep the stipulated promises, the covenant has been violated. If this happens, certain penalties or punishments may be imposed, or perhaps the covenant is simply rendered null and void. Whatever promises and obligations are involved, each party is understood as being accountable in acting to uphold his or her side of the covenant. Each party is an "agent," that is, one who has the ability and responsibility to act. The key claim I am making throughout this book and its description of God's covenantal relation with the Church is this: it is the Holy Spirit who acts as the effective agent of the Father in communicating Christ's benefits to us, *and* it is the Holy Spirit who acts as the effective agent in us to enable and strengthen our grateful human response.

In other words, the "covenant of grace" refers not just to God's Spirit-effected *giving* but also to our Spirit-effected *receiving* and our Spirit-effected *response*. It is as though, in effect, we are invited into a trinitarian dance in which the Spirit leads and also enables us to follow. The first step is God's saving gift to us, made known to us by the Spirit. Specifically, it involves God the Father's saving communication of Christ's benefits to us through the Spirit's power. The second step is our act of receiving it. Specifically, the Spirit joins with our spirits in our faithful acceptance of the giver and the gift. The third step is our own thankful response to God. On the face of it our own human agency might now seem to take precedence. But here, too, God is at work, because this active gratitude is our Spirit-enabled thankfulness and response in Christ to the Father, which includes our discipleship and obedience to the divine commandments. (One cautionary note: in delineating the movements of this dance metaphor, I don't mean to have you focus so much on your steps that you are never able to let go and move with the divine rhythm!) My key point in this image of the divine-human dance is to assert the pairing of covenantal grace and covenantal gratitude, with the initiative always coming from God, and to assert that our response—while truly our response—is likewise Spirit-enabled.

Another way of describing this is the Reformation principle that we are "justified by faith in God's grace." That is, we are "made right" or reconciled with God not on the basis of our own efforts but by simply trusting that what God the Father has done in Christ through the power of the Holy Spirit suffices. Our place is to believe, to have faith—and to know that that faithful acceptance of God's grace is *not* itself a human work. It is not a psychological state we must attain or a spiritual effort we must exert in order to merit or receive what God offers. Faith is itself a gift that God gives through the Holy Spirit so that we need not worry about meeting any preconditions. In human terms, faith is not an achievement but a surrender, a letting go, a trust in what God has promised, has accomplished, and is working out. It actually liberates us from any preoccupation or spiritual self-absorption with what we must do or think or feel.

In common usage, we are "saved" not by anything we can do but simply by acknowledging what God has done for us. But here we should be more precise in our theological language, namely, in describing the relation between justification, sanctification, and "glorification." Among many American evangelicals, answering "yes" to the question "Are you saved?" is frequently also followed by a description of one's personal conversion experience. The well-known hymn "Amazing Grace" speaks to this experience: "I once was lost, but now am found; was blind, but now I see." Technically, this sort of language describes the experience of justification, the recognition of having left behind one's sinful old life and being reconciled to God and given a new life. It is like being rescued from drowning or from some other life-threatening danger: you would say to your rescuer, "You saved me." In theological terms, this meaning of saving is the turning point—and yet it is also only the beginning. You have been justified; now what? While salvation is made available in Christ once and for all, nevertheless the individual's incorporation of salvation is not just something that happens once, nor is it simply the final goal. It is a new way of living that becomes deeper and richer over time (sanctification) until it reaches its final consummation (glorification). The language of salvation needs past, present, and future tenses: "I have been saved; I am being saved; I will be saved."

Having described the notion of "covenantal gratitude" above, I will flesh it out more fully by employing it to develop my understanding of the Reformed emphasis on the "third use of the law." In Calvin's *Institutes*,[23] he discusses the roles played by the law given by God to Moses. The first use of the law is to demonstrate the righteousness of God and to illustrate by contrast humanity's unrighteousness and its inability to keep the law. Despairing of our own abilities, we are driven to the grace of God. The second function of the law is

23. Calvin, *Institutes*, 2.7.6–15.

to control those who, unrestrained by pangs of conscience, will nevertheless be deterred from evil behavior by a fear of punishment. The third, and to Calvin principal and proper, use of the law is as an instrument of instruction and exhortation for believers to more thoroughly know and follow God's will for them. In the Lutheran tradition, by contrast, the emphasis was always on the first of the uses as the principal and proper one.

Covenant of Works and Covenant of Grace

So, where do I start? Let me begin where the tradition usually begins, with Adam and Eve, and give an example of how I will employ the covenantal framework. Were our first parents created under the covenant of grace or the covenant of works? While the tradition represented by the Westminster Confession says "works," a case can be made for both. Evidence for it being the covenant of works may be found in God's word to Adam, which certainly sounds like a laying down of the divine law: "And the LORD God commanded the man, 'You may freely eat of every tree of the garden; but of the tree of the knowledge of good and evil you shall not eat, for in the day that you eat of it you shall die'" (Gen. 2:16–17). Language such as "commanded" and "you shall not" seems self-evidently in the realm of the work required of this new human.

It comes across as a rather stern decree, but need we necessarily consider it as such? First of all, the Hebrew word translated by the English word "command" (*tsavah*) at root means "to constitute" or "enjoin." While "command" is the most common English translation in this verse, the original Hebrew term has connotations that might soften our English usage: to "appoint," to "bid," and to "commission" (for a task). What if we were to hear God's word to Adam not so much as a stern commandment but in more gentle tones, as encouraging and caring instructions—perhaps along the lines of a parent teaching a child to ride a bicycle? ("Keep your speed up, it'll help you keep your balance—and don't make any sudden turns or you will fall.") And besides that, note how the very first words to Adam are in fact not an injunction ("You shall not") but a *permission* ("You may freely eat . . ."). These words are more akin to explaining the use of a generous gift. Perhaps this should lead us to hear God's initial words to Adam less as a strict law, and more as a practical explanation of how things are in this new creation and how Adam may most fully fit into it. If this is the case, it seems as if the operative covenant here is that of grace. Indeed, perhaps both covenants are involved here, harmoniously intertwined in ways we tend to miss.

Let me follow another Reformation principle (of using Scripture to interpret Scripture) to explain myself further. How the apostle Paul understands the law and its role is suggestive here. In his letter to the Galatians, Paul writes that the law was "added because of transgressions" (Gal. 3:19). In his Letter to the Romans, he writes,

> If it had not been for the law, I would not have known sin. I would not have known what it is to covet if the law had not said, "You shall not covet." But sin, seizing an opportunity in the commandment, produced in me all kinds of covetousness. Apart from the law sin lies dead. I was once alive apart from the law, but when the commandment came, sin revived and I died, and the very commandment that promised life proved to be death to me. (Rom. 7:7–10)

What he describes is the way we experience the commands of the law—in my terms, when we are confronted by the covenant of works—within the context of our sin and estrangement from God. When Paul cries out a few verses later, "I do not understand my own actions. For I do not do what I want, but I do the very thing I hate" (Rom. 7:15), he gives voice to a sense of self-alienation that is perennially contemporary.

Yet this was not the context of our first parents, when they first received God's words. Our original and true human being was made to be grounded not in alienation and estrangement but rather in harmony with God, one another, and our surrounding environment. So even if we think of God's original word to Adam and Eve as a commandment, it certainly had a different character for them than the later commandments of the law would have for their fallen progeny. It seems rather that in the creation stories of Genesis we have both the covenant of grace and of works intertwined in harmony. This means that before the fall, and contrary to the tension described by Paul, the original pair initially did what God and their own being inclined them to as a matter of course. In their original creation, Adam and Eve had a built-in orientation to be and to act in alignment with God's intentions for and promptings of them. They did not experience God's command as an external, alien law because humanity's inner spirit was simply and without inner conflict receptive to the Spirit's orienting it toward its proper end. In this sense, humanity was truly free because it was not restrained *from* acting, or constrained *to* act, in any way *contrary to its deepest and true nature*. As originally created and oriented, humanity was in harmony with itself, with creation, and with God. This was the gracious gift humanity received in its creation that enabled its faithful response. In my reading of Scripture and the tradition, then, the covenant of grace comes first chronologically and theologically. The covenant of works is dependent upon and follows it, but was not initially experienced as an imposition, something that actually had to be worked at *against* our inclination. Rather, "working at it" was what humanity was originally and simply inclined to do—more akin to what we now construe as play than to labor.

This is not to say that the covenants of grace and works are equivalent with creation, that they are somehow embedded in the very being of creation. Creation, after all, can and did fall. It can, and did, become disoriented, corrupted, disordered. To borrow from Karl Barth, the covenant of grace is the (internal) basis of our creation, while God's act of creation is the external basis for the covenant of grace—but they are not two names for the same thing.[24] The fact *that* we exist is indeed a gift of God's gracious love. But that existence has a purpose, a telos: it has a journey that it is made to undertake. Therefore, it is not fully itself until that journey is completed. To illustrate what I mean by this, let me offer a "what if" thought experiment. What if Adam and Eve had not succumbed to the serpent's temptation? What if humanity had not fallen then or even in later generations? Based on the movement of the creation narratives, including the "assignments" given to all creatures, it seems we still would have had a future goal toward which to orient our lives and various tasks to complete in order to fulfill God's intentions for us.[25]

Many early Christian theologians, especially those in the East, understood our human goal, our telos, to be *theosis*, a "divinization," a being like God. They did not mean by this that we are to become gods, that our human substance or essence will be transformed into a divine substance or essence. This is ruled out by the requirement of Christian monotheism. Rather, they meant that as creatures, we have a destiny to become as perfectly aligned with God's will and purposes as our natures allow. One could say that our goal is to become the harmonics reverberating to the love and communion existing among the triune persons themselves. Yet we are finite and God is infinite; we are temporal and God is eternal. How can such an alignment or theosis be possible? In effect, these theologians answered: over time, asymptotically. That is, as creatures we remain fundamentally distinct in being from our Creator. But over *time*—which, with our *being*, we are also given at creation—we are granted the possibility of aligning our existence ever more closely and harmoniously with that of God and his purposes for us. Hence the label "asymptotic": it is a geometric term describing two points that are initially

24. See Karl Barth, *Church Dogmatics* III/1, *The Doctrine of Creation*, §41: "Creation and Covenant."

25. While the Reformed tradition typically avoids such speculative questions, in fact Calvin suggests something analogous when he states that the Son still would have had to become incarnate even without the fall: "Even if man had remained free from all stain, his condition would have been too lowly for him to reach God without a Mediator" (*Institutes*, 2.12.1, p. 465).

infinitely separate but that progressively approach each other even though they never finally merge.

So what does this have to do with my "what if" question? It makes the point that Adam and Eve represented the "infancy" of the human race and that even without the fall, God meant for us to have time to mature and reach the full potential originally intended in creation.[26] Now this should not be taken, in a condescending and literal way, to mean that our ancestors were immature or primitive and that only we moderns represent humanity "come of age" (as has too often been the claim in a secularized way since the Enlightenment). In matters technological perhaps we are more adept, but in matters spiritual we are frequently more naïve and superficial. Rather, it means that the full human story, whether individual or corporate, cannot be captured merely in a description of our origins or in a snapshot of some point along the way. We must allow the whole to unfold so that we may take the whole into account. It will not be captured in some terse definition but will be much more akin to a sprawling, nineteenth-century Russian novel. Such a trajectory, I am hypothesizing, would have been God's plan for creation and humanity even without the fall into disorder, alienation, and sin. And so it remains, even with humanity's fall, even with our collective original sin. In any case, this means that the full human story will be a narrative, with a beginning, a middle, and an end—just as the Bible has a beginning, a middle, and an end. It is a narrative that in fact starts in a garden with a man and a woman (Genesis), recounts human sinfulness and God's redemptive acts, and ends in a city—a particular city, Jerusalem— with its gates open to welcome all the nations of the world (Revelation). Only now, because of our disorientation and sin, when we encounter the covenant of works we inevitably experience it as an alien, external law, something that binds our freedom. And we are even suspicious of the covenant of grace because we sense it must be too good to be true: it must have hidden strings attached.

Three Biblical Images for the Church: Why These Three?

Now you are the body of Christ and individually members of it. (1 Cor. 12:27)

But you are a chosen race, a royal priesthood, a holy nation, God's own people, in order that you may proclaim the mighty acts of him who called you out of darkness into his marvelous light.

26. This understanding was first advanced with theological sophistication by Irenaeus of Lyons in his *Against Heresies*. A useful summary description is presented by John Hick, *Evil and the God of Love* (New York: Macmillan, 1966).

Once you were not a people,
> but now you are God's people;
once you had not received mercy,
> but now you have received mercy. (1 Pet. 2:9–10)

Or do you not know that your body is a temple of the Holy Spirit within you, which you have from God, and that you are not your own? For you were bought with a price; therefore glorify God in your body. (1 Cor. 6:19–20)

The notion of covenant is a very helpful and relevant theme running through the Bible, but to give it some concrete particularity I will explain it more precisely by employing three "images" of the Church derived from Scripture and the theological tradition. My goal is not to come up with some new and original understanding of the Church, but rather to reclaim, refresh, and interconnect traditional understandings in the hope of making them living and fecund options for our current context. These images will be unpacked in the following three chapters, describing how the Church is "the body of Christ," "the people of God," and "the temple of the Holy Spirit." Having made this choice, we could ask the questions, "Why three images rather than just one? And if more than one, why not two—or more than three? And if only three, why *these* three?"

The Diversity of Biblical Images for the Church

To begin with, it is important to know that the Christian faith has never had a singular definition or dogma of the Church analogous to the way it does, say, regarding the person of Christ or the Trinity. The orthodox definition of Jesus as the Christ is that he is fully human and fully divine, one person with two natures. Similarly, the Triune God is defined as being one nature in three persons. The most classic instance of such definitions is the Nicene Creed.[27] Its three articles or sections affirm the existence of God as Father, Son, and Holy Spirit, while its middle article devotes several lines to affirming and explaining the Son's divine nature (his human nature being presupposed). That the Church as such is included in the creed—specifically

27. More properly and awkwardly called the Niceno-Constantinopolitan Creed, in that the creed currently labeled the Nicene Creed was the product of an ecumenical council held in AD 325 that was later revised and expanded by another ecumenical council meeting in Constantinople in AD 381. And this does not address the unilateral addition (the "*filioque*" clause, i.e., that the Holy Spirit proceeds from the Father "*and the Son*") that began appearing in the Roman Catholic Church several centuries later. The *filioque* was both a symptom and a cause of the growing rift between the Latin-speaking Western and the Greek-speaking Eastern Church.

in the article dealing with the being and work of the Holy Spirit—does indicate that the Church's existence is in some manner an article of faith. That is, faithful Christians cannot simply choose to believe in God and decide not to believe that God also intends the being and work of the Church. But the Nicene Creed does not devote a similar amount of time to explaining what it means by "Church" apart from the terms that have come to be known as its four "marks" or "notes": the Church is one, holy, catholic, and apostolic. I will say more about these four marks below. But suffice it to say for now that in affirming these constitutive characteristics of the Church, the Nicene Creed does not unpack what they mean precisely. They are more a starting point for theological reflection than the conclusion of such reflection, in the way that creedal statements concerning the Trinity and Christology are. In other words, there is not just one ecumenically accepted, orthodox definition of "Church."

But this is not necessarily a problem. In fact, this seeming lack of specificity actually serves the variety of the biblical witness as well as displaying some practical wisdom for the Church's ongoing life and work. In this regard, it parallels the fact that there is no one orthodox understanding of Christ's *work*, even though there is one orthodox understanding of his *person*. The biblical witness makes clear that "Jesus saves" in a variety of complementary yet distinct ways.[28] At various times for diverse peoples, differing emphases may arise. Salvation may be redemption from an alien captivity or spiritual evil; it may be reconciliation with God overcoming one's own sin and guilt; it may be a spiritual enlightenment; or it may be some combination thereof. Scripture portrays God the Father's saving work in the Son through the power of the Holy Spirit as meeting the captive, the sinful, and the lost where they are—and then taking them beyond that. Similarly, the Bible describes the nature and work of the Church with an abundance of images and metaphors. Which ones are most aptly applied in a given situation depends upon listening to the Spirit and faithfully discerning among the available choices.

What are some of these various labels, analogies, and rubrics? A classic description of the diversity remains Paul Minear's book *Images of the Church in the New Testament*,[29] a work for which the author was commissioned by the World Council of Churches. On a quick perusal of the book, one is immediately struck by the enormous variety. He presents and discusses ninety-six distinct "images" for the Church, making clear, however, that not all the images

28. This is a key argument in my *King, Priest, and Prophet*.
29. Paul Minear, *Images of the Church in the New Testament* (Philadelphia: Westminster, 1960).

are of equal importance and usefulness. Of the thirty-two "minor" ones, he includes metaphors such as "salt of the earth," "a letter from Christ," "the ark," "branches of the vine," "God's planting," "God's building," "virgins," "bride of Christ," "citizens," and "exiles."[30] The remaining sixty-four images he groups together, discussing them under one of four general chapter headings: "The People of God," "The New Creation," "The Fellowship in Faith," and "The Body of Christ."[31] The sheer number of images is itself telling, for it suggests that no one image can be comprehensive and sufficient. Why? On the one hand, Minear explains that this is due in part to the nature of the reality being described. The Church is, in some fundamental sense, a mystery. As such, it can be spoken of only figuratively, and no one figure can exhaust all possible meanings of the reality. On the other hand, the purpose in selecting the particular image may have itself been limited. For example, it might have been chosen to assert a particular characteristic, to refute or correct a particular misunderstanding, to describe a particular function, or to enjoin a particular understanding or action for a specific time, place, or occasion. As for the interrelation of all the images, Minear calls for "at least three kinds of thinking, each quite difficult in itself": the "synoptic," the "reciprocal," and the "retroactive" or "depth thinking."[32] The first refers to seeing all the images at once in a kind of "single panorama." His point is for the faithful to have a general impression, an overall sense for the essence and character of the Church that these various images produce together. The second refers to the way that the individual images may overlap to a degree but also be distinct, thereby mutually reinforcing and expanding our understanding. And the third way of thinking refers to our effort to recover what the original author had in mind with a particular image.[33]

So how is this relevant for us today? And for this book in particular? Regarding the first question, the multitude of scriptural images gives the current Church an extensive vocabulary with which to understand and evaluate itself—but that understanding and evaluation is not automatic. This is why Minear says we must engage in "retroactive" thinking: we need to understand each image in its original context, rather than just hearing them according to our modern connotations. But the task is more than just one of historical reconstruction. We also need to open ourselves to the ancient Church's understanding of how the Spirit communicated through Scripture. In part, this means reclaiming the ancient practice of seeing life typologically "figured"

30. Ibid., 29–64.
31. Ibid., 66–104, 105–35, 136–72, 173–220.
32. Ibid., 221.
33. Ibid.

throughout the whole narrative of Scripture. The latter-day Church still bears the responsibility for listening to the Spirit while it reads Scripture, so as to discern which of the images best fit its own circumstances. This is where Minear's other two ways of thinking can help. The abundance of biblical images for the Church can serve as both an inspiration and a corrective as we seek to play our part in the unfolding drama presented there. Minear's three ways of considering the images cannot help but expand our own thinking about the nature and purpose of the Church.

Choosing the Best Images for Our Purposes

As for Minear's relevance to my own project, I too will focus on several of the primary biblical images he emphasizes (i.e., body of Christ, people of God, and temple of the Holy Spirit). And like him, I will also try to show their synoptic and reciprocal relation. I will suggest how together they give a broader picture of the Church than the sum of their parts might indicate, while also showing how some of the "lesser" images enrich and relate to the broader ones. But in the end, my project has a different purpose from that of Minear's book. His book is more a project in biblical and historical theology, while mine is more a constructive or systematic theology. More specifically, it is an ecclesiology, which is to say, a *theological* understanding of the nature and purpose of the Church—as opposed to a sociological, institutional, cultural, or political understanding and exposition. It presupposes that the Church is primarily a divine, and not a human, work. That is, in the first instance, the Church is that gathering "called forth" (i.e., *ekklēsia*) by God the Father, founded upon Christ "the cornerstone," and created and sustained by the Holy Spirit. While any thorough exposition of an ecclesiology may well include historical, sociological, institutional, and political analyses—as well as the theological recognition of our human fallenness—these aspects themselves should not be considered constitutive of that ecclesiology. This is so for the simple reason that these various worldly aspects of the Church are variable according to time and place. Instead, what is constitutive is the Church's animating source and principle, the Holy Spirit, who makes the Church the body of Christ, serving the purposes and goal of God the Father in creation and redemption. I will address this claim more fully in the chapters to come.

To be sure, just as Christ took flesh and was not a docetic apparition, so too will the "body of Christ" (the Church) have "fleshly" form. But that form itself will show some diversity to correspond to the diversity of human cultures in which it is "incarnated." The Church as it has actually existed down through the centuries and across cultures is not simply a clone of the "original" Church in Jerusalem. For just as one church itself has members who are not all the same, yet all belong to the body, so too does the Church universal have many members who are not all the same yet belong to the universal body. In other words, different churches will have different historical, sociological, institutional, and political forms, and no one of them is necessarily a truer church than the others on the basis of those forms alone. What constitutes them as a church has less to do with external forms than with a fundamental orientation, posture, and confession of faithfulness to what God has done in Christ through the power of the Spirit. That is why in the Protestant tradition the touchstones of what defines the "true Church" have been surprisingly minimalist.[34]

So why employ only three images to discuss the nature and purpose of the Church, when there are so many more scripturally available? For both practical and theological reasons. Consider the following circumstance from everyday life: a single occurrence of something is often not even noteworthy; twice may be construed as a coincidence; a third time suggests the beginning of a pattern. In a similar way, employing three different but complementary images to describe the Church should be enough to indicate that a single image really does not suffice, while also conveying the point that differing images both mutually reinforce and can correct one another. And I have chosen these three particular images because they also lend themselves to clarifying the Triune God at work in all understandings of Church. Stated more forcefully, I believe these three can serve to anchor ecclesiology to the Trinity and to the Church's eschatological purpose.

My first rubric, "the body of Christ," will focus on the Church's self-identity and thus the various ways in which the Church is internally constituted. It will discuss worship and the priesthood of all believers. Several key topics will

---

34. Thus, e.g., the Lutheran Augsburg Confession of 1530, in Article 7, states simply: "The Church is the congregation of saints, in which the Gospel is rightly taught and the Sacraments rightly administered." To be sure, Luther later expanded on this definition to include seven signs by which a "poor confused person" could identify "the holy Christian people" in this world. These included (1) possessing God's holy Word, (2) correct administration of baptism, (3) correct administration of the Lord's Supper, and (4) Church discipline (the "power of the keys") publicly administered. Moreover, the true Church (5) consecrates clergy to administer these, (6) has public worship and catechesis, and (7) lives a "theology of the cross," that is, a life of self-sacrifice like the life Christ lived (*Luther's Works* 41:148–64). John Calvin's brief definition, as found in his 1559 edition of the *Institutes*, was similar to that offered in the Augsburg Confession, with one key addition: "Wherever we see the Word of God purely preached *and heard*, and the sacraments administered according to Christ's institution, there, it is not to be doubted, a church of God exists" (*Institutes* 4.1.9, pp. 1011–24, emphasis added). Others in the Reformed tradition (e.g., Martin Bucer and the Scots Confession) expanded this to include the "power of the keys," but otherwise maintained a distinctly minimalist definition.

include a theology of infant baptism and the Lord's Supper as exemplifying the covenant of grace, with confirmation and "the priesthood of all believers" exemplifying the covenant of works. My second rubric, "the people of God," will place the Church in its broader covenantal and biblical context. It will develop around the biblical emphasis on God's sovereignty that traces like a red thread through both the Old and the New Testaments. This in turn will allow some important things to be said concerning the relation of Judaism and Christianity, and the ways in which both are subject to the covenants of grace and of works. This second rubric, therefore, will also be a bit of a hybrid, in that I will also combine the common theological label "the people of God" with the recurring emphasis in Jesus's preaching on the "kingdom" or "reign of God." One overarching point will be to emphasize that God's people are to be a blessing to the world. Finally, my third rubric, "the temple of the Holy Spirit," allows me a more biblical and concrete way of reintroducing the Spirit into the everyday life of the Church and of individual Christians. Among many, the Holy Spirit is the "missing" third person of the Trinity—and in that absence too many Christians in fact miss out on the joy and strength that is meant to be theirs. This third rubric will also allow me to counter an all-too-common tendency of using appeals to the Holy Spirit for what could be called antinomian purposes: that is, as a way of diluting or rescinding certain traditionally acknowledged requirements for Christian living. To the contrary, I will connect Pentecost and Sinai, and seek to reclaim and describe the tradition of "the power of the keys," that is, Church discipline.

3

The Body of Christ

The Spirit and God's Reconciling, Healing Purposes

Then came the day of Unleavened Bread, on which the Passover lamb had to be sacrificed. So Jesus sent Peter and John, saying, "Go and prepare the Passover meal for us that we may eat it." . . . So they went and found everything as he had told them; and they prepared the Passover meal.

When the hour came, he took his place at the table, and the apostles with him. He said to them, "I have eagerly desired to eat this Passover with you before I suffer; for I tell you, I will not eat it until it is fulfilled in the kingdom of God." Then he took a cup, and after giving thanks he said, "Take this and divide it among yourselves; for I tell you that from now on I will not drink of the fruit of the vine until the kingdom of God comes." Then he took a loaf of bread, and when he had given thanks, he broke it and gave it to them, saying, "This is my body, which is given for you. Do this in remembrance of me." And he did the same with the cup after supper, saying, "This cup that is poured out for you is the new covenant in my blood." (Luke 22:7–8, 13–20)

But when Christ came as a high priest of the good things that have come, then through the greater and perfect tent (not made with hands, that is, not of this creation), he entered once for all into the Holy Place, not with the blood of goats and calves, but with his own blood, thus obtaining eternal redemption. For if the blood of goats and bulls, with the sprinkling of the ashes of a heifer, sanctifies those who have been defiled so that their flesh is purified, how much more will the blood of Christ, who through the eternal Spirit offered himself without blemish to God, purify our conscience from dead works to worship the living God! For this reason he is the mediator of a new covenant, so that those who are called may receive the promised eternal inheritance, because a death has occurred that redeems them from the transgressions under the first covenant. (Heb. 9:11–15)

In the life, death, and resurrection of Christ the Son, God the Father has reconciled the world to himself. He has brought the old covenant to fruition and established a new one, overcoming the bondage, sin, and ignorance that have kept human beings from full and loving communion with him, with one another, and with creation. A new people has been created, with a new basis for its life, because those things that had separated humanity from God have been overcome. Christ accomplishes this reconciliation in his office as the mediating Priest, offering his own body and blood upon the cross.[1] This understanding is grounded in Jesus's ritual words and acts at the Last Supper, which explained the events that were to follow. Gathering his disciples together as faithful Jews to celebrate Passover, that holiday commemorating God's redemption of the people of Israel from their bondage in Egypt, Jesus had spoken of a new divine act, a new covenant. He told them of forgiveness of sins, newness of life, and the coming kingdom of God. No doubt, the disciples' hopes were raised and their hearts thrilled—only to be dashed with the seemingly catastrophic events of Jesus's arrest, trial, and execution. Yet God vindicated Jesus by raising him from the tomb, having put to death the "first Adam" and making available a fresh start for humanity through the "last Adam" (1 Cor. 15:45–49). This is the gospel—literally, the "good news" of God—which, when received with the faith that the Holy Spirit inspires, establishes a new creation and evokes both awe-filled joy and worship. Certainly Jesus's earliest followers responded this way when they encountered him following his resurrection,[2] and it is what bound them together as the first community of Christian faith, as the newborn Church. In his risen presence, the disciples knew that a new age had dawned.

Yet according to Christian scripture and tradition, Jesus Christ has ascended to sit "at the right hand of the Father," meaning that he is no longer present with his community the way he was with the original disciples. Does this differing circumstance put all later generations of Christians at a disadvantage when compared to his first followers? Does this mean that he is now just a figure from the past, available to his modern-day followers only through historical recollection or reconstruction? It might, if Jesus's mere physical

1. For an extended treatment of Christ's priestly work, see my *King, Priest, and Prophet: A Trinitarian Theology of Atonement* (New York: T&T Clark, 2004), chap. 4.
2. See, e.g., Matt. 28:8–9, 16–17; Luke 24:36–41, 50–52; John 20:19–20, 27–28.

presence were the decisive factor in communicating God's divine grace and the individual's grateful response. But as Jesus said to "doubting Thomas": "Have you believed because you have seen me? Blessed are those who have not seen and yet have come to believe" (John 20:29). Consider as well Paul, arguably the most influential of the apostles, who never knew the "historical Jesus" but was called through a heavenly revelation.[3] Besides, as the Gospels illustrate time and again, even the disciples misunderstood Jesus during his earthly life and did not immediately recognize him during his postresurrection appearances. Such recognition and understanding depend upon having the "eyes of faith."

And the "eyes of faith"—by which is meant a true perception of Jesus's life, words, and deeds—are a gift given by the Holy Spirit. This point was anticipated earlier in Jesus's lifetime by his response to Peter, following Peter's confession of him as the Messiah: "And Jesus answered him, 'Blessed are you, Simon son of Jonah! For flesh and blood has not revealed this to you, but my Father in heaven'" (Matt. 16:17). Jesus did indeed embody and enact the gospel, but it is *God* who enables the gospel's reception—and as I have clarified in the preceding chapter, the Father's enabling power is the Holy Spirit.[4] This was true during Jesus's earthly life two millennia ago, as evidenced by multiple scriptural passages describing how even he is "enabled" by the Spirit.[5] And it is still true today in the continuing mediation and intercession of Jesus at the Father's right hand. This is why the Son had the Father send an Advocate, the Holy Spirit,[6] so that God's reconciling work might have a living instrument here on earth until Christ's return. This Spirit forms for the Father and the Son a body, the Church, in order that the witness to the reconciliation and in-breaking new creation accomplished by Christ might have a continuing corporeal presence in the world. It is this people that is called and commissioned by God to witness to, embody, and enact, by means of the Spirit's animating and guiding power, this new reality.

When the Spirit works to convey the benefits of Christ, he does so within the bounds of a community—and not just a generic community, but a very specific

---

3. See Paul's own account of his conversion in Gal. 1:11–17 and a parallel account adding more details in Acts 9:1–22.

4. Consider, e.g., Matt. 10:19–20//Mark 13:11//Luke 12:11–12; Luke 10:21; 11:13; John 3:5, 34.

5. Note, e.g., that the Holy Spirit is the agent of Jesus's conception (Matt. 1:18//Luke 1:35), is the "commissioning agent" at his baptism (Matt. 3:16//Mark 1:10//Luke 3:22; cf. John 1:32), drives him into the desert to face temptation (Matt. 4:1//Mark 1:12//Luke 4:1) and fills him when he returns (Luke 4:14), is the one who enables both Jesus's proclamation (Matt. 12:18; Luke 4:18) and his ability to cast out demons (Matt. 12:28; cf. Luke 11:20), and is the one in whom Jesus rejoices regarding the Father's revelations (Luke 10:21).

6. John 14:16, 26; 15:26.

one, namely, the Church. This in no way negates the Holy Spirit's freedom to "[blow] where [he] chooses," as Jesus affirmed (see John 3:8). But neither is the Spirit's freedom capricious: it is directed by the Father's providential and covenantal purposes and informed by the Son's creative and redeeming work. The Spirit has the particular task of bringing to life and perfection that which the Father wills and the Son enacts. This gives the Spirit a special connection to the Church, one that binds him to the Church in unique ways, animating and guiding its life, identity, and mission in continuity with the first disciples. For this reason I have chosen to address first this rubric as the one most obviously and irreducibly Christian, namely, the Church as "the body of Christ." In one sense, the material covered under this heading may well be the most fundamental in the formation of the Church's—and the individual Christian's—unique identity. By contrast, in an increasingly post-Christian culture, the two ecclesial rubrics I will consider in the following chapters could, in isolation, be construed in generic terms that take them away from their particular Christian and biblical grounding.[7]

Of course, that does not imply that the other two rubrics are somehow subordinate or less important. In some pastoral situations, they may actually be more crucial to the Church's faithful life and witness. Recall what I said in the previous chapter, namely, that the various metaphors and images for the Church are meant to complement and mutually balance one another—and for very practical reasons. For instance, a Church community that has become too introspective or self-absorbed needs the broader perspectives required of it as the "people of God." Similarly, a congregation or denomination too lax or too institutionally captive to the surrounding culture needs the enlivening rigor described under the "temple of the Holy Spirit" rubric. In the same way that Jesus's atoning work takes several complementary forms, so too does the Holy Spirit's work in animating the Church take several mutually reinforcing forms. These various forms are all reflected in Scripture, so in that sense they have an equal legitimacy. But in actual practice, the different settings and needs confronting the Church must be allowed to have some influence: pastoral discernment that follows the Spirit's lead will often help determine how one emphasizes and relates each to the others in any given moment of the Church's life and work.

That said, the Church's basic recognition under the rubric "body of Christ" is as follows: in keeping with the Father's gracious purposes and covenantal

---

7. "The people of God" is certainly a label that, in itself, could be applied to the adherents of any monotheistic religion. And while "temple of the Holy Spirit" arises from very specific Pauline usage grounded in the centrality of the temple in Judaism, in contemporary parlance references to the "spiritual" or "spirituality" are notoriously elastic in meaning.

plan, the Holy Spirit knits together a particular community to be the continuing earthly "body" of its crucified and risen head, Jesus Christ, who is seated at the right hand of the Father as the world's Lord and Savior. Through the Spirit's animating power, the Church receives the "eyes of faith," by which it may see and be in intimate personal relation with its head, Jesus Christ. Thus, the Church is not the body of Christ in a merely natural sense. It is not an ethnic group or human association of like-minded individuals or a civic institution or a kind of cultural inheritance. But neither is it the body of Christ in a thoroughly supernatural sense. That is, it is not the historical continuation of the fully human–fully divine incarnation of the Son, as if the risen Christ were now somehow only a spectral figure who had to pass on his earthly embodiment to the Church. And the Church is certainly not "without sin," as the faith affirms of Jesus (Heb. 4:15).

Rather, the Church is a "mixed body." It is by no means perfect. On its own, in its continuing humanity, it is still prone to sin, both among the individuals composing it and as a collective entity. On its own, it possesses no special being or status. On its own, its mission and work can be disoriented or corrupted. But of course, God does not leave the Church on its own. The Holy Spirit animates this body, grounding its new life in Christ and growing it toward its final perfection according to the Father's eternal intention. It is the Holy Spirit who creates the collective spirit of this covenantal community and who unites with the spirits of individuals to establish and uphold them as the continuing body of Christ. The Spirit does this so that the Church might enjoy and promote communion with God now and bear witness to the sanctification and glorification that await the whole creation at the end of the age.

The "body of Christ" image plays a key role in the Church's understanding of itself because of this image's multiple uses in Scripture and how it was developed in such a rich and practical way by the apostle Paul. He employs the image in his letters to the Romans, the Ephesians, and the Colossians, and most famously in 1 Corinthians, of which the following is a substantial excerpt:

> For just as the body is one and has many members, and all the members of the body, though many, are one body, so it is with Christ. For by one Spirit we were all baptized into one body—Jews or Greeks, slaves or free—and all were made to drink of one Spirit.
>
> For the body does not consist of one member but of many. If the foot should say, "Because I am not a hand, I do not belong to the body," that would not make it any less a part of the body. And if the ear should say, "Because I am not an eye, I do not belong to the body," that would not make it any less a part of the

body. If the whole body were an eye, where would be the hearing? If the whole body were an ear, where would be the sense of smell? But as it is, God arranged the organs in the body, each one of them, as he chose. If all were a single organ, where would the body be? As it is, there are many parts, yet one body. The eye cannot say to the hand, "I have no need of you," nor again the head to the feet, "I have no need of you." On the contrary, the parts of the body which seem to be weaker are indispensable, and those parts of the body which we think less honorable we invest with the greater honor, and our unpresentable parts are treated with greater modesty, which our more presentable parts do not require. But God has so composed the body, giving the greater honor to the inferior part, that there may be no discord in the body, but that the members may have the same care for one another. If one member suffers, all suffer together; if one member is honored, all rejoice together.

Now you are the body of Christ and individually members of it. (1 Cor. 12:12–27)

The influence of the image does not arise just from Paul's extensive use, however. Another aspect of the image's continuing usefulness and power stems from the multiple, complementary meanings of references to Christ's body across the scriptural witness. In one context it harkens back to Jesus himself and the vicarious redemption he effects through his bodily death and resurrection (Rom. 6:6; 7:4; Heb. 10:5–12; 1 Pet. 2:24; cf. John 15:13), an effect made available to Christians in baptism (Rom. 6:3–5; 1 Cor. 12:13). In another context, the image connects to the bread used in the Lord's Supper, recalling Jesus's own words of institution (Matt. 26:26//Mark 14:22//Luke 22:19; 1 Cor. 10:16–17; 11:23–26). And in yet another, it refers to the Church community (1 Cor. 12:27; Eph. 4:12) or associates Christ's body with the locus of communal worship, the temple (John 2:13–22). This ambiguity is theologically significant because it helps capture the way in which the community and its members are joined with Christ by means of baptism and the Supper, a union effected by the Holy Spirit, to actually become in some real and continuing sense the body of Christ.

The Spirit effects a mystical union between Christ and his Church, such that the Church's truest reality is what the Spirit enables it to be in Christ. To be sure, this reality is not yet complete: it is yet being built up; it is yet maturing toward its fulfillment at the end of the age. And the Church may yet be distracted by the allurements of the world and the distractions of the flesh, and in so doing fall away from its truest reality. But the Church knows these to be disorders, an orientation away from its authentic reality and a diversion from the manner in which it is called to live. For this body to live and act in a way appropriate to its true vocation from the Father, it knows it must ground itself and continually renew itself in Christ through the Spirit. And it does this most fundamentally and deeply by means of its worship.

The Community's Formation: Members of the Body

Worship: Invoking God's Koinōnia

"For where two or three are gathered in my name, I am there among them." (Matt. 18:20)

"But the hour is coming, and is now here, when the true worshipers will worship the Father in spirit and truth, for the Father seeks such as these to worship him. God is spirit, and those who worship him must worship in spirit and truth." The woman said to him, "I know that Messiah is coming" (who is called Christ). "When he comes, he will proclaim all things to us." Jesus said to her, "I am he, the one who is speaking to you." (John 4:23–26)

What then, brethren? When you come together, each one has a hymn, a lesson, a revelation, a tongue, or an interpretation. Let all things be done for edification. (1 Cor. 14:26 RSV)

Then the angel showed me the river of the water of life, bright as crystal, flowing from the throne of God and of the Lamb through the middle of the street of the city. On either side of the river is the tree of life with its twelve kinds of fruit, producing its fruit each month; and the leaves of the tree are for the healing of the nations. Nothing accursed will be found there any more. But the throne of God and of the Lamb will be in it, and his servants will worship him; they will see his face, and his name will be on their foreheads. And there will be no more night; they need no light of lamp or sun, for the Lord God will be their light, and they will reign forever and ever. (Rev. 22:1–5)

Without worship, there is no Church. From this wellspring flow all aspects of the Church's life and work. Worship is the fundamental act that incorporates and animates this community as a body. This is so because worship is the community's continuing encounter and communion with God, where it receives its sustenance from God and its ever-renewed call to witness to God's redemptive purposes in the world. Of course, God's presence is not confined to worship. But worship is that occasion when the community knows it may rely on God's presence because Christ the Lord has made this promise: "For where two or three are gathered in my name, I am there among them" (Matt. 18:20). The Church's worship is not just those interactions between God and the community that may arise spontaneously, although it certainly does not exclude such moments. Worship is instead primarily the spiritual exercise undertaken on regular occasions to create and shape the body according to the rhythms and habits that God desires for it. Prayers of praise and petition; psalms and hymns lifted up with one voice; proclaimed words of instruction, challenge, and comfort; sacraments of water, bread, and wine: all of these contribute to the formation and strengthening of this body. The Church's worship is the means God has ordained for establishing and orienting this community toward him and its own ultimate purpose.

And in all this, worship is a triune activity. It is not merely a human act that God witnesses, the people involved being the performers while God is the passive audience. Rather, the congregation invokes the presence and power of the Holy Spirit, who unites it with its Lord, the risen Son of God, Jesus Christ, in order to praise, glorify, commune with, hear from, petition, and be guided by its heavenly Father. In so doing, the Holy Spirit also knits together the members of the congregation so that they might truly be one body in Christ, learning how better to love one another and to serve the furtherance of God's heavenly reign. To switch from the body metaphor to another, the foundation of Christian life is such corporate worship, while the foundation of individual Christian life is participation in corporate worship and personal prayer. And it is the Holy Spirit who is the power building this foundation (more on this image in chap. 5). Word and Sacrament form the heart of corporate worship, and from that heart flows the lifeblood of the individual's faithfulness.

Worship is also an eschatological event. That is, it is undertaken not merely with a faithful eye to the past, to what God has already accomplished. It also orients itself by what God will yet accomplish at the end of the age. The Church worships on the basis of its hope, as if that future reality were already fully present, living in the "already/not yet" of its risen Lord's reign. With Christ's resurrection a new age has dawned; and while that new age has not yet reached its culmination in Christ's return, the joy of worship anticipates it. As upheld and animated by the Holy Spirit, worship both offers a foretaste of the final heavenly communion and also sustains and encourages the community in its ongoing pilgrimage. Thus does the Holy Spirit ever and again incorporate this body of Christ into the covenantal purposes of the Father.

Worship Forms the Body

Because worship constitutes the Church and is its most basic identifying characteristic, it also becomes the Church's first obligation and thereby the basis for its freedom as a people. Recall the words that God gives to Moses at the burning bush to speak to Pharaoh: the Hebrew people are to be redeemed from their slavery that they might worship God at the mountain in the wilderness.[8] Having been freed from their bondage in Egypt, the people are led by Moses to Mount Sinai. There they receive the law, the covenantal prescriptions that will constitute and guide them as God's people. The foundation of the people's obligations to God is proper worship, as carved by "the finger of God"[9] in the stone of the law's first tablet. The Lord God commands,

> You shall have no other gods before me.
> You shall not make for yourself an idol, whether in the form of anything that is in heaven above, or that is on the earth beneath, or that is in the water under the earth. You shall not bow down to them or worship them. . . .
> You shall not make wrongful use of the name of the LORD your God, for the LORD will not acquit anyone who misuses his name.
> Remember the sabbath day, and keep it holy. Six days you shall labor and do all your work. But the seventh day is a sabbath to the LORD your God; you shall not do any work—you, your son or your daughter, your male or female slave, your livestock, or the alien resident in your towns. For in six days the LORD made heaven and earth, the sea, and all that is in them, but rested the seventh day; therefore the LORD blessed the sabbath day and consecrated it. (Exod. 20:3–11)

At a fundamental level, all these commandments are rooted in worship, for they have to do with the community's and individual's right orientation toward, yielding to, and joyful communion with God—and that is precisely what worship is about. Worship is where the community and individuals learn and practice the meaning of these commandments, and thus worship forms and constitutes the people at the deepest level. True, the third commandment, perhaps more widely remembered as "not taking the Lord's name in vain," may not obviously relate explicitly to worship, and the full meanings of the other three are not restricted to worship services. Fair enough. Nevertheless, the gathering of a people to praise and glorify God in worship also has the intended aftereffect of orienting that people in everything else each member does beyond worship.

Stated more generally, by their worship the people receive their bearing. They come to know their truest reality and purpose in relation to God, with one another, and with the whole of creation. They learn where they have come from and where they are going, their origin and their goal. This is

---

8. Exod. 3:12; 4:23; 7:16; 8:1, 20; 9:1, 13; 10:3.
9. See Exod. 31:18, Deut. 9:10, and, tellingly, cf. Luke 11:20 with its parallel in Matt. 12:28, where the finger of God/Spirit equivalence becomes clear.

what the apostle Paul meant when he said that worship should be "for edification" (1 Cor. 14:26 RSV). Worship should "build up" the congregation in
its knowledge of, and relation to, God, others, and our ultimate end. In this
sense, worship helps Christians to be formed—or, rather, "transformed by
the renewal of your mind" (Rom. 12:2 RSV). Similarly, worship transforms
and directs the Christian's desire, the orientation and sincerity of the heart:
"But what does it say? 'The word is near you, on your lips and in your heart'
(that is, the word of faith which we preach); because, if you confess with your
lips that Jesus is Lord and believe in your heart that God raised him from
the dead, you will be saved. For man believes with his heart and so is justified, and he confesses with his lips and so is saved" (Rom. 10:8–10 RSV). As
this passage indicates, the substance and details of worship are inextricably
linked to, and grounded in, Jesus Christ. Christ is the Mediator, the one
through whom we have access to God the Father and the one by whom the
Holy Spirit is sent to join us with him. By the power of the Holy Spirit, we
are incorporated into Christ's body, joined to him and fellow Christians that
we might have access to the benefits he has achieved: redemption of our old
selves and reconstitution as new selves, as a new communion. Joined with the
incarnate and risen Son, we receive adoption as children of God and become
joint heirs with him (Rom. 8:14–17).

Of course, this incorporation and adoption entails not just the benefit of
"self-realization," as that is all too often narrowly understood nowadays. It
also entails a reorientation to witness and service—its own kind of benefit—
toward a goal that may bring with it suffering along the way. More on this
below. Nevertheless, as Paul writes:

> I consider that the sufferings of this present time are not worth comparing with
> the glory about to be revealed to us. For the creation waits with eager longing
> for the revealing of the children of God; for the creation was subjected to futil-
> ity, not of its own will but by the will of the one who subjected it, in hope that
> the creation itself will be set free from its bondage to decay and will obtain the
> freedom of the glory of the children of God. We know that the whole creation
> has been groaning in labor pains until now; and not only the creation, but we
> ourselves, who have the first fruits of the Spirit, groan inwardly while we wait
> for adoption, the redemption of our bodies. (Rom. 8:18–23)

The Spirit incorporates the Church in Christ, the Spirit orients the Church's
compass toward him, and on this basis the Church truly experiences communion with God. But the full attainment of Christ's promised *koinōnia*
remains ahead of it.

NEW CREATION, NEW DAY

While many Christians might not realize it, this dynamic between "the already" and the "not yet" is manifested in the very day common to Christian worship: Sunday. Why does the Church worship on Sunday? After all, it is not the traditional seventh day of the week, the Sabbath, consecrated because it was the day God rested from his labors of creation (Exod. 20:8–11). As pious Jews, Jesus and his original disciples typically gathered on the traditional day for the community's worship, prayers, and teachings, namely, the Sabbath. Yet very early on in the Christian community's history (precisely when remains unclear), Sunday became the primary day when the Church gathered for its communal worship, and according to the biblical creation accounts (and contemporary calendars that have not succumbed to the fashion of putting Saturday and Sunday at the end of the seven-day sequence to make the modern "weekend"), Sunday is the *first* day of the week, the day when God *began* creating. So why do Christians traditionally worship together on Sunday morning?

Because it is the *Lord's* Day, the day of *resurrection*. On this day, the women first discovered the empty tomb and, according to Matthew 28:9–10, encountered the risen Jesus himself (cf. Mark 16:9 and John 20:11–16). On this day, the risen Christ appeared to the eleven remaining disciples and at least several other followers.[10] On this day, for the first time, all that had been written about Jesus in Moses, the Prophets, and the Psalms had been fulfilled (Luke 24:44)—and the most common response of those encountering him was worship. In all this, Sunday came to be understood not simply as the Christian replacement of the Jewish Sabbath but as its *fulfillment*. Sunday was not just the mundane first day of the old creation but the first day of the *new* creation. Sunday became the eschatological "eighth" day, the day when the new age of God's glorious reign first began by revealing itself in Christ's victory over death. A symbolic expression of this may be found in the structure of many traditional baptismal fonts: they are octagonal, representing that those baptized are made a new creation in Christ. God's glorious future reaches back into the present, that the community may no longer be imprisoned by the past but may live from God's ultimate intentions for us rather than from our own sinful heritage.

This recognition of a new day and a new creation also finds symbolic expression in the use by Jesus and the early Church of wedding imagery: parables of bridegrooms, brides, banquets, attendants, and guests. Such imagery was, of course, used frequently in the Old Testament to emphasize the intimacy

10. Matt. 28:16–17; Mark 16:12–14; Luke 24:28–41; and John 20:19–20.

of God with his chosen people, but it was also employed to express the over-flowing joy of the wedding day, that day of new beginnings. Consider the first reference, in Genesis 2:21–24, which describes God making Eve from the rib of Adam. Adam exultantly recognizes her as bone of his bones, flesh of his flesh, and Scripture then states: "Therefore a man leaves his father and his mother and clings to his wife, and they become one flesh." Captured in these few brief verses are the dynamic of leaving one's previous life and relations behind, embracing a new life and relation, and discovering a joyous intimacy with the exclamation, "This is what I was made for!" The prophets used this image and that of marriage to describe the joy that the people will feel in their deliverance from exile and their renewed relation with God,[11] even while they also used the image of unfaithfulness in marriage to express the breakdown of the covenant and its consequences.[12]

With this scriptural heritage as background, Jesus focuses on the wedding itself: being prepared for it (and warning against being ill prepared),[13] emphasizing the joy of being with the bridegroom,[14] even miraculously producing great quantities of new wine at one.[15] The early Church built on this background to understand the Church to be the bride of Christ,[16] with all that that entails: love, devotion, faithfulness, all based on the new reality that two have become one. Portraying the Church as the bride of Christ became a common theological trope, perhaps reaching its epitome in the Middle Ages with Bernard of Clairvaux's famous allegorical sermons on the Old Testament Song of Solomon, with its highly charged love poems between the bride and groom.[17] Joined with Christ as a bride to her bridegroom, the Church is a community that has left behind its old life and entered into a new and joyous reality. In this way, it echoes and is reinforced by the well-known saying of Jesus that one must be "born again/from above" to enter the kingdom of God. For as it is with this "second birth,"[18] so too is it with this spiritual marriage: it does

11. E.g., Isa. 54:5–9; 61:10; 62:5; Jer. 33:10–11; Hos. 2:19–20.

12. E.g., Jer. 3:1–5, 20; Ezek. 16:32; Hos. 1:2–8.

13. E.g., Matt. 22:1–14 (the parable of the king's wedding banquet for his son); 25:1–10 (the parable of the wise and foolish bridesmaids); Luke 12:35–38 (the servants prepared for their master's return from the wedding banquet); 14:8–11 (not presuming to take a place of honor at the wedding banquet).

14. Matt. 9:15//Mark 2:19–20//Luke 5:34–35; John 3:27–30.

15. The wedding at Cana, described in John 2:1–11.

16. 2 Cor. 11:2; Eph. 5:21–33; Rev. 19:7–9.

17. While later Christians could not be blamed for thinking that Bernard pushed his allegorical interpretation a bit too far, the image of the bride and the groom becoming one remains a very fruitful source for understanding what it means to say that the Church is "the body of Christ."

18. The phrase "born again" comes from John 3:3, 7, where Jesus tells Nicodemus that one may see the kingdom of God only if one is "born from above/again." The Greek term that Jesus

not come naturally but is the special work of the Holy Spirit. Like Adam, we are no longer left alone but have become one body with Christ to become his grateful, joyous Church.

The Spirit in the Form of Liturgy

Indeed, the special work of the Spirit is presupposed in the whole of Christian worship and gives it its internal logic and coherence. Consider the diverse elements that, with certain variation among Christian traditions, often appear in the content and structure of worship. The service begins with a call to worship and an invocation: the former gathers the people together, then the latter invokes God's presence. In other words, this will be an intentional and humble engagement with God that the congregation also recognizes is utterly grounded in God's prior graciousness. These initial moments of worship may also contain a prayer of confession and words of forgiveness and reassurance, although this element of the liturgy may also appear later, often as a preparation for the celebration of the Lord's Supper. In either location, confession and forgiveness signal the acknowledgment that the beginning of faithfulness is repentance. On our own, we recognize how our sinfulness must prevent us from entering near to God's holiness. But our recognition of this fact is met by God's overflowing grace and forgiveness, granting us in Christ through the power of the Spirit the access we can never achieve on our own. The natural response to such a gift is to rejoice and glorify God's goodness—and the liturgy gives voice to this when what comes next is words of praise repeated from Scripture and/or a joyous hymn of praise and thanksgiving. Thus prepared, the congregation is then ready to listen to God, through Scripture lessons and the sermon (or, in briefer form, the "homily").

Then, when the congregation has praised God and listened and learned from God, the next element in worship often entails its response to God. This takes the form of corporate prayers and the collection and presentation of the offering. Then, if the Lord's Supper is to be celebrated in this particular service (many Protestant denominations celebrate weekly, others less frequently), it follows at this juncture. Regardless of the particular tradition, the placement of the Lord's Supper at this stage in the liturgy makes it the high point of the service, the moment of the participants' deepest communion with God and with one another. When it is concluded, it is usually followed only by a closing hymn and a benediction, the "good word" sending the members

---

uses, *anōthen*, has the double meaning of "from above" and "again" or "anew." Nicodemus, assuming the second meaning, asks how he can enter again into his mother's womb. Jesus clarifies that it is not a second natural birth but a new spiritual one.

of the congregation back into the world renewed for their continuing life of discipleship.

Now this emphasis on the Word certainly reflects a Protestant rather than a Roman Catholic sensibility. A common distinction noted between Roman Catholic and Protestant worship is the centrality of the Eucharist in the former and of preaching in the latter. This difference is often reflected even in church architecture, in that the altar is typically the most prominent interior feature in Catholic sanctuaries, while the pulpit is usually the most prominent in Protestant sanctuaries. There are historical and theological reasons for these different emphases. Within the Reformed tradition itself, explanations of the Last Supper's meaning range from a memorial ritual to a "mystical" communion. Even to grasp the reasoning behind these different understandings—let alone choosing sides—requires a deep familiarity with the biblical narrative. To understand the Lord's Supper, one needs to know the story, the gospel of Jesus Christ.

The Word

In the beginning was the Word, and the Word was with God, and the Word was God. He was in the beginning with God. All things came into being through him, and without him not one thing came into being. What has come into being in him was life, and the life was the light of all people. The light shines in the darkness, and the darkness did not overcome it. . . .

And the Word became flesh and lived among us, and we have seen his glory, the glory as of a father's only son, full of grace and truth. . . . From his fullness we have all received, grace upon grace. . . . No one has ever seen God. It is God the only Son, who is close to the Father's heart, who has made him known. (John 1:1–5, 14, 16, 18)

And Peter opened his mouth and said: "Truly I perceive that God shows no partiality, but in every nation any one who fears him and does what is right is acceptable to him. You know the word which he sent to Israel, preaching good news of peace by Jesus Christ (he is Lord of all), the word which was proclaimed throughout all Judea, beginning from Galilee after the baptism which John preached: how God anointed Jesus of Nazareth with the Holy Spirit and with power; how he went about doing good and healing all that were oppressed by the devil, for God was with him. And we are witnesses to all that he did both in the country of the Jews and in Jerusalem. They put him to death by hanging him on a tree; but God raised him on the third day and made him manifest; not to all the people but to us who were chosen by God as witnesses, who ate and drank with him after he rose from the dead. And he commanded us to preach to the people, and to testify that he is the one ordained by God to be judge of the living and the dead. To him all the prophets bear witness that every one who believes in him receives forgiveness of sins through his name."

While Peter was still saying this, the Holy Spirit fell on all who heard the word. And the believers from among the circumcised who came with Peter were amazed, because the gift of the Holy Spirit had been poured out even on the Gentiles. (Acts 10:34–45 RSV)

Yet among the mature we do impart wisdom, although it is not a wisdom of this age or of the rulers of this age, who are doomed to pass away. But we impart a secret and hidden wisdom of God, which God decreed before the ages for our glorification. None of the rulers of this age understood this; for if they had, they would not have crucified the Lord of glory. But, as it is written,

> "What no eye has seen, nor ear heard,
> nor the heart of man conceived,
> what God has prepared for those who love him,"

God has revealed to us through the Spirit. For the Spirit searches everything, even the depths of God. For what person knows a man's thoughts except the spirit of the man which is in him? So also no one comprehends the thoughts of God except the Spirit of God. Now we have received not the spirit of the world, but the Spirit which is from God, that we might understand the gifts bestowed on us by God. And we impart this in words not taught by human wisdom but taught by the Spirit, interpreting spiritual truths to those who possess the Spirit. (1 Cor. 2:6–13 RSV)

All scripture is inspired by God and is useful for teaching, for reproof, for correction, and for training in righteousness, so that everyone who belongs to God may be proficient, equipped for every good work. (2 Tim. 3:16–17)

The Spirit animates the heart of the worship of God by bringing to life the mediating Word. This Word, of course, is the Word of God, incarnate as Jesus Christ, the Mediator and Intercessor through whom the world was made, by whom that world was redeemed, and in whom its consummation will be accomplished. In the Church's use of the term, "the Word" also functions as a form of theological shorthand for all that Christ represents and has accomplished, that is, the good news or gospel of Christ's saving work on behalf of the Father. The Church may be assured that this Word—Christ himself and all he has done as Savior—is indeed present to all who worship because the power of the Holy Spirit makes it so. In more than just a poetic sense, the Spirit is the breath (in Hebrew *ruach*, in Greek *pneuma*) who gives the Word voice and who enables the Word to be heard. Indeed, the Holy Spirit not only animates the Word that God speaks to us but also enables the speech that we then offer up in response to God. From the opening words of invocation to the closing words of benediction, when two or three gather in Jesus's name, it is the Holy Spirit who enables him to be present with them and they with him as together all give glory to the Father. All of this is simply another way of making the point stated before, namely, that worship is a trinitarian event, in which the Holy Spirit joins with the spirits of those assembled to bring them into communion with the Father through the mediating work of the Son.

Worship is the Church "living into the Word": living into Christ, living into the gospel (which is to say, the new reality he opens to us), living into God's covenant community, living into the whole sweep of the biblical story. Christians are called to inhabit this story, recognizing themselves in it and having it re-create and reorient them toward their own truest, God-given selves. Worship is informed by the shape, content, rhythms, and trajectory of the biblical story, and its purpose is to "take us out of ourselves" and embed us in these things, so that the worshiping community might also be informed by them.

So where are we in that story? In one sense, we know ourselves to have a particular location and calling in the biblical time line, namely, with most of the written story "behind" us. That is, the contemporary Church lives between the book of Acts and the various New Testament epistles, on the one hand, and the end-time vision of John in the book of Revelation, on the other. And yet in another sense, we also see ourselves in the recurring types and patterns evident throughout the whole of the Bible. We recognize these people, these stories and events, as revealing our own lives. The characters become our contemporaries; they become us and we them. Consider as one example Dietrich Bonhoeffer's description of the effects of the classic Protestant practice of *lectio continua*:

> Consecutive reading of Biblical books forces everyone who wants to hear to put himself, or allow himself to be found, where God has acted once and for all for the salvation of men. We become a part of what once took place for our salvation. Forgetting and losing ourselves, we, too, pass through the Red Sea, through the desert, across the Jordan into the promised land. With Israel we fall into doubt and unbelief and through punishment and repentance experience God's help and faithfulness. All this is not mere reverie but holy, godly reality. We are torn out of our own existence and set down in the midst of the holy history of God on earth. There God dealt with us, and there He still deals with us, our needs and our sins, in judgment and grace. It is not that God is the spectator and sharer of our present life, howsoever important that is; but rather that we are the reverent listeners and participants in God's action in the

sacred story, the history of the Christ on earth. And only in so far as we are *there*, is God with us today also.[19]

With this in mind, we recognize that one of the worst habits the Church can develop is a preoccupation with making the Bible "relevant," that is, bending and tailoring the biblical story to fit our preoccupations, assumptions, desires, and agendas. That absorbs and dissipates the Bible into *our* culture, rather than having the Bible acculturate us into *its* reality. The Spirit enables the biblical story to come alive within us, encompassing our prior individual and collective stories in a new light and context. The biblical story may lead us to renounce certain aspects of our prior stories. Or it may cause us to redouble efforts in ways previously neglected. Or it may cause us to seek out entirely new paths for our unfolding stories. I recall one contemporary observer of the Church stating that he was less concerned with the Church learning to read the signs of the times than with its writing some of them.[20]

One irreplaceable way that Scripture gives the worshiping community a voice is through the Psalms. From the earliest centuries of the Church's existence, the Psalms have provided the hymns and poetry with which to praise God, to thank God for his abundant blessings, to petition God, and to express laments, even anger and frustrations. And this happens on both a personal and a communal level. As Ronald Heine points out: "The unique element of the book of Psalms is that it allows the reader to get inside the personalities and events of the Old Testament as a participant; or, perhaps better said, it allows those personalities and events to get inside the reader as an emotive factor in shaping his or her life in accordance with the teachings found there."[21] Repeating the words of the Psalms helps bridge the historical distance separating the ancient and the contemporary faithful, joining them into one chorus. And this is as true for a single individual reading a Psalm in her private devotion as it is for a congregation echoing them in communal worship, whether through a responsive reading, plainsong, or some other form. It is especially powerful when the Psalm flows from the lips by memory. I can testify to this reality from attending funerals at my local church: when the pastor leads the congregation in reciting the Twenty-Third Psalm, one can hear and feel how deeply its words are being said "by heart," bringing comfort and assurance.

19. Dietrich Bonhoeffer, *Life Together*, trans. John Doberstein (New York: Harper & Row, 1954), 53–54.
20. Sadly, I cannot remember to whom I should attribute this quip.
21. Ronald E. Heine, *Reading the Old Testament with the Ancient Church: Exploring the Formation of Early Christian Thought* (Grand Rapids: Baker Academic, 2007), 147.

The primary way in which the worshiping community learns to place itself within the story of Scripture is, of course, through the weekly lessons and preaching. This is especially true if a congregation follows a lectionary schedule of readings, cycling through the whole of Scripture in a regular, commonly three-year, rotation of Old and New Testament passages. The lectionary provides both a discipline and a framework: it disciplines the preacher and the congregation to encounter the whole sweep of the Bible, including those passages they might otherwise ignore or avoid.[22] It also frames the reading of Scripture within the rhythm of the Church year—from Advent to Christmas to Epiphany to Lent to Holy Week and Easter to Pentecost to the "Ordinary Time" that leads again to Advent.[23] Such framing helps the faithful discern the covenantal patterns within the mass of the biblical material and also distinguish between major and minor themes. Indeed, it is an invaluable aid in enabling the faithful to hear the Bible *christologically*, that is, as a testimony to what God has done in Christ for the salvation of the world, rather than merely *historically*, say, as simply a collection of ancient Near Eastern religious wisdom.

But what is the theological rationale or "theo-logic" that enables Christians to understand the Bible this way? That is, not just as human insights but as God's own Word? Swiss theologian Karl Barth is well known for describing the threefold form of God's Word: as preached, written, and revealed.[24] To begin with, the Word *preached* is the good news of Christ presented in proclamation, the gospel announced by a living voice so that others may hear it. This personal interaction of proclaimer and listener is meant to reflect, indeed, enable—through the work of the Holy Spirit—the personal encounter of Christ and believer. The Word *written* refers to the Holy Scriptures, understood to have been inspired by God's Holy Spirit so that they may be recognized as reliable witnesses to God's saving deeds. These written words are the basis and "raw material" for the word preached, while also serving as a canon or rule for that proclamation. Yet the Word written, while the standard for Christian faith and life, does not possess its authority intrinsically. Rather, it becomes authoritative insofar as it is made such by the Word *revealed*, which is to say, by the divine Word himself, Jesus Christ. For even the written word remains a creature until Christ, enlisting the animating power of the Holy

22. Unfortunately, this discipline does have gaps, in that the committees drawing up the lectionaries too frequently abridge passages that are deemed too controversial!

23. For a fuller discussion of the Christian year and its liturgical implementation, see Hoyt L. Hickman, Don E. Saliers, Laurence Hull Stookey, and James F. White, *The New Handbook of the Christian Year* (Nashville: Abingdon, 1992).

24. Karl Barth, *Church Dogmatics* I/1 (Edinburgh: T&T Clark, 1975), §4.

Spirit, makes it his own living Word and presence. This actually mirrors how people encountered Jesus in his days on earth. Recall what I said about the "eyes of faith": without them, Jesus's contemporaries would meet him merely as the carpenter's son, the rabbi.

In Barth's description of this threefold character, his key concern was to emphasize the dynamic and living relation between the three forms, while also maintaining a definite chain of authority. Without preaching, the word remains inert; yet preaching must never consider itself free with regard to its content. Such proclamation is bound to the word written as source and norm. Yet neither is the word written its own Lord, possessing its own autonomy. It is not self-interpreting but must be understood in light of the Word revealed. That is, the living Word himself, Jesus Christ, remains the Lord, and thus Lord of the word written and proclaimed. And all of this becomes active and enabled only through the effective work of the Holy Spirit.

That is why, in many traditions, the reading of Scripture is preceded by a prayer asking the Spirit to enable the congregation to hear the words of Scripture as the living Word of God, followed by a prayer of acknowledgment and thanks when the lesson concludes. In the Reformed tradition, with its understanding of the very high place of preaching, the sermon is also encompassed within this prayer for illumination. This is so because the sermon is not meant to represent the preacher's own personal or even "expert" opinion but is to be offered up as an instrument for the Spirit's clarification and application of the biblical lessons previously read. This does not mean that the preacher's personal gifts and professional skill are to be rejected. Indeed, in the Reformed tradition there has been a historical respect and emphasis on the "learned ministry." The point is rather that the preacher's gifts and skill are always to be guided by, and placed in service of, the Spirit's work.

Faithful preaching may take many forms and is not restricted to only certain styles. Textbooks on preaching often distinguish among different kinds of sermons: expository or exegetical ones (unpacking in detail a particular biblical passage), doctrinal ones (expounding one or more key teachings of the Church), and thematic ones (addressing a particular concern or issue), among others. Similarly, the style of sermon presentation may be more or less formal, presented from a pulpit or among the pews, related by means of stories and illustrations or by using broader concepts and ideas. The touchstone in choosing one approach over another ought to be the example of Jesus himself, who consistently tailored his message to the audience he was addressing. This is not to say he always said what his listeners wanted to hear. Quite the contrary! But he did always say what they *needed* to hear, which, depending upon the circumstance, could be a word of comfort or challenge, a word of encouragement or reorientation, a word of enlightenment or judgment. In many instances, this word was heard and heeded. In many others, it was neither heard nor heeded. And in all cases, the Gospel accounts make clear that in his message Jesus was consistently serving the larger purposes of the One who sent him, from his initial preaching of the coming kingdom of God to his prayer of submission in the garden of Gethsemane to his passion and final agony on the cross. The apostle Paul famously summarized Christ's humility in his letter to the Philippians as a "self-emptying" (Phil. 2:5–11).

My point here is that the preacher undertakes a similar "emptying" of his or her own personal preoccupations, concerns, favorite ideas, and/or annoyances in order to allow the Spirit and the Word to do their work. This is not to say that the preacher is merely passive, but rather that the Spirit and Word will employ the preacher's biblical meditation, prayerful study, and theological reflection to offer a sermon that can edify those who hear it. A mark of such upbuilding is that the sermon should offer the congregation—and the individual faithful composing it—some thought or challenge or insight or encouragement that more deeply connects them to the biblical story as their own story. At its best, preaching provides a glimpse of the new reality we have become in Christ and sparks the desire to live ever more fully into that new reality.

John Calvin understood the *essence* of "Word and Sacrament" as being the same, the only difference being the form of its presentation. He makes a particularly helpful and practical point when he describes the sacraments as being a wonderful example of God's "accommodation" to our creaturely nature.[25] God's grace and will are indeed more *precisely* communicated through the divine word: it is by this means that God's promise is most clearly made. But our limitations and bodily existence may hamper reception of that word. Knowing that we humans are creatures who interact with our world not just through hearing but through all our senses, God provides the sacraments as the means by which we may more *wholly* receive his divine graciousness.

Baptism

In those days Jesus came from Nazareth of Galilee and was baptized by John in the Jordan. And just as he was coming up out of the water, he saw the heavens torn apart and the Spirit descending like a dove on him. And a voice came from heaven, "You are my Son, the Beloved; with you I am well pleased." (Mark 1:9–11)

25. John Calvin, *Institutes of the Christian Religion*, ed. John T. McNeill, trans. Ford Lewis Battles, Library of Christian Classics 20 and 21 (Philadelphia: Westminster, 1960), 4.14.3, p. 1278.

And Jesus came and said to them, "All authority in heaven and on earth has been given to me. Go therefore and make disciples of all nations, baptizing them in the name of the Father and of the Son and of the Holy Spirit, and teaching them to obey everything that I have commanded you. And remember, I am with you always, to the end of the age." (Matt. 28:18–20)

For in Christ Jesus you are all children of God through faith. As many of you as were baptized into Christ have clothed yourselves with Christ. There is no longer Jew or Greek, there is no longer slave or free, there is no longer male and female; for all of you are one in Christ Jesus. And if you belong to Christ, then you are Abraham's offspring, heirs according to the promise. (Gal. 3:26–29)

As the body of Christ, the Church lives into the Word not merely by hearing but also by doing. The gospel message specifically, and the biblical story more generally, are not just proclaimed; they are enacted. Indeed, there are two specific actions by which the Spirit engrafts and nurtures Christians as members of this body, namely, the sacraments of baptism and the Lord's Supper.

A sacrament is a corporate ritual, a liturgical drama enacted by Jesus Christ and effected by the Holy Spirit as a tangible sign and seal of God the Father's gracious will, promise, and saving acts on our behalf, and of our corresponding trust in and allegiance toward God. It is a covenantal interchange between God and the worshiping community. This may make it sound as if there is divine initiative on one side and a purely human response on the other. But recalling what I have written earlier, we should recognize sacramental activity as trinitarian on both sides of the equation. On the one side, both baptism and the Lord's Supper were initiated by the Son and made objectively effective signs of the Father's will and work in him through the power of the Holy Spirit. On the other side, our subjective human reception of them mirrors and is enabled by this triune activity. Or perhaps rather than using the language of "sides," it would be more accurate to say that these sacramental activities take place within the compass of the Triune God. It is the Holy Spirit who enkindles our trust in and allegiance toward the Father by uniting us with our Savior and Lord in baptism and his Supper, in such a way that it is proper and accurate to affirm that Christ truly is present with and among the worshiping community.[26]

The communal character of the sacraments deserves more explanation. The sacraments are a covenantal sign and seal of God's graciousness toward

---

26. Those familiar with the Reformed tradition will recognize that my description here aligns more with Calvin's "real presence" understanding of the sacraments than Zwingli's "memorial" view.

us, of God's saving deeds on our behalf. That is, as "signs" they point to God's gracious saving acts, and as "seals" they convey God's solemn pledge that their benefits will be ours. Therefore, they should not be understood only introspectively or retrospectively. That is, they are not merely signs and seals of God's grace toward us individually, and they do not just refer to what God has already done. They are rituals that themselves ever and again continue to knit us together as the body of Christ. They are also signs that God's gracious will and activity ultimately encompass the whole of humanity, indeed all creation, and that that will and activity continue to unfold. This becomes clear when we recognize how the Church's sacraments are actually an aspect of God's larger covenantal purposes. God's initiating act was his covenant with Abraham; his constituting act was his covenant with Moses and Israel at Sinai; God's realizing act is the life, work, death, and resurrection of Jesus Christ; and the culminating act will occur at the end of the age with Christ's return and the emergence of the new heaven and earth. And just as the first covenant with Abraham was ritually signified with circumcision and as the journey to Sinai commenced with Passover, so too does Jesus give his followers two ritual markers to signify the benefits and responsibilities entailed in his new covenant. These markers become the ritual reenactments and liturgical means by which individuals and the community may know that, through the animating power of the Holy Spirit, they have been brought into and given a part to play in the unfolding drama of salvation.

In this sense, the sacraments are in essence no different from the word of God proclaimed in preaching. They are "the good news" presented in concrete and tangible form, the visual aids of the divine promise made in the proclamation (the *kērygma*). This is, of course, a very Reformed move to make, and in comparison to Roman Catholic tradition it does downplay the centrality of the sacraments—especially the Eucharist—while elevating that of preaching. But my underlying concern is not a partisan desire to promote a particular stream of Protestantism over against Catholicism or over against other branches of the Protestant tradition. It is instead a self-consciously theological one, which seeks not to subordinate the sacraments to preaching but to subordinate both sacraments *and* preaching to God's graciousness toward us. In this sense, both preaching and sacraments are signs, pointing not to themselves but to God: to the Father's action on our behalf in Christ, made available to us through the power of the Holy Spirit. The focus of the Church's faith and trust is to be on God; preaching and the sacraments are the divinely instituted instruments that the Spirit wields in order to serve that end.

In this role, the sacraments (as well as worship more generally and preaching more particularly) become both an accommodation *and* an obligation for the Christian community. Jesus has ordained them as the "ordinary" means by which the Holy Spirit nurtures and maintains Christian fellowship, incorporating members of the body into the Father's covenant and the covenant community in order to make that community's history and purpose the individual's new history and purpose.[27] Practically speaking, this is reflected in part by there being an appropriate "chronology" or order to the sacraments, which mirrors the unfolding history of the covenant. Baptism, which comes first, communally represents and liturgically effects the individual's joining to Christ's body, his or her initiation into God's covenant and community of grace, while the Lord's Supper, which comes afterward, represents and liturgically sustains the ongoing life of Christian discipleship within the community. Simultaneously evocative and tangible, these sacraments embed us in the Christian narrative of repentance and rebirth, of redemption and reconciliation, in a manner that incorporates the whole person, and not just our hearing or our head. As noted above, they are a wonderful and gracious accommodation by God to our creaturely nature, helping us know the promise of, and our accountability to, the gospel through all our senses by means of our active participation. For all this, God is not restricted to working solely through the sacraments—even though we are simultaneously allowed and obliged to cleave to them as divine ordinances. As such they represent both a surety and a mandate.

Baptism Precedes the Supper

First, then, how does the relation of baptism and the Lord's Supper to each other help determine their meaning? The barest outline of the gospel narrative offers our first clue: baptism comes first, and the Supper comes later. This order may seem so obvious that it is not worth mentioning, but contemporary insistence by some that communion be open even to the unbaptized indicates that this order is not self-evident to everyone. Nevertheless, the pattern recurs several times in several ways in the New Testament writings. The most obvious is the pattern offered by Jesus himself. Each of the four Gospels portrays Jesus undergoing baptism at the start of his public ministry, whereas his institution of the Supper occurs toward the end of his public ministry.

Similarly, the pattern of baptism first and only then sharing communion is also portrayed in the Acts of the Apostles. Indeed, the priority of baptism is indicated in part by the fact that it is mentioned or described far more often than is "the breaking of the bread." Nevertheless, the pattern is established early in the apostles' ministry that baptism comes before communion, as the

27. See Matt. 26:26–29; 28:18–20. Cf. John 21:15–19; Acts 2; 1 Cor. 11:17–34.

order described in Acts 2:37–42 attests. Similarly, Paul apparently presupposed the same order. While the tone of Paul's rhetoric in the opening chapter of 1 Corinthians might seem to downplay the significance of baptism, the point of contention is not baptism per se but that it does not matter who administered it, just as long as it has been administered—because its real agent is not the human involved but the Holy Spirit. Thus, that the Corinthian community has been baptized by someone is simply taken for granted—and presupposed in everything Paul has to say about the proper celebration of the Lord's Supper (see 1 Cor. 1:10–17). Later, Paul more clearly implies a specific sequence as he recounts the scriptural prefiguring of the Israelites passing through the waters of the (Red) Sea before partaking of the spiritual food and drink (1 Cor. 10:1–4).

So the scriptural narrative suggests a similarly narrative pattern for us: baptism precedes participation in the Lord's Supper. This does not preclude the possibility that there might have been exceptions. But it does suggest that there is, in fact, a customary order. Yet why should this be the case? What inner logic is revealed about the nature of both baptism and the Lord's Supper by maintaining this one-directional sequence? Why is baptism ordinarily at the beginning and the Lord's Supper farther along in the biblical narrative, as well as in the narrative order of our own Christian pilgrimages?

Jesus's Baptism as a Model

Let us consider Jesus's own baptism. All four Gospels testify that Jesus himself was baptized at the beginning of his ministry. Yet each Gospel presents the precise details of Jesus's baptism quite differently, especially with regard to the relation between Jesus and John the Baptist. Mark's account tersely states: "In those days Jesus came from Nazareth of Galilee and was baptized by John in the Jordan" (Mark 1:9). Matthew also recounts Jesus's baptism by John but adds that "John would have prevented him, saying, 'I need to be baptized by you, and do you come to me?' But Jesus answered him, 'Let it be so now; for it is proper for us in this way to fulfill all righteousness.' Then he consented" (Matt. 3:14–15). Luke's Gospel implies that John could not have administered Jesus's baptism, having been locked up in prison by Herod (Luke 3:20), and leaves unspecified who did administer it ("Now when all the people were baptized, and when Jesus also had been baptized . . . ," Luke 3:21). By contrast, the Gospel of John returns the Baptist to the scene, bearing witness to Jesus as the one who will baptize with the Holy Spirit, yet this Gospel account does not actually state that Jesus was himself baptized. It recounts John saying, "I saw the Spirit descending from heaven like a dove, and it remained on him" (John 1:32), which in the Synoptics is linked with the moment of Jesus's baptism. But the Gospel of John does not make this connection explicit.

So what are we to make of this divergence in accounts? Historical-critical scholars have long postulated that early Christians, perhaps in a certain rivalry with followers of John the Baptist, were discomfited by the apparent subordination of Jesus to John the Baptist. Why should the Messiah be baptized by someone "beneath" him? The perceived need arose to explain—or sidestep—this apparent subordination, a perception that shows itself in the apologetic accounts of Matthew, Luke, and John. Because Mark's rendition does nothing to avoid this embarrassing implication, so this theory goes, then his account must be the most historically accurate. Jesus was, in fact, baptized by John. From this bare fact, historical reconstruction then typically appeals to a developmental explanation, namely, that Jesus grew into a sense of his mission, first becoming a follower of John before striking out on his own.

Yet accepting the historical accuracy of Mark's account does not necessarily lead to this "developmental" answer as to why Jesus would submit to baptism by John. While such theories may appeal to our modern psychologizing inclinations, I suggest that a theological explanation better fits the various testimonies of Scripture. The key is suggested in the Matthean verse cited above, which portrays John subordinating himself while elevating Jesus's status. Jesus refuses John's gesture, saying, "'Let it be so now; for it is proper for us in this way to fulfill all righteousness.'" Simply put, that Jesus would submit to John's baptism is not a denigration of his messianic work but in fact an epitome of it. All the Gospels testify to the human tendency—in Jesus's own time as well as all subsequent eras—to want a Messiah who is triumphant, not humble. Yet Jesus consistently follows the path of humility, both as an embodiment of God's own gracious "stooping down" to us and as a model that Christians themselves are to imitate. This messianic humility is demonstrated again in the final hours before Jesus's crucifixion, in John's account of Jesus washing the feet of his disciples and his admonition that they must follow his example (John 13:3–17). And the same theme is sounded again in the famous passage from Philippians 2:1–11, which emphasizes how Jesus's humbling himself on the cross is but the culmination of a humbling that began with his incarnation:

> If then there is any encouragement in Christ, any consolation from love, any
> sharing in the Spirit, any compassion and sympathy, make my joy complete:
> be of the same mind, having the same love, being in full accord and of one
> mind. Do nothing from selfish ambition or conceit, but in humility regard

others as better than yourselves. Let each of you look not to your own interests, but to the interests of others. Let the same mind be in you that was in Christ Jesus,

> who, though he was in the form of God,
>   did not regard equality with God
>   as something to be exploited,
> but emptied himself,
>   taking the form of a slave,
>   being born in human likeness.
> And being found in human form,
>   he humbled himself
>   and became obedient to the point of death—
>   even death on a cross.
> Therefore God also highly exalted him
>   and gave him the name
>   that is above every name,
> so that at the name of Jesus
>   every knee should bend,
>   in heaven and on earth and under the earth,
> and every tongue should confess
>   that Jesus Christ is Lord,
>   to the glory of God the Father.

So if Christ himself submits to baptism in order "to fulfill all righteousness" and as a sign of his humility, should not the followers of Christ likewise be willing to submit to baptism?

One word in this question likely explains our reluctance: "submit." In our modern Western culture especially, we do not relish submitting to others. If we do reluctantly recognize its necessity, we might be willing to submit to God in the privacy of our own conscience and piety. But we hardly relish the prospect of doing it publicly, much less in a formal ritual that effectively authorizes others to hold us accountable to certain norms of belief and behavior in the future. Yet such submitting, such letting go—especially in a public and declarative manner—is the only way we can truly enter the story, the biblical story that reveals to us a whole new world. We know this to be true in other areas of our lives. Consider how telling friends of our intention to change some bad habit or undertake some new positive behavior helps us keep our resolve. Consider how learning a new skill often requires us to "forget everything we know" in order to allow the instructor to build up our ability from scratch. Baptism is a multilayered ritual that signifies our entry into a divinely ordered new way of being, perceiving, and acting.

THE MEANING OF BAPTISM

So what does baptism mean? Scripture describes it with a number of interlocking and mutually enriching images, with various New Testament passages often linking it with a variety of Old Testament passages. A very useful summary of these meanings was compiled in the ecumenical document *Baptism, Eucharist and Ministry*.[28] This booklet lists five different images, even while those five also include within them distinguishable nuances and associations. The first understands baptism as a participation in the life, death, and resurrection of Jesus. Just as Jesus showed solidarity with us by undergoing baptism and being the fulfillment of the Suffering Servant, so too are we joined with him in his death (which buries our sins) and resurrection (which liberates us to new life here and now, and at the end of the age to a glorious resurrection like his).[29] The second understanding overlaps but also adds to this: it sees baptism as a conversion, pardoning, and cleansing. In this, Christian baptism is linked with that of John the Baptist by joining the demand for repentance with the gift of absolution.[30] The third likewise overlaps and enriches these understandings by recognizing baptism as bestowing the gift of the Holy Spirit. Just as Jesus received the anointing of the Spirit at his baptism, so too do Christians receive the Spirit at their baptisms.[31] It is this Spirit who nurtures the life of faith in believers until their final deliverance.[32] Fourth, baptism incorporates the individual into the body of Christ, that is, the Church. It is a sign and seal of common discipleship and union with believers of every time and place.[33] Fifth, baptism stands as a sign of God's kingdom, both as an in-breaking reality and as a sign of the life of the world to come.

This brief summary illustrates some of the diverse yet intertwined understandings of baptism in the New Testament, even while more images and associations are available.[34] I would like to highlight two points in relation to these diverse images. The first is the way in which all of them together are threads weaving the Christian ritual of baptism into the fabric of the scriptural story. The New Testament writers understood baptism to be prefigured in a number of Old Testament events, while these writers also clarified the

28. World Council of Churches, *Baptism, Eucharist and Ministry*, Faith and Order Paper No. 111 (Geneva: World Council of Churches, 1982), 2–3. This paragraph is my paraphrase of the material presented there, including the scriptural references.

29. See Matt. 3:15; Mark 10:38–40, 45; Rom. 6:3–11; Eph. 2:5–6; and Col. 2:12–13.

30. Mark 1:4; Acts 22:16; 1 Cor. 6:11; and Heb. 10:22.

31. Mark 1:10–11 and Acts 2.

32. 2 Cor. 1:21–22; Eph. 1:13–14.

33. Eph. 4:4–6.

34. E.g., baptism as a new birth (John 3:5), as a rescue from the waters of the flood (1 Pet. 3:20–21), or as passing through the waters of a new exodus (1 Cor. 10:1–2).

true covenantal significance of those earlier occurrences. What had been foreshadowed was now made clear—as well as broadened to include the gentiles. The other observation has to do with the thesis guiding this whole book, namely, that while "the gift of the Spirit" is listed above as one of five different understandings, in a deeper sense it is the one that in fact enables all the others. It is the Spirit who enables our participation in the crucified and risen Christ. It is the Spirit joining with our spirits who sparks our repentance, cleanses us, and nurtures us in the new life of faith. It is the Spirit who incorporates us into Christ's body, making us members of the covenant people. (It is this divine initiative that is so clearly demonstrated in the practice of infant baptism, a sign that salvation depends utterly on God's grace.) Finally, it is the Spirit who invokes in us the sense of God's present and coming reign.

And it should come as no surprise that the Spirit works in exactly the same manner when the Church celebrates the Lord's Supper, which we will consider next.

The Lord's Supper

When the hour came, he took his place at the table, and the apostles with him. He said to them, "I have eagerly desired to eat this Passover with you before I suffer; for I tell you, I will not eat it until it is fulfilled in the kingdom of God." Then he took a cup, and after giving thanks he said, "Take this and divide it among yourselves; for I tell you that from now on I will not drink of the fruit of the vine until the kingdom of God comes." Then he took a loaf of bread, and when he had given thanks, he broke it and gave it to them, saying, "This is my body, which is given for you. Do this in remembrance of me." And he did the same with the cup after supper, saying, "This cup that is poured out for you is the new covenant in my blood." (Luke 22:14–20)

And he said to them, "O foolish men, and slow of heart to believe all that the prophets have spoken! Was it not necessary that the Christ should suffer these things and enter into his glory?" And beginning with Moses and all the prophets, he interpreted to them in all the scriptures the things concerning himself.

So they drew near to the village to which they were going. He appeared to be going further, but they constrained him, saying, "Stay with us, for it is toward evening and the day is now far spent." So he went in to stay with them. When he was at table with them, he took the bread and blessed, and broke it, and gave it to them. And their eyes were opened and they recognized him; and he vanished out of their sight. They said to each other, "Did not our hearts burn within us while he talked to us on the road, while he opened to us the scriptures?" (Luke 24:25–33 RSV)

The cup of blessing that we bless, is it not a sharing in the blood of Christ? The bread that we break, is it not a sharing in the body of Christ? Because there is one bread, we who are many are one body, for we all partake of the one bread. (1 Cor. 10:16–17)

For I received from the Lord what I also handed on to you, that the Lord Jesus on the night when he was betrayed took a loaf of bread, and when he had given thanks, he broke it and said, "This is my body that is for you. Do this in remembrance of me." In the same way he took the cup also, after supper, saying, "This cup is the new covenant in my blood. Do this, as often as you drink it, in remembrance of me." For as often as you eat this bread and drink the cup, you proclaim the Lord's death until he comes.

Whoever, therefore, eats the bread or drinks the cup of the Lord in an un-worthy manner will be answerable for the body and blood of the Lord. Examine yourselves, and only then eat of the bread and drink of the cup. For all who eat and drink without discerning the body, eat and drink judgment against themselves. (1 Cor. 11:23–29)

As I did with my consideration of baptism, let me first consider Jesus's words and deeds in instituting this meal. The accounts of the Last Supper presented in each of the Synoptic Gospels make clear two crucial points. First, they all indicate that this meal is a Passover Seder.[35] Thus, it is not merely a meal, but a *ritual* meal, a meal that remembers and helps form the identity of a particular people, young and old alike. Embedded in this meal are all the memories associated with Israel's original exodus, as well as hopes for the future. These memories and yearnings form the context for Jesus's celebra-tion of this meal, even while he bestows new meaning upon it through his own life, ministry, impending death, and expectations regarding God's reign.[36] Second, unlike the meals he shared with "publicans and sinners" or with the multitudes in the fields, this is not a public meal. It is rather an "insider" meal, one shared only with his disciples,[37] the twelve,[38] held privately in "the upper room."[39] The Last Supper's character as a disciples' meal, rather than just a sign of God's graciousness and "hospitality," is reinforced immediately by Jesus's strong words regarding how they are to act and serve others. They are not to act as the gentile rulers do, exercising their authority by lording it over others. Rather, they are to deny themselves, becoming great by being

35. Matt. 26:17–19//Mark 14:12, 14, 16//Luke 22:7–8, 11, 13, 15.
36. Matt. 26:26–29//Mark 14:22–25//Luke 22:15–20.
37. Matt. 26:18//Mark 14:14//Luke 22:11.
38. Matt. 26:20–25//Mark 14:17; cf. Luke 22:14.
39. Mark 14:15//Luke 22:12.

the servant of all—just as Jesus himself (the Son of Man) came not to be served but to serve.[40]

The Fourth Gospel, despite its indication that Jesus's last supper with his disciples was not a Passover Seder (because John instead portrays Jesus as the new Passover lamb sacrificed for the whole world; see John 1:29, 36 and 19:30–31), nevertheless reinforces the points just made in reading the Synoptic accounts. That is, Jesus has concluded his public ministry, withdraws with his disciples alone to share a supper before the impending events of his passion (13:1–2), and uses this meal not as simply one last occasion to demonstrate hospitality but to enact and proclaim his significance in God's redemptive purposes and to instruct his disciples how they are to be his true disciples: by imitating him, becoming servants to one another (13:3–17), and loving one another (13:34–35).

Of course, Gospel passages describing Jesus's *Last* Supper do not explain everything we need to know about the *Lord's* Supper, for the simple reason that his passion and resurrection had not yet occurred. Yes, the Last Supper does carry with it all the memories and associations of the old covenant community's liberation from bondage under Pharaoh; yes, it was the old covenant community's meal of national identity and obligation. But as Jesus celebrated this meal with his disciples, he also knew that God was undertaking a new work of liberation, creating a new people and a new way of faithfulness. *He* was aware of this, in establishing this new communal meal of the new covenant community—but the disciples did not fully realize it until *after* their encounters with the risen Christ. Luke 24 makes clear that the disciples did not grasp the significance of everything that had happened in Jesus's passion and death. Even when, "beginning with Moses and all the prophets, he interpreted to them in all the scriptures the things concerning himself" (Luke 24:27 RSV), they did not understand—until they recognized him in his blessing and breaking of the bread (24:30–31). Once this happened, and following the coming of the Holy Spirit at Pentecost (Acts 2), the disciples began to make the scriptural connections themselves, as their various sermons to Jewish audiences in the Acts of the Apostles illustrate.[41]

Paul makes a similar linkage between the events of the old covenant and the new when he writes the following to the Church at Corinth: "I want you to know, brethren, that our fathers were all under the cloud, and all passed through the sea, and all were baptized into Moses in the cloud and in the sea,

40. Matt. 20:25–28//Mark 10:42–45//Luke 22:24–27.
41. See Peter's sermons (Acts 2:14–40; 4:8–12), Stephen's sermon (7:2–53), and Paul's sermon (13:16–41).

and all ate the same supernatural food and all drank the same supernatural drink. For they drank from the supernatural Rock which followed them, and the Rock was Christ" (1 Cor. 10:1–4 RSV). While Paul does not link the "supernatural food" to Jesus in this passage, the Gospel of John does when it cites Jesus as saying he is "the bread of life," of which one may eat and gain eternal life, unlike the manna in the wilderness (John 6:48–51). The one generalization that seems obvious from these connections with Passover and the wilderness wanderings is that this meal illustrates and embodies our need to have divine sustenance for the journey.

This observation and these various passages raise the more general question (akin to our earlier one regarding baptism), what does the Lord's Supper entail more fully? I have already considered some of the ways its significance comes from its echoing of Passover traditions, but here again the ecumenical document *Baptism, Eucharist and Ministry* (BEM) offers a rich and succinct summary of the Supper's intertwining meanings.[42] First, it is understood as a great thanksgiving to God the Father for all that he has done, is doing, and will do: creation, redemption, sanctification, and bringing about the kingdom. This understanding is most clearly expressed when the word used for the Supper is the "Eucharist," derived from the Greek word for thanksgiving. It is a sacrifice of praise in which the celebrating community is joined with Christ its Lord by means of the Spirit in offering itself up to God in gratitude. Second, the Supper is understood as a memorial of the crucified and risen Christ's sacrifice, accomplished once and for all on the cross on behalf of all humanity. To call it a "memorial" points to this "once and for all" character of Christ's work; it does not mean that he and his benefits remain somehow in the past. To the contrary, Christ himself is present in this memorial celebration, so that on the basis of what he has done and his continuing intercession on our behalf, we may also proclaim what the future will hold. (Of course, how Christ is understood as present is a matter of much theological debate and Church division. I will address this issue below.) At this point, the BEM document also notes that this memorial celebration of communion also "properly includes proclamation of the Word,"[43] because the preached Word is the very content of the memorial. Third, the Lord's Supper entails an invocation of the Spirit, an *epiclēsis*, which makes the crucified and risen Christ really present in this meal. Fourth, the Eucharist or Lord's Supper is understood as a communion of the faithful. Here the sharing of the common loaf and cup signifies the unity of all believers in all times and all places. Of course, in signifying this unity,

42. See World Council of Churches, *Baptism, Eucharist and Ministry*, 10–15.
43. Ibid., 12.

the Supper may also call us to account for all the things that divide us in our ecclesial, social, economic, and political lives. Thus, the unity at the heart of the meal challenges us to live lives of reconciliation, generosity, justice, and peace. Finally, the Lord's Supper is understood as a meal of the kingdom, a foretaste of the messianic feast that will be celebrated with the full realization of God's reign at the end of the age. In this regard, the meal is not so much a memorial of things past but the in-breaking of things future, of God's new reality. By participating in the meal in this way, the faithful may become better witnesses of God's redemptive purposes for the whole of creation: "The eucharist is precious food for missionaries, bread and wine for pilgrims on their apostolic journey."[44]

One observation I would make about these five points is similar to the one I made regarding *BEM*'s treatment of baptism: while the invocation of the Spirit is listed third among the meanings of the Lord's Supper, it is in fact the one that enables all the others. It is the Holy Spirit who makes the crucified and risen Lord present to us; it is the Spirit who unites us with Christ in our praise of the Father; it is the Spirit who unites us as one communion of the faithful and grants us a foretaste of the messianic banquet. The whole of the Lord's Supper is in fact a trinitarian event, and our participation in it depends entirely upon the Spirit as the effective agent joining us into this communion. *BEM* follows the traditional theological order in its list because it is the Father who sends the Son, and the Son who commissions the Spirit. But from the human point of view, the order is actually reversed, because it is the Spirit whom we first encounter, joining us to Christ our Savior and Mediator, through whom we may approach the Father.

Some Thoughts on Sacramental Disagreements

The sacraments are the most foundational and also among the most moving and meaningful of Christian acts. And probably for this very reason, they are also among the most controversial subjects in Church life—and not just among theologians. They all too easily become the flash point for theological disputes among laypeople because they are the place where personal piety and the Church's traditional practice most keenly intersect. Among faithful Christians, the possibilities for controversy are many. How many sacraments are there? Who may legitimately celebrate them? Who may legitimately receive them? Do they actually accomplish something, and if so, what? May infants be baptized? Or only those capable of making their own confession of faith?

44. Ibid., 15.

Are the physical elements of bread and wine of the Lord's Supper supernaturally transformed? Or are they only natural, if meaningful, signs? Indeed, what does one properly call this ritual meal? The Eucharist? Communion? The Lord's Supper? Are the sacraments necessary? If so, necessary for what? Salvation? Assurance? As a sign of allegiance? As a sign of hospitality? Pity the poor pastor reluctant to baptize the baby at the grandparents' urging, when the parents are an unchurched couple who apparently have no intention of raising that child in the community of faith. Pity the poor pastor who, in an age of emphasizing "self-esteem," suggests that a confession of sin might be a necessary prerequisite to receiving the bread and wine of the Supper.

It appears that many misunderstandings and debates concerning the sacraments may arise from the tendency to conceive them abstractly. On the one hand, "sacrament" becomes a generic category ("an outward and visible sign of an inward and invisible grace")[45] of which, in principle, there may be multiple specific examples. The notion of "sacrament" becomes free-floating, attachable to a variety of ritual or meaningful acts. As the nature and number of sacraments expand, the focus can tend to shift toward a more "natural" spirituality and away from the concrete particulars of the biblical narrative. Consider how restricting the label of "sacrament" to baptism and the Lord's Supper (the Protestant practice) roots that label more obviously in the New Testament accounts of these activities, whereas including confirmation, penance, marriage, ordination, and anointing of the sick (formerly known as last rites or extreme unction) under this rubric (Roman Catholic practice) seems to orient the notion of sacrament more toward the life milestones of individual Christians. To put it starkly, seven sacraments seems more a topic in theological anthropology (albeit a "sanctified" anthropology), while two sacraments seems more obviously christological. Both approaches have their theological merits.

But merely affirming the christological basis of the sacraments of baptism and the Lord's Supper is not enough. In today's highly individualistic context of personal, indeed, private piety, this affirmation too can be easily misconstrued. One danger is that, for all practical purposes, the sacramental act is viewed as a neutral, "mystical" doorway enabling a one-on-one relationship between the believer and God. Such a view assumes that the sacraments' meaning is open ended, derived from the individual's personal pious experience, rather than concrete, derived from the sacraments' instrumental particularity grounded in the narrative of God's saving acts. As a result, in an odd sort of post-Christian

---

45. This is a definition common, with only slight variation in wording, across denominational lines, dating back at least to Saint Augustine.

manner, the sacramental form is maintained, perhaps with a lingering sense that it is a "means of grace," but its full meaning and significance are left for the individual participant to determine. "After all," proponents of this view say, "who am I to judge what's going on between God and this person, and exclude her even though she finds it meaningful?" Such rhetoric fails to recognize that the sacraments do not need to have their meaning supplied by the participants, because their meaning is already supplied by the biblical story.

Indeed, such rhetoric fails to recognize who is the active agent in the sacraments and who is the recipient. For not only do the sacraments provide their own meaning; they actually embed meaning in those who participate. That is, participants do not incorporate the sacraments into their own autobiographical constellation of meaning; rather, the sacraments are intended to incorporate those who partake of them into a preexisting, scripturally illuminated narrative meaning. This is so because the sacraments are not merely a human ritual but primarily an activity of the Father, Son, and Holy Spirit into which we are invited. Thus, to counter any and all idiosyncratic understandings of the sacraments, we must ground them explicitly in the providential unfolding of the divine economy of salvation from whence the purpose, power, and meaning of the specific sacraments derive. In that sense, our understanding of the sacraments needs to be not only christological but also fully trinitarian.

In this regard, the "milestone" character of Roman Catholic practice does offer a suggestive lesson (even if, to my Reformed frame of mind, it seems more anthropocentric than theocentric): in the sacraments we are to recognize that there is a divinely established order of things. Yet this is so not merely on a personal level but on a communal and historical level. This means that baptism and the Lord's Supper cannot be understood properly apart from their ordered relation to each other. Additionally, this ordered relation cannot be understood properly apart from its role in the life of the Church. Finally, this ecclesial role cannot be understood properly apart from the place of the Church in the larger divine economy of salvation.

So regarding the question of the order of baptism first, then the Supper, we have both the example of Jesus's ministry itself and also the prefiguring image of the Israelites passing through the "baptism" of the Red Sea, then later receiving manna in the wilderness. This is why partaking of the Lord's Supper without first being baptized either misunderstands or ignores how as Christians we are to live into the biblical story and the covenant community. It is equivalent to wanting to live an ahistorical, untethered life, and represents a failure to acknowledge our embeddedness in time and salvation history, where baptism is a beginning only to be consummated at the last day. As noted above, we are sojourners and pilgrims. The Lord's Supper is not the messianic banquet, but only a foretaste. It is food for the journey, to sustain the people of God on the way—a way that is obscured unless one recognizes that it has a beginning (signaled with each baptism) as well as an end.

Some may notice that in describing the sacraments I emphasize the action involved in the overall sacramental ritual rather than focusing on the elements involved. I do this because experience has taught me that far too many Christians conceive of God's grace as some sort of substance that God "pours" into us by means of the sacraments and that believers passively receive. That is, divine grace somehow inheres in the physical elements of baptism and the Lord's Supper in such a way that they become some sort of holy "stuff." No doubt this derives from a rather basic understanding of the Catholic doctrine of "transubstantiation." By contrast, the Reformed tradition, from which I write, suggests it is far more appropriate and helpful to understand God's grace not as akin to a substance, but as God's gracious attitude and activity on our behalf. In other words, divine grace is "located" not in the elements so much as in the Holy Spirit acting in and through the *whole* of the sacramental act, communicating divine grace and enabling our human response. Grace as it is available in the sacraments is not a noun but a verb.

To my mind, the traditional Roman Catholic notion of transubstantiation and the Lutheran notion of "consubstantiation," developed in the sixteenth century, both rely on certain Aristotelian metaphysical assumptions that in our current context can be more confusing than clarifying. That is why I find more helpful the Reformed approach, which upholds God's "real presence" in the sacraments without seeking to explain the metaphysical particulars of how that occurs—except to maintain that it is the agency of the Holy Spirit which makes that presence real. Sacraments are not conduits of a holy substance. Their efficacy is not intrinsic to them but resides (1) in God's promise to be gracious to us in the atoning work of Jesus Christ and (2) in the efficacious application of that work through the power of the Holy Spirit. This means that the sacraments do not "stand on their own" but are instruments that God uses. Hence, they are in no way magic, having an efficacy independent of God's attitude toward and work in us.[46] Indeed, this is one of the reasons that sacraments are called "signs," because signs don't point to themselves. Instead, they point away from themselves to something else, in this case, God's promise, accomplishment, and continuing activity. But, having made

---

46. Consider one possible etymology of the phrase "hocus pocus," which has to do with magic and conjuring and can have rather negative overtones. The term was apparently coined in the 1600s, and some think it is a satirical play on the Latin words "Hoc est corpus meum"—"this is my body," a sarcastic reference to "magical" understandings of the Mass.

this statement, one may also add that they are instruments that help *effect* that to which they point.

Medieval theologian Duns Scotus made a similar distinction when he explained that the sacraments themselves don't cause grace; rather, it is God who causes grace through them. But my position is actually more Protestant than that. The Roman Catholic position of Scotus and Augustine holds that the sacraments are indispensable to the communication of grace. Yet does this understanding imply a limitation on God, as if God could not be gracious to us except by means of the sacraments? To my mind, this goes against the logic of grace as described in Scripture. God does not need sacraments to be gracious, but, practically speaking, the sacraments are needed by us, who, as embodied, social, and historical beings, ordinarily become who we are through tangible and social interactions over time. To put it another way, the sacraments are not a necessity to God, but they *are* the way God has ordained to unite and sustain the "body of Christ," the Church with its living Lord, through the ongoing work of the Holy Spirit. Here the understanding and sentiments of John Calvin are helpful. Had Calvin had his druthers, the churches of Geneva would have celebrated communion every Sunday. For all his reputation as a dry, intellectualist theologian, Calvin was quite sensitive to the need humans have for the tangible and tactile. He knew it could be very helpful for people's faith to have communion frequently, indeed, weekly. But the other leaders of Geneva, who wanted to avoid any semblance to weekly Mass, outvoted him.

Regarding this emphasis on the sacrament's "tangibility," theologian Colin Gunton raises another concern. To his mind, that traditional definition of a sacrament mentioned above—"an outward and visible sign of an inward and spiritual grace"[47]—actually creates certain unnecessary problems that it would be better to avoid. On the one hand (as I have already noted), it "encourages a broadening of what counts as a sacrament, effectively diluting the importance of what can, for want of a better expression, be called the gospel sacraments of baptism and the Lord's Supper."[48] On the other hand, "the dualism also tends to call attention away from the outward and material dimensions, whose reference rather should be primarily not to something going on *within* the believer but to concrete material and historical realities. Jesus's life and death are not the outward sign of something invisible, but the invisible become visible, God in action not only inwardly but also outwardly."[49] Sacraments are

47. Colin Gunton, *The Christian Faith: An Introduction to Christian Doctrine* (Oxford: Blackwell, 2002), 129.
48. Ibid.
49. Ibid., 129–30.

tangible means for incorporating individuals and a community into a concrete reality, namely, the redemptive activity of the Triune God in the world and its unfolding history. In other words, the sacraments are a means by which the gospel message may be communicated more effectively.

All these divergences, even controversies, in worship and sacramental practice should not overwhelm the recognition that under the headship of Christ, we are called to be one body. In this regard, Paul's warning to the Corinthians in the first century is as relevant to us today: "For any one who eats and drinks without discerning the body eats and drinks judgment upon himself" (1 Cor. 11:29 RSV). Many Christians over the centuries have understood this to mean discerning the body in the sacramental elements themselves. But given the context of Paul's admonitions chastising the divisions within the congregation at Corinth, it seems just as likely that he was saying judgment would come upon those who proceeded with the ritual without seeking first to overcome those divisions of the body. For being formed as one body, in increasing conformity with Christ, is in actuality one of the deep functions of the sacraments in particular and communal worship in general. Worship shapes us and orients us at the deepest levels, both by calling us out of ourselves and re-creating us into our true selves. Worship sets before us the vision of God's ultimate communion, even as it fosters that communion. In so doing, it tells us *who* we are, as God has intended from before creation. The recurring words and rhythms and patterns and music of worship ingrain such identity in ways that are frequently emotive and subconscious. But they are also only part of knowing fully who we are. At some point, our identity will have to become more explicit, so that a deep sense of who we are is also coupled with a clear sense of what we believe and what we stand for.

Priesthood of All Believers: Responsibilities of Office

> Like living stones, let yourselves be built into a spiritual house, to be a holy priesthood, to offer spiritual sacrifices acceptable to God through Jesus Christ. (1 Pet. 2:5)

The previous paragraphs have considered the worship of the community, including the centrality of Word and Sacrament. Through the power of the Holy Spirit, worship becomes a direct experience of the gathered body's communion with God. It includes personal address to God and the personal presence of God. Its speech is therefore "first order" language: of hearing God speak to us through Scripture, preaching, and the words of the liturgy and of us speaking to God through hymns, prayers, and other words of the liturgy. Worship itself has a formational effect upon the body and its members because its words and rituals orient and shape us in particular ways. Worship has a logic that becomes our logic; it has rhythms that become our rhythms; it has stories that become our stories. When we are truly worshiping, we usually practice these things unselfconsciously because they have become second nature to us.

A Body Must Know What *It Believes: Doctrine*

He was praying in a certain place, and after he had finished, one of his disciples said to him, "Lord, teach us to pray, as John taught his disciples." (Luke 11:1)

Judas (not Iscariot) said to him, "Lord, how is it that you will reveal yourself to us, and not to the world?" Jesus answered him, "Those who love me will keep my word, and my Father will love them, and we will come to them and make our home with them. Whoever does not love me does not keep my words; and the word that you hear is not mine, but is from the Father who sent me.

"I have said these things to you while I am still with you. But the Advocate, the Holy Spirit, whom the Father will send in my name, will teach you everything, and remind you of all that I have said to you." (John 14:22–26)

And his gifts were that some should be apostles, some prophets, some evangelists, some pastors and teachers, to equip the saints for the work of ministry, for building up the body of Christ, until we all attain to the unity of the faith and of the knowledge of the Son of God, to mature manhood, to the measure of the stature of the fulness of Christ; so that we may no longer be children, tossed to and fro and carried about with every wind of doctrine, by the cunning of men, by their craftiness in deceitful wiles. Rather, speaking the truth in love, we are to grow up in every way into him who is the head, into Christ, from whom the whole body, joined and knit together by every joint with which it is supplied, when each part is working properly, makes bodily growth and upbuilds itself in love. (Eph. 4:11–16 RSV)

Hold to the standard of sound teaching that you have heard from me, in the faith and love that are in Christ Jesus. Guard the good treasure entrusted to you, with the help of the Holy Spirit living in us. (2 Tim. 1:13–14)

All scripture is inspired by God and is useful for teaching, for reproof, for correction, and for training in righteousness, so that everyone who belongs to God may be proficient, equipped for every good work. (2 Tim. 3:16–17)

But even if you do suffer for righteousness' sake, you will be blessed. Have no fear of them, nor be troubled, but in your hearts reverence Christ as Lord.

Always be prepared to make a defense to any one who calls you to account for the hope that is in you, yet do it with gentleness and reverence; and keep your conscience clear, so that, when you are abused, those who revile your good behavior in Christ may be put to shame. (1 Pet. 3:14–16 RSV)

If the stories, rhythms, and logic of worship have so shaped us as to have become *second* nature to us, this also means they have been *learned* at some point. That is, they are not instinctual; they have been taught. Being *this* body (the Body of Christ), worshiping in *this* way (as daughters and sons of our heavenly Father, empowered by the Holy Spirit) necessarily presupposes that at some point we will have learned who we are and what we are doing.

THE CHURCH AS MOTHER

Yes, infants and children present in worship may participate in ways of which they are unaware. Yes, worship itself will form them subconsciously. The Spirit can indeed work directly and through the mediation of the congregation. I attended worship in a Russian Orthodox congregation some years back where a mother with an infant in her arms placed the baby's lips on the icon and then moved the baby's hand in the sign of the cross. Later, the same mother brought the infant to commune, and the priest gave the baby a small sip of consecrated wine with a petite spoon made for that purpose. I am convinced that all three acts will prove to be formational for the infant in some deep and subconscious way, and I was moved by observing them. But growing and maturing in the faith does require that at some point individual Christians and the congregation as a whole understand the basic tenets of what the Church believes, in order to worship fully and faithfully as well as to witness to and defend the gospel.

We human beings are not a precocious species, able to fend for ourselves instinctually from the moment of birth. The individuals of some species are so able: they do not require the care and nurture of parents. Young humans, of course, do require such nurture and care. And what holds true from the moment of our biological birth holds true for Christians from their spiritual rebirth in the waters of baptism. Christian faith does not come naturally; it must be taught and learned. Just as conscientious biological parents nurture their offspring in the knowledge, skills, and personal responsibilities necessary for adult life, so too does the Church nurture in its members a mix of the knowledge, skill, and responsibilities needed for membership in this community and participation in its witness. The venerable practice of assigning godparents to aid the biological parents of newly baptized children is one sign of the Church recognizing its responsibilities in this regard. Even more broadly, the role of the whole Church in such nurture is one of the implications that have grown out of the ancient saying of Cyprian of Carthage (d. AD 258): "He cannot have God as his Father who does not have the Church as his Mother."[50]

Indeed, some Protestants might be surprised that even the sixteenth-century Reformers, for all their complaints against the Catholic Church of their day, still extolled the necessary role the Church has in giving birth to and nurturing faith in its members. John Calvin wrote the following with regard to the "visible church" (i.e., the institutional Church here on earth) as "mother of believers":

> Let us learn even from the simple title "mother" how useful, indeed how necessary, it is that we should know her. For there is no other way to enter into life unless this mother conceive us in her womb, give us birth, nourish us at her breast, and lastly, unless she keep us under her care and guidance until, putting off mortal flesh, we become like the angels [Matt. 22:30]. Our weakness does not allow us to be dismissed from her school until we have been pupils all our lives. Furthermore, away from her bosom one cannot hope for any forgiveness of sins or any salvation, as Isaiah [Isa. 37:32] and Joel [Joel 2:32] testify. Ezekiel agrees with them when he declares that those whom God rejects from heavenly life will not be enrolled among God's people [Ezek. 13:9]. On the other hand, those who turn to the cultivation of true godliness are said to inscribe their names among the citizens of Jerusalem [cf. Isa. 56:5; Ps. 87:6]. For this reason, it is said in another psalm: "Remember me, O Jehovah, with favor toward thy people; visit me with salvation: that I may see the well-doing of thy chosen ones, that I may rejoice in the joy of thy nation, that I may be glad with thine inheritance" [Ps. 106:4–5; cf. Ps. 105:4, Vg., etc.]. By these words God's fatherly favor and the especial witness of spiritual life are limited to his flock, so that it is always disastrous to leave the church.[51]

50. Saint Cyprian of Carthage, "On the Unity of the Church," chap. 6 in *On the Church: Select Treatises*, trans. Allen Brent, Popular Patristics Series 33 (Crestwood, NY: St. Vladimir's Seminary Press, 2006), 157. To be sure, in the context of this treatise Cyprian employed the phrase as a polemic against schismatics rather than as, say, a justification for catechesis. Nevertheless, when he describes the "mothering" work of the Church, he echoes the sorts of things we would consider Christian nurture. And over the centuries, the saying has become a catchphrase understood and developed in a variety of ways. For example, when *The Catechism of the Catholic Church* describes the human profession of faith, it states the following in paragraph 181: "'Believing' is an ecclesial act. The Church's faith precedes, engenders, supports and nourishes our faith. The Church is the mother of all believers. 'No one can have God as Father who does not have the Church as Mother' (St. Cyprian, *De unit.* 6: PL 4, 519)." See http://www.vatican.va/archive/ccc_css/archive/catechism/p1s1c3a2.htm.

51. Calvin, *Institutes*, 4.1.4, p. 1016 (bracketed Bible citations are original to the Battles translation).

As Philip Butin comments, this passage shows Calvin's awareness "that the crucial role of the church in the divine-human relationship is as the matrix in which the grace of God is seen in and communicated to human beings."[52] His use of the term "matrix" here is not incidental: it is the Latin word for "womb." It is within this matrix of the Church—a concrete, historical entity—that God the Father through the work of the Holy Spirit knits us together with the risen Son, nurturing us into one body with him.

CATECHESIS

One aspect of this nurture is instruction—the traditional word is *catechesis*—in the faith. The necessity and practice of instruction is evident early on in scriptural accounts of the Church. In one sense, of course, the apostles' preaching was itself a form of instruction, following the lead of Jesus himself—especially the postresurrection instruction explaining everything written about him in the Law, the Prophets, and the Psalms (Luke 24:27, 44). As described in Acts 2, Peter's sermon at Pentecost is an exposition and interpretation of the Jewish scriptures in light of Jesus's life, death, resurrection, and ascension and an exposition of the role of these events in God's covenantal and redemptive purposes. And this sermon—along with the response it evokes—is hardly unique, in that the other sermons recounted in the book of Acts tend to follow the same basic pattern, regardless of who delivers them, and to evoke the same response. Philip's interaction with the Ethiopian eunuch makes explicit the connection between Scripture, instruction, and entry into the body (Acts 8:26–39). The Ethiopian is reading from Isaiah 53:7–8 when Philip runs up to him in his chariot and asks, "Do you understand what you are reading?," to which the Ethiopian replies,

"How can I, unless someone guides me?" And he invited Philip to get in and sit beside him. Now the passage of the scripture that he was reading was this:

"Like a sheep he was led to the slaughter,
   and like a lamb silent before its shearer,
      so he does not open his mouth.
In his humiliation justice was denied him.
   Who can describe his generation?
      For his life is taken away from the earth."

The eunuch asked Philip, "About whom, may I ask you, does the prophet say this, about himself or about someone else?" Then Philip began to speak, and

---

52. Philip W. Butin, *Reformed Ecclesiology: Trinitarian Grace according to Calvin*, Studies in Reformed Theology and History 2.1, ed. David Willis-Watkins (Princeton: Princeton Theological Seminary, 1994), 13.

starting with this scripture, he proclaimed to him the good news about Jesus. As they were going along the road, they came to some water; and the eunuch said, "Look, here is water! What is to prevent me from being baptized?" He commanded the chariot to stop, and both of them, Philip and the eunuch, went down into the water, and Philip baptized him. (Acts 8:31–38)

This passage anticipates a pattern that will later become common: instruction or catechesis first, and then baptism into the body of Christ, which is to say, union with the risen Christ and full membership in the Church community. Of course, in later Church practice the catechesis would last far longer than described in this episode.

Yet this pattern of adult instruction and baptism is not the only one evident in Scripture, as references to whole households being baptized (including, presumably, children)[53] and excerpts from 2 Timothy indicate. In the opening thanksgiving of that letter, Paul expresses his gratitude for Timothy's faith: "I am reminded of your sincere faith, a faith that lived first in your grandmother Lois and your mother Eunice and now, I am sure, lives in you" (2 Tim. 1:5). It seems clear that this is not a coincidental sequence, but that Timothy was in fact nurtured in this faith by his mother and grandmother. Now one might argue that this nurture was only informal, or that Timothy's faith grew simply as a result of watching and imitating the godly living of these two women. Yet a later passage renders such a reading unlikely. Warning of the wickedness and persecutions Timothy is likely to face, Paul admonishes him with these words:

> But as for you, continue in what you have learned and firmly believed, knowing from whom you learned it, and how from childhood you have known the sacred writings that are able to instruct you for salvation through faith in Christ Jesus. All scripture is inspired by God and is useful for teaching, for reproof, for correction, and for training in righteousness, so that everyone who belongs to God may be proficient, equipped for every good work. (2 Tim. 3:14–17)

This passage indicates that Timothy's childhood also included formal instruction and learning the Scriptures. And the obvious implication is that he received this instruction from his mother and grandmother, a conclusion given more weight when coupled with the brief description of Timothy in Acts 16:1, that he was "the son of a Jewish woman who was a believer; but his father was a Greek"—and presumably an unbeliever. These two types of example illustrate that regardless of one's chronological age when entering into the

53. Acts 16:15, 31–34; 18:8; 1 Cor. 1:16.

fellowship of the Church, one needs instruction, one needs to be raised up in the faith, to grow from "infancy" to "maturity" in the body.

Of course, such instruction usually means catechesis, which has typically been understood as meaning instruction in doctrine. But one must recognize that the Church's nurture of believers includes more than this, namely, formation in right desire and practice in good works. (I will speak more fully to such formation in chap. 5.) Recall from our discussion of baptism that one of its scriptural images is that we are "clothed in Christ," that we "put on" his righteousness. As one young theologian observed, these clothes do not immediately fit because we need to "grow into them."[54] This point is reinforced by the contrast appearing several times in Scripture between the "milk," or food fit for children, given in the early stages of Christian life and the "meat" that more mature Christians are able to digest.[55]

After all, Jesus himself sought out instruction (Luke 2:41–52) before he became a teacher, a "rabbi," who interpreted Scripture and taught through word, action, and example—although he was of course much more than just a teacher. Similarly, the apostle Paul, who himself clearly undertook serious study before his conversion (Phil. 3:4–6), speaks to the need for Christians to know certain things and to be rather sophisticated in that knowledge, in a variety of ways: by "maturing" in the faith, by "upbuilding" and "equipping," by being given sound teaching, by holding firm to sound doctrine, not being swayed by fashions and new teachings.[56] Does this mean that every Christian must become a professional theologian? No—but becoming at some level a *professing* theologian might not be too far off the mark. Recall the admonition of Peter: "Always be prepared to make a defense to any one who calls you to account for the hope that is in you, yet do it with gentleness and reverence" (1 Pet. 3:15). Here too, the Holy Spirit has a key role to play, as Jesus told his disciples: "These things I have spoken to you, while I am still with you. But the Counselor, the Holy Spirit, whom the Father will send in my name, he will teach you all things, and bring to your remembrance all that I have said to you" (John 14:25–26 RSV). Latter-day Christians, of course, have a different relation to Jesus's memory than the disciples to whom he first said this. The Spirit would call to mind their own memories of his words, while the Spirit

54. Martin Earnhardt, a seminarian at Princeton Theological Seminary, in a children's sermon delivered at Messiah Lutheran Church on Sunday, June 14, 2009. He illustrated this idea by having a young girl in the congregation put on an adult-size robe.

55. Confirmation is the common "rite of passage" that signifies this maturation, indicating that one has personally acknowledged and embraced that faith, and committed to be a living witness to it in thought, word, and deed.

56. 1 Cor. 2:6; 14:20; Eph. 4:11–15; Phil. 3:15; Col. 1:28; 4:12; 1 Tim. 1:3–11; 4:6–8; Titus 2:1–8.

reminds us through illuminating the Word of Scripture. At its most basic, this means being able to describe and affirm one's place in God's story: knowing what God has done, is doing, and will do for the world and for each of us, and knowing how God calls us to respond as a result. All Christians should be familiar with the basic outline of Scripture, the story of what God the Father is doing through his "two hands," the Son and the Spirit, for Israel, for the Church, and ultimately for the whole creation.

CREEDS

And this basic outline is typically what catechesis offers, and what the creeds present in even more summary form: a condensed statement of the basic tenets of the Christian faith and an outline for reading the Bible. The English word "creed" derives from the opening Latin word of these statements: "*Credo*" ("I believe . . .") or "*Credimus*" ("We believe . . ."). The two most familiar in the Western Church are the Nicene and the Apostles' Creeds. While this is not the place for a full historical consideration of their origins, it is important to know that the creeds emerged for two distinct but complementary reasons. The first was to be clear on the essentials when the faith was challenged by persecution or theological developments that threatened to derail or subvert the original gospel message. The second was to instruct new Christians in the fundamentals of the faith so that they knew what they were affirming at their baptism. Thus, for example, even in the apostolic era there was concern about "false teaching,"[57] and this only increased in the following centuries, which prompted a number of early Church fathers to offer succinct rebuttals or affirmations to refute such false teaching. Ignatius of Antioch, in countering the view typical of "docetism" that Jesus was a sort of "spirit person" and not a flesh-and-blood human, wrote this in the early 100s: "Be deaf, therefore, whenever anyone speaks to you apart from Jesus Christ, who is of the stock of David, who is of Mary, who was truly born, ate and drank, was truly persecuted under Pontius Pilate, was truly crucified and died in the sight of beings of heaven, of earth and the underworld, who was also truly raised from the dead."[58]

Similar sorts of summaries were offered by other early Church theologians,[59] and in all of them, one can hear precursors to the content and structure of the Nicene Creed of 325. This should come as no surprise, in that the creed produced by the Council of Nicaea likewise sought to repudiate "false teaching,"

---

57. Rom. 16:17–18; Eph. 4:11–15; 1 Tim. 6:3–5; 2 Tim. 4:3–4; Titus 1:9–11.
58. Quoted in John H. Leith, ed., *Creeds of the Church*, rev. ed. (Richmond: John Knox Press, 1973), 16–17.
59. Such as Justin Martyr, Irenaeus, Tertullian, and others. See Leith, *Creeds*, 18–22.

namely that of Arius, who held that Jesus was not fully divine. The orthodox position rejected this view, and not because it claimed special metaphysical insight into the inner being of Jesus. Rather, the orthodox position recognized, first, that if Jesus was not fully divine, then the worship of countless Christians directed toward him as Lord was not only misplaced but blasphemous, and, second, that because only God can save, if Jesus was not divine, he could not accomplish what the Church had always proclaimed he had!

The creeds also arose due to the catechetical needs of the growing Church. As converts from gentile, rather than Jewish, backgrounds began to predominate, they had to learn the history and identity of the covenantal family they were joining. More specifically, they needed to be able to make their baptismal vows fully informed on what they were affirming. In the baptismal rite, catechumens were asked a series of three questions concerning the faith, to which they were to answer, "I believe." According to the *Apostolic Tradition* of Hippolytus, a liturgical manual for clergy with roots in the third century, the process was for the catechumen to be taken down into the font with a deacon, while the presiding bishop or priest stood by and asked: "Do you believe in God, the Father Almighty . . . ?," to which the catechumen replied, "I believe." At this point, the deacon lowered him or her into the water once. Then the priest asked, "Do you believe in Christ Jesus, the Son of God, who was born from the holy Spirit from the Virgin Mary, and was crucified under Pontius Pilate, and died, and rose again on the third day alive from the dead, and ascended into heaven, and sits at the right hand of the Father, and will come again to judge the living and the dead?" The catechumen replied, "I believe," and the deacon lowered him or her again into the water. Then the priest asked: "Do you believe in the holy Spirit and the holy Church and the resurrection of the flesh?" When the person being baptized said again, "I believe," she or he was lowered a third time into the water by the deacon and then brought up out of the font and anointed with oil.[60] Anyone familiar with the Apostles' Creed will immediately recognize how these questions, reframed in the form of a tripartite statement, serve as the heart of that later affirmation.

Why is it important to know and affirm these things? Most basically, because Jesus commanded it: "You shall love the Lord your God with all your heart, and with all your soul, and with all your strength, and with all your *mind*" (Luke 10:27, emphasis added). One cannot truly love what one does not know, and the creeds—as well as the catechetical instruction they presuppose— help clarify who it is that the Church worships and adores. In this sense, the

60. *Hippolytus: A Text for Students*, with introduction, translation, commentary, and notes by Geoffrey J. Cuming (Nottingham: Grove Books, 1987), 19–20.

creeds are not ancillary to worship but serve to inform the faithful so that we may worship more fully and truly. In one sense, the creeds are the product of thoughtful, deep, and critical reflection upon the words and assumptions of Christian worship itself. They help clarify the necessary presuppositions that make Christian worship Christian. In another sense, when the creeds are themselves recited in worship, they help nurture and sustain the body over time as the body of *Christ*. To be sure, the creeds were the product of centuries of theological reflection, discussion, debate, and even acrimony, but over even more centuries they have been a source of guidance, reassurance, comfort, and unity. When generations of Christians have affirmed their faith using these traditional phrases, it is good to keep in mind the words of the apostle Paul: "Therefore I want you to understand that no one speaking by the Spirit of God ever says 'Jesus be cursed!' and no one can say 'Jesus is Lord' except by the Holy Spirit" (1 Cor. 12:3). They may be human words, but they can still be an instrument of the Holy Spirit, helping the body more fully know and live its faith.

A Body Must Know How It Is Put Together: Church Constitution

For as in one body we have many members, and all the members do not have the same function, so we, though many, are one body in Christ, and individually members one of another. Having gifts that differ according to the grace given to us, let us use them: if prophecy, in proportion to our faith; if service, in our serving; he who teaches, in his teaching; he who exhorts, in his exhortation; he who contributes, in liberality; he who gives aid, with zeal; he who does acts of mercy, with cheerfulness. (Rom. 12:4–8 RSV)

And his gifts were that some should be apostles, some prophets, some evange-lists, some pastors and teachers, to equip the saints for the work of ministry, for building up the body of Christ, until we all attain to the unity of the faith and of the knowledge of the Son of God, to mature manhood, to the measure of the stature of the fulness of Christ; so that we may no longer be children, tossed to and fro and carried about with every wind of doctrine, by the cunning of men, by their craftiness in deceitful wiles. Rather, speaking the truth in love, we are to grow up in every way into him who is the head, into Christ, from whom the whole body, joined and knit together by every joint with which it is supplied, when each part is working properly, makes bodily growth and upbuilds itself in love. (Eph. 4:11–16 RSV)

It is through the creating and sustaining work of the Holy Spirit that this body of Christ is—as the Nicene Creed puts it—one. (Just as it is the Holy Spirit who ensures the other creedal "marks" of the Church as well: holy, catholic, and apostolic—but more on that below.) The Church has its unity, indeed its very being, from the Holy Spirit—but unity does not mean uniformity or homogeneity. The "body of Christ" image for the Church is most fully developed in the apostle Paul's first letter to the Corinthians, although the image also appears in Romans 12:4–8; Ephesians 3:6; 4:11–16; 5:23; and Colossians 1:24; 3:15. While Paul's key concern in writing to the Corinthians was to help them overcome the culturally inherited divisions rending their church, in these various passages he clearly recognizes that the Church necessarily has diverse members with a variety of gifts. The social standings the Corinthians bring with them threaten to sunder the body; the gifts the Spirit provides unite and strengthen the body. Compiling a list from 1 Corinthians, Romans, and Ephesians, we can say that Paul recognizes how the Spirit gives some "the utterance of wisdom" and others "of knowledge"; some have a special gift of faith and others the discernment of spirits. It is a gift that some are apostles, prophets, teachers, or miracle workers, while others are healers, assistants, leaders, tongue speakers, exhorters, givers, the compassionate, evangelists, and pastors. Note also that Paul's discussion of the "one body/many members" metaphor in 1 Corinthians 12 is grounded in a trinitarian context throughout. In this light, he makes it clear that the diverse gifts are not intrinsic to the individuals themselves; rather, they are gifts bestowed by the Spirit following baptism "for the common good" (1 Cor. 12:7).

Paul holds that the various gifts of the Spirit are meant to complement and reinforce one another for the mutual good of the whole body. In so doing, he also makes it clear that they are not meant to be ranked, as if some had more spiritual status than others—and thus their recipients had a higher spiritual status than others, too. Rather, all are equally necessary to the one body. Indeed, in an echo of Jesus's teaching that the first will be last and the last first, Paul writes:

> On the contrary, the members of the body that seem to be weaker are indispensable, and those members of the body that we think less honorable we clothe with greater honor, and our less respectable members are treated with greater respect; whereas our more respectable members do not need this. But God has so arranged the body, giving the greater honor to the inferior member, that there may be no dissension within the body, but the members may have the same care for one another. (1 Cor. 12:22–25)

The body's connection to Jesus is made explicit in passages found elsewhere in the Pauline letters, passages that describe Christ as the head of the body,[61]

61. Eph. 1:22–23; 4:15–16; 5:23; Col. 1:18; 2:19.

who even with this status so loved the Church that he "gave himself up for her" (Eph. 5:25). In other words, the various gifts bestowed upon the diverse members of the Church are not meant to indicate different levels of status. But that is only part of Paul's concern. The other concern is, how are they to be used?

At first, it might appear that Paul gets sidetracked, when chapter 12 is followed by Paul's famous hymn to love: "If I speak in the tongues of men and of angels, but have not love, I am a noisy gong or a clanging cymbal" (1 Cor. 13:1–13 RSV). The hymn does indeed have a quality and coherence that allows it to stand on its own. Yet in the context of Paul's discussion of unity in the Church, it also establishes the principle that the use of the Spirit's gifts must always be grounded in love. The passage thus forms the backdrop for Paul when he resumes his more obviously ecclesiological questions and advice in 1 Corinthians 14. He offers a number of particular examples of how these gifts should be exercised, from which one may conclude they are to be used by the members of the Church in ways that avoid both conflict and chaos, while edifying the Church as a whole. He accentuates the complementary nature of the gifts, and how God intends for them to function together harmoniously for the common good (see Rom. 12:16). In the words of the Ephesians passage, they are "to equip the saints for the work of ministry, for building up the body of Christ" (Eph. 4:12). In the Corinthians passage he closes with an admonition that has become particularly famous in the Reformed theological tradition: "But all things should be done decently and in order" (1 Cor. 14:40).

Later tradition, based on the affirmations of the Nicene Creed, summarized the character of the true Church under what have come to be known as the Church's four "notes" or "marks": the Church is "one, holy, catholic, and apostolic." While these marks have relevance for any structure a particular church body may take (I will speak more about this below), they are primarily theological. Institutional interests should always serve the Church's God-given theological purposes, and not vice versa. So what do these marks mean? To begin with, the Church is "one" because God is one. And this oneness implies a derivative unity down the line. Recall Ephesians 4:4–6 (RSV): "There is one body and one Spirit, just as you were called to the one hope that belongs to your call, one Lord, one faith, one baptism, one God and Father of us all, who is above all and through all and in all." The Church has its unity not through any work of its own but because it has been incorporated by the Spirit into the communion of the one Triune God.

Similarly, the Church is "holy" because God is holy. The Church does not "institute" itself or belong to itself. It is, and remains, the work of the Triune God. Just as Israel would not exist were it not for God's call, so too the Church does not exist except as it is called forth, separated and dedicated to God's will and work. Etymologically, "set apartness" belongs to the very notion of "holy" itself.

Next, the Church is "catholic" (or "universal," which is what the original Greek word *katholikos* means) because God's act of reconciliation in Christ is universal. Christ's work was and is done for all humanity, and therefore the Church's character and service should likewise be universal. This also means that a true church cannot claim any essentially independent status vis-à-vis other churches, as if it had its own unique character and mission from God. It must in theory always be open to the claims and corrective of the "Church universal."

Finally, the Church is "apostolic" because God's revelation in Christ was and is, through the agency of the Holy Spirit, contained in one gospel entrusted to the apostles and summarized in their proclamation and writings. In other words, there is one faith, one basic message for the whole Church. This claim about the apostolic proclamation serves as the historical anchor, the affirmation that keeps the Church from drifting away when subjected to differing winds of doctrine (Eph. 4:14).

The preceding observations serve as an important starting point when we are considering the actual structure the Church as the body of Christ assumes. Yes, the God-given theological purposes of the Church should shape its institutional form—but it will still need an institutional form. This is evident from the scriptural witness, which also gives evidence of a certain structural flexibility and evolution. The pattern begins with Jesus himself, when he calls disciples to assist him in his ministry.[62] The fact that there are twelve of them, corresponding to the original number of Israel's tribes, clearly suggests that some divine purpose is unfolding. Following Jesus's ascension—and the death of Judas—the disciples felt compelled by scriptural prophecy to restore their number. Peter states that one of the men who have followed Jesus and the disciples from the beginning should be selected. Two are proposed, and after praying, they cast lots and Matthias is added to the eleven apostles (Acts 1:15–26).

The selection process is governed by theology. A modern reader might miss the theological assumptions guiding this selection process. First, Peter addresses the assembled believers with a reflection upon the Holy Spirit's foretelling certain events through Scripture, including the need for a new apostle. He reasons that the candidate should be not just anyone but rather someone drawn from among those long associated with the movement. In

---

62. Matt. 4:18–22; Mark 1:16–20; Luke 5:1–11; John 1:35–51.

response, the group proposes two names. In a sense, this back-and-forth between Peter and the assembly operates on a thoughtful but rather mundane
level. Yet then the group in effect consecrates their own process by praying,
turning the decision over to the Lord. Then they cast lots—which of course
is *not* understood as leaving things "to chance" or "the luck of the draw."
Rather, it is understood as allowing divine providence to decide, a practice
dating back at least as far as the ancient Hebrew practice of the Urim and
Thummim.[63] In other words, the decision depended on Scripture, a balanced
input of individual and group thoughtfulness, and experience, prayer, and
trust that the Holy Spirit was involved in the whole process.

A similar, though not identical, process was involved later with the selection
of the first deacons, described in Acts 6:1–7. The impetus is the complaint of
the "Hellenists" (i.e., later gentile converts) against the Hebrews (i.e., the more
established, earlier Jewish Christians) that their widows are being neglected
in the daily distribution of food. The "institutional structure" of the early
Church could not keep up with its ever-increasing numbers, which apparently
has prompted the two camps to fall back on old ethnic habits and suspicions.
So the apostles call the whole community together, Hellenists and Hebrews,
stating in effect that a new "office" needs to be created to serve the poor, so
that the apostles can continue their service to the Word. They call on the assembly to select seven from among themselves, "men of good standing, full
of the Spirit and of wisdom" (Acts 6:3), whom the apostles will appoint to
this task. After the group chooses them (two of Jewish background and five
of Greek, if their names are any indication), the apostles pray over them and
commission them through the laying on of hands. As with the last example,
note the balanced approach: apostolic authority is assumed, but it is open to
a change in current structure as well as to the input of the whole group. The
actual decision is made by the group itself, but the final decision is consecrated
with prayer and apostolic recognition.

Again in Acts 13 the Church adapts to the requirements of its call, commissioning Paul (still "Saul" at this point) and Barnabas for their first missionary
journey. The church at Antioch has several "prophets and teachers" among its
members. During a period of worship and fasting, the Holy Spirit says, "Set
apart for me Barnabas and Saul for the work to which I have called them"
(Acts 13:2). This they do, and following more fasting and prayer, members
of the church lay their hands on the two and send them off (Acts 13:3). This
episode has a more ad hoc character to it than the establishment of a new
"office," but the manner in which the process included a variety of leaders,

---

63. See e.g., Exod. 28:30; Num. 27:21; 1 Sam. 14:41; Ezra 2:63.

some spiritual disciplines, and an apparently requisite laying on of hands is noteworthy.

Later in Acts, what appears to be, in fact, a new ecclesial "office" does emerge, namely that of "elder" (*presbyteros*).[64] This position is a carryover from the Church's Jewish heritage, and as the name implies, an elder is the senior leader of a local congregation, respected for his presumed wisdom and experience. It is mentioned that Paul and Barnabas appointed a number of elders "with prayer and fasting" (Acts 14:23) on their missionary travels,[65] but it is not clear how other elders attained their position. At the mother church in Jerusalem, they hold a position of authority just under the apostles and are fully involved in the deliberations of the "Jerusalem Council" described in Acts 15. Of course, mention of elders is not confined to the Acts of the Apostles; references to this position are also made in the letters of 1 Timothy, Titus, James, 1 Peter, and 2 and 3 John and in the book of Revelation. The position evidently became an established part of the early Church's structure around the Mediterranean, although details on how one became an elder and what responsibilities it entailed remain somewhat ambiguous.

This contrasts starkly with the status and character of any who would "aspire" to a position of oversight (*episkopos*, that is, become a "bishop" or "overseer"). The position has apparently become a formal "office," and to even be considered for it, one must meet an extensive list of job qualifications, as outlined in 1 Timothy 3:1–7:

> The saying is sure: whoever aspires to the office of bishop desires a noble task. Now a bishop must be above reproach, married only once, temperate, sensible, respectable, hospitable, an apt teacher, not a drunkard, not violent but gentle, not quarrelsome, and not a lover of money. He must manage his own household well, keeping his children submissive and respectful in every way—for if someone does not know how to manage his own household, how can he take care of God's church? He must not be a recent convert, or he may be puffed up with conceit and fall into the condemnation of the devil. Moreover, he must be well thought of by outsiders, so that he may not fall into disgrace and the snare of the devil.

Scholars often point to this passage as an indication that the early Church has moved from a charismatic form of leadership to a more institutionalized form of structure and authority. There is no doubt truth in this observation,

---

64. Acts 11:30; 14:23; 15:2, 4, 6, 22–23, among other passages.
65. Cf. Titus 1:5. Intriguingly, such authorizing could be reciprocated, such as when a group of elders "commissioned" Timothy through the laying on of hands. See 1 Tim. 4:14.

yet one should also notice that the earlier, charismatic approach still echoes in the advice given to Timothy directly later in the letter. Paul admonishes him to set a good example in his words, faith, and deeds, and to attend to his duties of public Scripture reading, preaching, and teaching. For us, the heart of the matter is summarized in the words: "Do not neglect the gift that is in you, which was given to you through prophecy with the laying on of hands by the council of elders" (1 Tim. 4:14). In other words, the pattern is not so different from earlier instances described in Acts: the individual has certain gifts or skills from the Holy Spirit, and the Church recognizes them and confirms the individual's fitness for leadership through a laying on of hands. There is continuity in the fact that, from its earliest years, the Church has always been open to the guidance of the Holy Spirit in choosing and maintaining its leadership. Certainly, the process had a more ad hoc character in the beginning, which became more institutionalized as the generations passed. But the structure was there, with an essential balance between the prompting of the Spirit and the discernment of the individuals and the Church. While it is anachronistic to describe these as "ordinations" in our sense of the term, the precedent of a dual recognition by the Spirit and the Church, followed by a ritual affirmation or commissioning, is a succinct summary of what the modern Church does in choosing its leaders.

And it is crucial to recognize the need for such structures of leadership and oversight. It is naïve—and may in fact be a demonic lie—to assert that the Church does not need structure, that it need not and should not be "institutional." If the Church is to be embedded in a social context, if it is to exist from one generation to the next, it must have concrete forms and offices that enable it to maintain its identity and integrity in different places over time. This is not to say that these institutional structures are immune to stagnation or even abuse—the Church's history sadly shows that they can be and have been. But the appropriate response to such inertia or abuse ought never to be to disregard the need for structure altogether. Rather, the answer is to create in-built structures of accountability and renewal that, like the Church of the New Testament, remain open to the Holy Spirit's guidance and correction.

A Body Must Know Why *It Is: Ministry*

While spiritual and catechetical formation serves the individual's own life with God, it is never intended merely for the individual's "self-realization." Realizing one's true self is indeed a fruit of a maturing relationship with the Father through Christ by means of the Spirit. But a true faith also turns one outward, toward witness and works that help the Church serve God's greater covenantal mission in the world. Jesus himself set the standard, in coming "not to be served but to serve" (Matt. 20:25–28; Mark 10:42–45) and telling his disciples: "If I then, your Lord and Teacher, have washed your feet, you also ought to wash one another's feet. For I have given you an example, that you also should do as I have done to you. Truly, truly, I say to you, a servant is not greater than his master; nor is he who is sent greater than he who sent him" (John 13:14–16 RSV). And Jesus does indeed send them, and the Church, for we are under his commission: "All authority in heaven and on earth has been given to me. Go therefore and make disciples of all nations, baptizing them in the name of the Father and of the Son and of the Holy Spirit, teaching them to observe all that I have commanded you; and lo, I am with you always, to the close of the age" (Matt. 28:18–20 RSV). The Church's role in God's greater purposes can best be explained by considering it within the larger context of his covenantal people, to which I now turn.

4

The People of God

The Spirit and God's Sovereign Eschatological Purposes

> The LORD says to my lord:
> "Sit at my right hand,
> till I make your enemies your footstool."
>
> The LORD sends forth from Zion
> your mighty scepter.
> Rule in the midst of your foes! (Ps. 110:1–2 RSV)

Again the high priest asked him, "Are you the Messiah, the Son of the Blessed One?" Jesus said, "I am; and

> 'you will see the Son of Man
> seated at the right hand of the Power,'
> and 'coming with the clouds of heaven.'" (Mark 14:61–62)

In the first book, Theophilus, I wrote about all that Jesus did and taught from the beginning until the day when he was taken up to heaven, after giving instructions through the Holy Spirit to the apostles whom he had chosen. After his suffering he presented himself alive to them by many convincing proofs, appearing to them during forty days and speaking about the kingdom of God. While staying with them, he ordered them not to leave Jerusalem, but to wait there for the promise of the Father. "This," he said, "is what you have heard from me; for John baptized with water, but you will be baptized with the Holy Spirit not many days from now."

So when they had come together, they asked him, "Lord, is this the time when you will restore the kingdom to Israel?" He replied, "It is not for you to know the times or periods that the Father has set by his own authority. But you will receive power when the Holy Spirit has come upon you; and you will be my witnesses in Jerusalem, in all Judea and Samaria, and to the ends of the earth." (Acts 1:1–8)

> Therefore God also highly exalted him
> and gave him the name
> that is above every name,
> so that at the name of Jesus
> every knee should bend,
> in heaven and on earth and under the earth,
> and every tongue should confess
> that Jesus Christ is Lord,
> to the glory of God the Father. (Phil. 2:9–11)

For since death came through a human being, the resurrection of the dead has also come through a human being; for as all die in Adam, so all will be made alive in Christ. But each in his own order: Christ the first fruits, then at his coming those who belong to Christ. Then comes the end, when he hands over the kingdom to God the Father, after he has destroyed every ruler and every authority and power. For he must reign until he has put all his enemies under his feet. The last enemy to be destroyed is death. For "God has put all things in subjection under his feet." But when it says, "All things are put in subjection," it is plain that this does not include the one who put all things in subjection under him. When all things are subjected to him, then the Son himself will also be subjected to the one who put all things in subjection under him, so that God may be all in all. (1 Cor. 15:21–28)

In the life, death, and resurrection of Jesus Christ the Son, God the Father has liberated the world from those powers that have kept human beings— indeed, the whole of creation—in bondage to sin and death. Christ accomplishes this victory in his office as God's anointed King, heir to the throne of David, offering himself up on the cross to sin and death and vanquishing them through his glorious resurrection.[1] Recognizing this great work of God, the early Christian Church proclaimed that "Jesus is Lord." He is the crucified and risen Son of God, the Royal Messiah, whose victory over sin and death

---

1. For an extended treatment of Christ's royal work, see my *King, Priest, and Prophet: A Trinitarian Theology of Atonement* (New York: T&T Clark, 2004), chap. 3.

has broken their unjust sovereignty and fundamentally altered the world and its history. He is the King who has defeated Satan and once again revealed and reclaimed the Father's sovereignty over all creation. And this lordship is not merely something asserted or exercised in the past, something only associated with those few days following the first Easter Sunday. Rather, the Church knows it to remain in effect even now because of Jesus's ascension and his promise to return at the end of the age.

The Meaning of Jesus's Lordship in the Church

In this regard, contemporary Christians cannot understand fully what it means to say that "Jesus is Lord" and to be the people of God under his reign without first recognizing the significance of one of the most frequently cited scriptural passages in the emerging New Testament: "The LORD says to my lord, 'Sit at my right hand until I make your enemies your footstool.'" The quotation comes from Psalm 110:1, and it is used or alluded to in Matthew, Mark, Luke, the Acts of the Apostles, Romans, Ephesians, Colossians, Hebrews, and 1 Peter.[2] That so many New Testament writers echo this passage indicates its centrality and importance in explaining the risen Christ's status and role. And, of course, this usage is the basis for the later inclusion of this language in the Nicene Creed, first in affirming that following his resurrection, Jesus "ascended into heaven and is seated at the right hand of the Father," and then that "he will come again in glory to judge the living and the dead, and his kingdom will have no end." But what does the citation mean, as used in the New Testament and summarized in the creed? And why is it so central, so important, to affirm these things about Jesus in order to understand the Church as "the people of God"?

To begin with, saying that the risen Jesus sits at the right hand of God is simply another way of proclaiming that through Jesus, God exercises divine sovereignty over creation. The risen Jesus is the Father's royal Messiah, his anointed plenipotentiary. In the common English phrase, he is God's "right-hand man," through whom he governs the cosmos and through whom he will ultimately judge and perfect his good creation. The Son's incarnation and resurrection as Jesus Christ is both the act and the sign assuring us that God will not abandon creation to sin, death, and ultimately meaninglessness. Instead, he makes these enemies Jesus's "footstool," a poetic way of saying that Jesus will redeem the world from them, realigning it with the course that God had originally intended for it. God does not forsake the world but

2. See Matt. 22:41–46; Mark 12:35–37; 16:19; Luke 20:42–44; 22:67–70; Acts 2:30–36; 5:30–31; 7:55–56; Rom. 8:34; Eph. 1:20–22; Col. 3:1; Heb. 1:8–13; 8:1; 10:12–13; 12:2; 1 Pet. 3:21–22.

reclaims and renews it, incorporating it into the sphere of "the kingdom of God" or "kingdom of heaven." To say that "Jesus is Lord," that he is "seated at the right hand of God the Father," and that he will "come again to judge the living and the dead" means that God's reign is far larger than the Church. Divine sovereignty extends over all that God has made, from its origin to its ultimate end. But this hardly means that the Church has only a secondary role in this grand divine drama. Several points need to be made to place the Church's work in context.

First, we need to lay aside any literalistic fixation on the "metaphysical geography" of this affirmation of Jesus's location. As with all theological language, such an affirmation is analogical or metaphorical in character. But this is not to say it is "merely" analogical or metaphorical. The analogical and metaphorical are as capable of conveying truth as more straightforwardly literal language—and in certain cases they are even more capable. (Sadly, this is not the place for a fuller discussion of such capabilities.) So, stipulating that Jesus is seated at God's right hand, what does it mean? To begin with, saying that Christ is the Church's risen Lord occupying this place next to the Father is another way of saying that Jesus is transcendently living and present to the Church. He is not merely a figure of the past, no matter how inspiring and "alive" in the Church's memory. (And in the present context, with its amazing and often contradictory collection of authors claiming to offer *the* "historical Jesus," this is a relief!) The Church recognizes that Jesus is not "located" back then but is present here and now. Jesus is not just the revered originator of a religious movement; rather, he continues to be its living head. Yet for many, it might seem that "up there" in heaven is just as inaccessible and distant to us as "back then" in history is—so how does the Church overcome this gulf?

The short answer is, the Church doesn't. Instead, locating Jesus at the right hand of the Father means, second, that it is the Holy Spirit alone who makes the living Lord present to the Church: the Church does not possess or control the risen Christ but must ever and again receive him through the work of the Spirit. Recognizing this reality both humbles and exalts the Church. It humbles the Church because, like any other human collective or institution, it, too, is embedded in the world's fallenness, in original sin. As such, it too is subject to disorientation, disorder, and sinful behavior. In particular, it is prone to think too highly of itself, by confusing itself with what it proclaims. Indeed, as Karl Barth observes, religions can be the most egregious sinners precisely because they have to do with divine things. Self-idolatry crouches ever ready by the door. But when the Church humbly submits itself to God and to God's intentions for it, it is indeed exalted. It obtains intimate communion with its Lord and is enabled to blossom and grow in unexpected, even miraculous, ways. The Church knows its Lord's gracious mercy and transforming power and holiness. Opening itself to this Spirit-given reality also exalts the Church in that it receives the awe-inspiring responsibility of being the Spirit-wielded instrument continuing the Son's witness to the Father's in-breaking reign.

Third, as the people whose living Lord will come again, the Church is given its telos, its purpose and goal. As the people of God's reign, the Church was not merely given life at the first Pentecost and launched into the stream of history, leaving later generations to direct it according to their best lights. It is the Holy Spirit who sustains this people toward the fulfillment of the reign that Jesus proclaimed and initiated in keeping with the Father's eternal purposes, and that goal offers the Church a criterion by which it may measure its faithfulness toward—or deviation from—that end. The Holy Spirit grants the Church the tools of discernment it requires to be a responsible instrument. All this presupposes and explains further the claim I made in chapter 2 about the Church being the particular work of the Holy Spirit. The period between Christ's ascension to the right hand of the Father and his return to judge the living and the dead is precisely that time in which the Spirit is active as the enlivening and sanctifying mediator of Christ to the Church. The Church cannot be the Church unless it affirms Jesus as its Lord; it cannot affirm Jesus as Lord unless it affirms his exaltation to the right hand of the Father; and it cannot affirm this exaltation unless it opens itself to the inspiration and guidance of the Holy Spirit. As Paul writes: "Therefore I want you to understand that no one speaking by the Spirit of God ever says 'Jesus be cursed!' and no one can say 'Jesus is Lord' except by the Holy Spirit" (1 Cor. 12:3 RSV).

The Spirit and Our New Allegiance

Why is all this so important? Because far too many Christians still tend to think that Jesus's inquiry of his disciples ("But who do you say that I am?") remains an open question. We know Peter's famous confession ("You are the Christ, the Son of the living God"),[3] yet like Peter, we also too easily miss the full meaning of this confession. We are prone to slide into old patterns of thinking, our versions of the expectations in Jesus's own day. There were various currents of hope and expectation among the Jews of Jesus's time that a messianic figure would appear to save the people. Certain Zealots hoped that a descendent of the Davidic line would usher in a new political order by defeating the Romans and establishing an independent nation-state. The highly ascetic Essene community near the Dead Sea had more otherworldly

3. See Matt. 16:15–16//Mark 8:29//Luke 9:20.

hopes, believing God's messiah would be an apocalyptic figure descending from the heavens. And some thought that Jesus himself might be this new leader. Witness how they acclaimed his entrance into Jerusalem with palm branches, reminiscent of the Hasmonean dynasty from Israel's last period of independence following the Maccabean Revolt. Peter's confession and Jesus's response make clear what had been implicit in Jesus's words and actions up to that point, that he was indeed God's messiah.

And yet Jesus continually confounded expectations, especially in his insistence on his future suffering, death, and resurrection.[4] Even when it all came to pass, his disciples and followers had difficulty giving it credence or making sense of it. In Matthew's account, the eleven remaining disciples encounter the risen Christ; most worship him, "but some doubted" (Matt. 28:17). In Mark's account ending at 16:8, the women flee from the empty tomb saying nothing to anyone, "for they were afraid." The longer ending of Mark recounts further unbelief on the part of the disciples.[5] In a passage we have already partly considered, Luke's Gospel tells how the two followers walking on the road to Emmaus recount to the (by them unrecognized) risen Jesus all the events that had occurred in Jerusalem the past few days, and how they cannot make sense of it all. This prompts Jesus to reply, "'Oh, how foolish you are, and how slow of heart to believe all that the prophets have declared! Was it not necessary that the Messiah should suffer these things and then enter into his glory?' Then beginning with Moses and all the prophets, he interpreted to them the things about himself in all the scriptures" (Luke 24:25–27). After inviting him into their lodging for the evening meal, they do finally recognize him in the breaking of the bread—but Jesus vanishes. A similar event occurs shortly thereafter, as this first group of followers rush back to Jerusalem to relate to the eleven disciples what has happened. Once again Jesus appears—provoking fear, wonder, and disbelieving joy—and once more explains,

> "These are my words that I spoke to you while I was still with you—that everything written about me in the law of Moses, the prophets, and the psalms must be fulfilled." Then he opened their minds to understand the scriptures, and he said to them, "Thus it is written, that the Messiah is to suffer and to rise from the dead on the third day, and that repentance and forgiveness of sins is to be proclaimed in his name to all nations, beginning from Jerusalem. You are witnesses of these things. And see, I am sending upon you what my Father promised; so stay here in the city until you have been clothed with power from on high." (Luke 24:44–49)

4. Matt. 16:21//Mark 8:31//Luke 9:22.
5. Mark 16:11–14.

The Gospel of John reiterates this same point regarding how one must learn—or, more accurately, must be taught—to see the risen Christ, because the meaning and implications of his messianic role are not self-evident. Mary Magdalene does not recognize the risen Jesus on her own; she recognizes him only when he addresses her by name.[6] Thomas refuses to believe the testimony of the other disciples and insists on having his own personal empirical experience. Jesus provides it—provoking Thomas's confession, "My Lord and my God!"—but implicitly upbraids Thomas by blessing those who believe without seeing.[7] Moreover, the commission that the disciples receive under Jesus's lordship does not align with any worldly expectations. Appearing to a group of disciples, Jesus says, "As the Father has sent me, so I send you" (John 20:21), breathing upon them and telling them to receive the Holy Spirit, with the accompanying words: "If you forgive the sins of any, they are forgiven; if you retain the sins of any, they are retained" (John 20:23 RSV; cf. Matt. 16:19; 18:18). Yet faithfully following this commission can hardly be expected to lead to worldly power and eminence. Indeed, given Jesus's words to Peter ("Very truly, I tell you, when you were younger, you used to fasten your own belt and to go wherever you wished. But when you grow old, you will stretch out your hands, and someone else will fasten a belt around you and take you where you do not wish to go" [John 21:18]), disciples must instead be prepared for martyrdom.

In sum, the early disciples had their preconceptions of how Jesus was the Messiah, preconceptions that had to be done away with and reforged by Jesus and the events of his crucifixion, death, resurrection, and ascension. In a similar manner, preconceptions about what it meant to be "the people of God" also had to be done away with and reforged according to the events of Jesus's crucifixion, death, resurrection, and ascension. That is, if Jesus was not to be conceived as a worldly king, then his reign was not to be conceived as a worldly kingdom. If his reign was a reign of God, a "kingdom of heaven," then the "people of God" could no longer be understood as just one more nation among the nations. Its call is instead to be a "holy nation" and a "royal priesthood" (Exod. 19:6; 1 Pet. 2:9), a commission first given by God to Moses and the people at Sinai and now made possible through the outpouring of the Holy Spirit.

The Church's basic recognition here is as follows: in keeping with the Father's gracious purposes and covenantal plan, the Holy Spirit summons a particular community to become the "people of God," now defined by their

6. John 20:11–17.
7. John 20:24–29.

allegiance to God's heavenly reign, as proclaimed and enacted by Jesus, his incarnate and risen Son. To belong to the Church means to belong to a people whose ultimate allegiance is to a Lord not of this world who lived, died, and was raised for the sake of this world. To belong to the Church means to be an alien people in a strange land, even while being citizens of the new commonwealth in which that land will discover its truest fulfillment. To belong to the Church means to belong to a people that lives in two worlds: the world created by God but fallen into sin, despair, and death and the world intended by God, namely, that same world redeemed, made whole, and given new life in Christ through the power of the Holy Spirit. To belong to the Church is to belong to that people who knows that in Christ's resurrection God has achieved the victory that ultimately reclaims the world from the powers of evil and darkness and begins its salvation and glorification. The Church is that people of God which, through the power of the Holy Spirit poured out upon it, acknowledges and has experienced the kingdom proclaimed by his Son Jesus, and which, by that same Spirit's power, knows itself to be an instrument of the furtherance of God's reign.

In all this, the Church recognizes that it has been incorporated into the covenantal promise first made to Abraham and Sarah, namely, that through them will all the nations of the world be blessed (Gen. 12:1–3). The Church recognizes that it has been incorporated into the liberation from Egypt and the covenant obligation laid down at Sinai (Exod. 19:1–6). And the Church recognizes that Jesus has also been made heir to the dynastic promise given to David, that God would raise up an offspring after him and "establish the throne of his kingdom forever" (2 Sam. 7:12–16), the basis and a prophecy of Jesus's elevation to sit at God's right hand as Lord.

The Community's Mission: A Holy Nation, a Royal Priesthood

> Now the LORD said to Abram, "Go from your country and your kindred and your father's house to the land that I will show you. And I will make of you a great nation, and I will bless you, and make your name great, so that you will be a blessing. I will bless those who bless you, and him who curses you I will curse; and by you all the families of the earth shall bless themselves." (Gen. 12:1–3 RSV)

> Then Moses went up to God; the LORD called to him from the mountain, saying, "Thus you shall say to the house of Jacob, and tell the Israelites: You have seen what I did to the Egyptians, and how I bore you on eagles' wings and brought you to myself. Now therefore, if you obey my voice and keep my covenant, you

shall be my treasured possession out of all the peoples. Indeed, the whole earth
is mine, but you shall be for me a priestly kingdom and a holy nation. These
are the words that you shall speak to the Israelites." (Exod. 19:3–6)

> "And in that day, says the LORD,
>   I will answer the heavens
>   and they shall answer the earth;
> and the earth shall answer the grain, the wine, and the oil,
>   and they shall answer Jezreel;
>   and I will sow him for myself in the land.
> And I will have pity on Not pitied,
>   and I will say to Not my people, 'You are my people';
>   and he shall say, 'Thou art my God.'" (Hos. 2:21–23 RSV)

But you are a chosen race, a royal priesthood, a holy nation, God's own people,
that you may declare the wonderful deeds of him who called you out of darkness into his marvelous light. Once you were no people but now you are God's
people; once you had not received mercy but now you have received mercy.
(1 Pet. 2:9–10)

The Church is not just an aggregate of individuals but a body: persons knit
together into an assembly, a congregation, a people. This is so because God
calls individuals not in isolation but as members of this people, a "communion
of saints." And this is so because redemption itself has a social character: it
is not just an individual's reconciliation to God, but also each individual's
reconciliation with his or her estranged fellow creatures. Through his redemptive acts, God the Father gives this people a new reality and identity in
Christ, which in the power of the Holy Spirit evoke in them praise and thanks
and joy. But this new reality and identity also entail a task and a goal: to be a
people "set apart," a "city on the hill" witnessing to God's being and larger
purposes in and for the world. The Church must know who it is, must know
the essence and implications of its reality and identity. And this is necessary
not just for its own self-edification, not just so it can be introspective, curved
in upon itself in self-referential preoccupation. Rather, it is necessary so that
it may fulfill its role as a holy nation and royal priesthood enlisted in the work
of God's unfolding covenantal promises.

A premise of this book is that many Christians in America—mainline and
evangelical Protestants in particular, but even Roman Catholics insofar as they
have absorbed the ethos of American individualism—need to regain a sense
of the Church as the locus of our common culture, of both our communal
and individual identity. For certain segments of the population, this would be

a hard sell. For them, the Church is the problem, not the answer. Particular scandals—be they sexual, financial, or something else—and a general sense that the Church is behind the times, out of touch, and a hindrance to human progress and self-realization all contribute to this disregard. For others, namely Christians whose lives are already centered very much in Church activities, this prescription may seem unnecessary. Yet they may not realize the degree to which their church life has itself been infiltrated by assumptions and behaviors that are ultimately inimical to the ideals and long-term health of the Church. One example is the degree to which various denominations and individual churches simply reflect rather than seek to reconcile or transcend the various divisions existing in the surrounding society, whether they are based on ethnic, racial, political, economic, generational, educational, or other characteristics. One's church affiliation runs the risk of becoming nothing more than a marker of one's "identity politics." In a benign form, it is an unconscious and uncritical mirroring of one's place in the surrounding society. In a more pernicious form, it is the Church being co-opted by other ideologies.

Culture does not exist in a vacuum, and neither can it exist on a merely "spiritual" level. It also cannot exist for long compartmentalized as something merely personal. For it to thrive, it must be embedded in the material world and have its own rich and complex ecology to sustain it over time. Western Christianity used to exist in such a cultural ecosystem, but over against the patterns and forces of modernity, this ecology has been thinned and undermined. Now, in many parts of American society, Christianity occupies a small, highly specialized niche. Therefore, it has become susceptible to collapse with only the slightest of changes in the surrounding environment. This may seem counterintuitive, given the number of church buildings that still dot the American landscape, the still-large majorities of Americans who identify themselves as Christian when polled,[8] the continuing pervasiveness of Christian religious language in civic discourse, and the abiding strength of Christian sensibilities in moral and legal matters. Yet all of these are also less dominant than they might first appear: many of those church buildings are often more empty than full; Christian identification may still be pervasive, but it is often superficial; and Christian language and sensibilities are hotly

8. According to a January–November 2011 Gallup poll, 78 percent of Americans pick Christianity as their "religious preference." That said, compared to sixty years ago, when only 1 percent of respondents said they had no formal religious identity, this poll found that that number had increased to 15 percent. Note that "preference" implies it is a choice along the lines of a consumer decision, a matter of personal taste rather than a recognition of a fundamental reality or truth. Available at http://www.gallup.com/poll/151760/Christianity-Remains-Dominant-Religion -United-States.aspx?utm_source=Christianity&utm_medium=search&utm_campaign=tiles.

contested in the public realm. Religion is increasingly seen as something that is and should be a private matter, and also as something rather fluid. It is not unusual to hear individuals describing personal spiritual journeys that include various episodes in which they self-identified as a Christian, an atheist, a Buddhist, something else, or some eclectic combination.

Not Pluralism but Fragmentation

All of this reflects the fact that, as Jonathan R. Wilson describes, Americans live in a culture that is no longer pluralistic but rather fragmented.[9] A pluralistic culture is

> made up of coherent, integral communities, traditions, or positions that can be clearly differentiated from one another. Although they disagree and may often be in conflict, where the disagreements are located and why they arise are generally clear to everyone. One's identity—as an individual or community—is clear, the convictions that constitute that identity are coherent, and the life that follows from those convictions is determined.[10]

Examples of such communities could be American Roman Catholics in the 1950s; the Amish; current self-contained Hasidic Jewish, Muslim, or Hindu communities in some large cities; or certain immigrant ethnic groups that have not assimilated into "mainstream" American culture. There is a clear sense of personal identity grounded in a group identity, of that group identity existing in clear contrast to the surrounding culture, and of a way of life that will unfold in a manner different from, or even at odds with, the dominant culture. One's identity is inherited, assumed, and "grown into" in a manner that is both organic and reinforced in multiple ways.

A fragmented culture, by contrast, does not ground the individual in a clear and coherent community with a set tradition and ethos. A fragmented culture is one in which the individual inhabits multiple cultures sequentially and simultaneously. One's identity is not so much inherited as personally invented or selected. Such fragmentation finds the individual afloat in a sea of cultural options from which he or she chooses, and one's identity is presumed to be most authentic when it is a product of this self-creation. And yet without a coherent ground from which to make those choices, our acts easily become

9. Jonathan R. Wilson, *Living Faithfully in a Fragmented World: Lessons for the Church from MacIntyre's* After Virtue, Christian Mission and Modern Culture (Harrisburg, PA: Trinity Press International, 1997), 26–38. As Wilson's title makes clear, his analysis borrows directly from the philosopher Alasdair MacIntyre.

10. Ibid., 27.

merely arbitrary, indeed, reactive. That is, they are not so much grounded in deep-seated and time-tested principles as they are a response to the most recent or most dominant stimuli we encounter. Consider the implications of the fact that the word "feel" so often replaces the word "think": when asked for an opinion or a response to some situation, how often do individuals say, "I feel this or that" rather than "I think this or that." It seems less a matter of considered reflection than an unconscious and reactive impulse or reflex. Or perhaps this is not entirely accurate, because there may indeed be deep-seated habits at work, namely, individuals responding in ways to which they have been conditioned. Perhaps they are making consumer-minded decisions, having been accustomed to prefer the new and different, or they are making value judgments based on norms absorbed from the vagaries of popular culture.[11]

What Is a People?

It may well be that many in modern North American culture simply do not know what it means to be a "people." What constitutes a "people"? No single, obvious definition offers itself because the answer depends so heavily on context and presupposition. Many in contemporary culture probably understand it in merely grammatical terms as the plural for "person": "Go stand next to that group of people over there" in contrast to "Go stand next to that person." "People" simply refers to a collection of individuals with nothing necessarily identifying them with one another. Other persons may recognize it as a collective term but differ in defining the underlying commonality that forms these particular individuals into this specific group. One people might be defined by their shared citizenship in the same country; others by their common language or culture; others by a shared ethnicity or race; others by a common ancestry; others by a particular ideology; yet others by a shared geography. These various commonalities may overlap, but they may also be in tension.

The United States is a nation of immigrants: what does it mean to be an "American," that is, a member of the American "people"? The question itself has become highly politicized. One inherited image is that of the "melting pot," where our various ethnic, racial, cultural, and linguistic particularities are blended together under a shared allegiance to certain ideals, such as democracy, "liberty and justice for all," personal responsibility, "land of opportunity," and the like. Others say this image conceals certain vested interests, masks

---

11. A very insightful investigation into the impact of modern and secular "cultural liturgies" is James K. A. Smith, *Desiring the Kingdom: Worship, Worldview, and Cultural Formation*, Cultural Liturgies 1 (Grand Rapids: Baker Academic, 2009).

certain entrenched ideologies, and privileges certain power groups within the whole. To counter these, they promote the alternative image of the "patchwork quilt," which helps preserve some of the ethnic, racial, and cultural distinctives of the given groups that make up the American population. But this raises the question, with which "people" do these subgroups most identify? Such a question is currently a hot-button one in our context, raising debates about "identity politics"—but it might draw a look of blank incomprehension in another context. How could one's membership in a people be a matter of choice? Isn't it simply a given? In societies with more cultural, racial, and linguistic homogeneity—Japan, for example—who is or is not a member of the people is typically understood as self-evident.[12]

Of course, living in a homogeneous, inherited culture is itself no guarantee of harmony and justice. Cultures can themselves be disordered, just as received traditions may be more evil than good. Indeed, as discussed in chapter 1, sin and evil embedded in culture are typically more pernicious than individual sin and immorality because they can be largely invisible, simply assumed as the way things are. Individuals cannot see them because they surround them externally and inform them internally. They just become a part of who people are and how they view life. This is why I have argued for the necessity of maintaining the Christian doctrine of original sin, because without it we lose a key tool for recognizing the insidious nature of sin when it becomes systemic. But I have also argued that the only way one can resist culturally embedded sin is with a counterculture. Individuals alone simply do not have the capacity for withstanding the pressure and power of a culture set against them. But this presents our current postmodern, fragmented American Church with a dilemma. It sounds as if we are being called to create a new culture, to invent a new tradition. Yet for a tradition to truly function, it must be received, not invented; it must be inherited as a given and not be the product of our own creativity and imagination. After all, if it is something we make up ourselves, how can it be binding? What's to prevent us from arbitrarily changing it in the future, since it is our creation in the first place? This is the paradoxical dead end into which our current cultural fragmentation has led us, into a self-referential loop that cannot escape itself, that thinks reality is its own invention.

12. Of course, such "self-evidence" is not necessarily always benign in its consequences, as people of Korean heritage will testify regarding Japan's behavior toward them during World War II. The United States government's treatment of American citizens of Japanese heritage during the same time frame is another example of actions taken on the basis of "self-evident" assumptions made by one group about another—assumptions that we now recognize as clearly racist.

Growth of Humanity, Growth of Sin

And yet such self-reference is nothing new in human existence. "Inventing our own reality" actually has a long history. Indeed, our present fragmented, disordered reality is just a variation on a common human theme. This is the truth to which the Genesis story of humanity's creation and fall speaks. I described this in chapter 1, but let me add some further thoughts. Adam and Eve get into trouble in the garden by turning away from the reality that God designed and gave them, seeking instead to invent a better reality on their own terms. Their expulsion from the garden is, in effect, God giving them what they desired: the opportunity to build a life according to their own lights. Of course, God does not abandon them, as indicated in Genesis 3:21 by his making garments of skin to clothe them. Yet the story that immediately follows this account illustrates the repercussions of that initial rupture. Modern parlance speaks of the "butterfly effect" ("a butterfly flapping its wings in Africa can cause a hurricane in the Gulf of Mexico"), as if we had just discovered how seemingly insignificant occurrences can ripple along to disproportionate consequences. Yet the Bible long ago recognized how the breaking of trust between Adam and Eve and God grew to infect the relationship between Cain and Abel, and how Cain's murdering Abel corrupted the relationship of humanity with the earth. Yet again, when God judges and punishes the offender, he also declares that he will be the offender's protector, marking him so that all will know that God will be his avenger should any harm befall him.

At this juncture in the biblical story come two terse, crucial verses: "Then Cain went away from the presence of the LORD, and dwelt in the land of Nod, east of Eden. Cain knew his wife, and she conceived and bore Enoch; and he built a city, and called the name of the city after the name of his son, Enoch" (Gen. 4:16–17 RSV). This is the first city mentioned in the Bible, and the list of Cain's descendants also describes the invention of musical instruments, of tools of bronze and iron, and apparently also the vendetta.[13] In other words, with the founding of the city, human culture emerges. Is it reading too much into these words to conclude that, now that Cain has left the Lord's presence, this city Cain builds will be a godless place? Perhaps. Following this brief history of Cain's fate, the story returns to Adam and Eve and their third son, Seth, who in turn has a son, Enosh. The account then concludes with the statement: "At that time people began to invoke the name of the LORD" (4:26b). So maybe it is more appropriate to say that a yearning for God remains, even while the increase of humanity through the generations makes its resistance to God all the more intractable:

13. Gen. 4:18–24.

The Lord saw that the wickedness of humankind was great in the earth, and that every inclination of the thoughts of their hearts was only evil continually. And the Lord was sorry that he had made humankind on the earth, and it grieved him to his heart. So the Lord said, "I will blot out from the earth the human beings I have created—people together with animals and creeping things and birds of the air, for I am sorry that I have made them." (6:5–7)

Thus commences the story of Noah, the ark, and the flood, as well as the covenant that God makes with Noah, his family, and all creation. This will be a fresh start: from Noah's three sons will come all the people of the earth (9:19).

Yet immediately following this statement, Scripture then describes Noah as the first tiller of the soil. What does he plant? A vineyard—and the account wastes no time saying he partakes of its wine, becomes drunk, and passes out naked in his tent. His son Ham discovers his father in this disgraceful state and tells his two brothers. They manage to cover their father without looking. When Noah awakes and discovers what has happened, he actually pronounces a curse upon Ham's son Canaan, that he will be a slave to his two uncles, Shem and Japheth (Gen. 9:20–27). After a genealogy of the descendants of Shem, Ham, and Japheth (chap. 10), there immediately follows the story of the construction of the tower of Babel and the effort of the men involved to make a name for themselves (11:1–4). The Lord witnesses this undertaking and recognizes that the human unity and power involved actually pose a threat, so he confuses their language and scatters them across the face of the earth (11:5–9).

These stories illustrate that as human culture grows, increases its skills, and becomes more complex, so too does human sin. As new generations are born into what has come before, they inherit the assumptions, the tendencies, and the predilections of their ancestors. And the same, of course, is true for us as well. It is simply the human story. Embedded as every individual is in fallen human culture, it is hardly likely that our release from sin will come from within culture itself. And that is why Scripture, when describing the beginning and sustaining of the people that God would make a blessing for all the nations, characterizes that beginning and sustaining as a *call* rather than as the conclusion of human experience or reflection. That is why Scripture recounts God breaking *into* everyday reality to summon individuals and peoples *out* to a new reality: Abraham and Sarah, Jacob, Moses, David, the prophets, the women at Jesus's tomb, the disciples gathered in the upper room and then at Pentecost, the apostle Paul, and the seer of Revelation. To be holy means to be set apart. And it is the holy God who does the setting—and the continual resetting. Scripture makes this point by showing God repeating his call and covenantal blessing of Abraham[14] and reaffirming it to his descendants: first to Isaac,[15] then to Jacob,[16] and then it passes to Joseph (Gen. 39:5) and radiates out from him (48:15–16). God is not just the God of Abraham but, as the tradition recognized, "the God of Abraham, the God of Isaac, and the God of Jacob" (Exod. 3:6, 15; 4:5). In a manner analogous to legal testimonies that require two or three witnesses,[17] this suffices to confirm the matter. The call and blessing are in that sense cumulative, building with each generation.

Church as Counterculture

This cumulative pattern is one reason why the new covenant in Christ should not be understood as a replacement of the old covenant, as somehow superseding it. The new covenant broadens and deepens that original covenant, unveiling and realizing what was implicit in it. But its essence remains constant. Recall Jesus's encounter with the disciples on the road to Emmaus and later with those in Jerusalem, and his saying: "'These are my words which I spoke to you, while I was still with you, that everything written about me in the law of Moses and the prophets and the psalms must be fulfilled.' Then he opened their minds to understand the scriptures" (Luke 24:44 RSV). Clarification of this same reality then provides the basis for the apostolic preaching throughout the book of Acts, the letters of Paul, the Letter to the Hebrews, indeed, the remainder of the New Testament. In other words, the Church does not invent or create this reality; it is summoned, rather, to recognize it. Our call is to live into this recognition, this covenantal reality that God has already established, is providentially guiding, and will ultimately bring to full fruition. The Church is to be a counterculture, one that resists the inroads of fallen human norms and attitudes.

To be sure, a concern regarding this way of thinking is that an "us against them" mentality may develop, rekindling a dangerous form of group division and strife. Yet resources are available to avoid such strife without denying a need for a solid group identity. If we forsake such a communal identity, this simply means we have laid ourselves open to uncritically and perhaps unconsciously accepting the norms of other cultural groups: consumer capitalism, political parties of the left or the right, academic or professional elitism, our various work environments, popular culture, and the like. Since we are

14. Gen. 12:1–3; 18:18–20; 22:15–18.
15. Gen. 25:11; 26:2–5, 24.
16. Gen. 28:13–14; 35:9–15. Cf. Gen. 28:3–4; 32:24–32; 48:3–4.
17. See Deut. 17:6; 19:15; Matt. 18:16; 26:60; John 8:17; 2 Cor. 13:1; 1 Tim. 5:19; Heb. 10:28; Rev. 11:3.

irreducibly social beings, our lives abhor a cultural vacuum. It will be filled by something. Consider how a culture shapes and informs the people within it and the characteristics it has in order to maintain its identity over time. In our current situation, our Christian responsibility is to enable our communal life together to remain and become a culture that aligns itself with God's larger purposes. To echo the psalmist, we need a rock, a stronghold from which to evaluate the cultural claims around us, as well as to withstand their increasingly destructive assaults. What theologians such as Jonathan Wilson, Stanley Hauerwas, Barry Harvey, and others are calling for is the Church to re-embrace a sense of its own cultural identity, its own communal particularity, as a way of resisting the corrosive effects of our current fragmentation. And, of course, one of the most obvious sources the Church has regarding the culture God intends for it to be and proclaim is Jesus's teachings on the kingdom of God.

Jesus and the "Kingdom of God"

Now after John was arrested, Jesus came into Galilee, preaching the gospel of God, and saying, "The time is fulfilled, and the kingdom of God is at hand; repent, and believe in the gospel." (Mark 1:14–15 RSV)

But when Jesus saw it he was indignant, and said to them, "Let the children come to me, do not hinder them; for to such belongs the kingdom of God. Truly, I say to you, whoever does not receive the kingdom of God like a child shall not enter it." (Mark 10:14–15 RSV)

Jesus said to him, "No one who puts his hand to the plow and looks back is fit for the kingdom of God." (Luke 9:62 RSV)

"Whenever you enter a town and they receive you, eat what is set before you; heal the sick in it and say to them, 'The kingdom of God has come near to you.' But whenever you enter a town and they do not receive you, go into its streets and say, 'Even the dust of your town that clings to our feet, we wipe off against you; nevertheless know this, that the kingdom of God has come near.' I tell you, it shall be more tolerable on that day for Sodom than for that town." (Luke 10:8–12 RSV)

He said therefore, "What is the kingdom of God like? And to what shall I compare it? It is like a grain of mustard seed which a man took and sowed in his garden; and it grew and became a tree, and the birds of the air made nests in its branches."

And again he said, "To what shall I compare the kingdom of God? It is like leaven which a woman took and hid in three measures of flour, till it was all leavened." (Luke 13:18–21 RSV)

Someone asked him, "Lord, will only a few be saved?" He said to them, "Strive to enter through the narrow door; for many, I tell you, will try to enter and will not be able. When once the owner of the house has got up and shut the door, and you begin to stand outside and to knock at the door, saying, 'Lord, open to us,' then in reply he will say to you, 'I do not know where you come from.' Then you will begin to say, 'We ate and drank with you, and you taught in our streets.' But he will say, 'I do not know where you come from; go away from me, all you evildoers!' There will be weeping and gnashing of teeth when you see Abraham and Isaac and Jacob and all the prophets in the kingdom of God, and you yourselves thrown out. Then people will come from east and west, from north and south, and will eat in the kingdom of God. Indeed, some are last who will be first, and some are first who will be last. (Luke 13:23–30)

And when the hour came, he sat at table, and the apostles with him. And he said to them, "I have earnestly desired to eat this passover with you before I suffer; for I tell you I shall not eat it until it is fulfilled in the kingdom of God." And he took a cup, and when he had given thanks he said, "Take this, and divide it among yourselves; for I tell you that from now on I shall not drink of the fruit of the vine until the kingdom of God comes." And he took bread, and when he had given thanks he broke it and gave it to them, saying, "This is my body which is given for you. Do this in remembrance of me." (Luke 22:14–20 RSV)

Jesus answered him, "Very truly, I tell you, no one can see the kingdom of God without being born from above." Nicodemus said to him, "How can anyone be born after having grown old? Can one enter a second time into the mother's womb and be born?" Jesus answered, "Very truly, I tell you, no one can enter the kingdom of God without being born of water and Spirit." (John 3:3–5)

Early in this chapter I wrote: "To say that 'Jesus is Lord,' that he is 'seated at the right hand of God the Father,' . . . means that God's reign is far larger than the Church" (p. 126 above). Christians who have a merely privatistic or ecclesial sense of the kingdom's scope need to broaden their horizon. Of course God's sovereignty rules over the Church; the Church knows this through its covenant with God established in Christ. But it would be a grave error to say that the kingdom of God is simply equivalent to the Church or extends no further than the Church.

The Church Reveals the Kingdom

Divine sovereignty extends over all that God has made. The task of the Church is to witness to this reality by allowing God's risen Son to exercise his lordship in and through it as "the people of God" by means of his Holy Spirit. When the Church truly surrenders itself to the Holy Spirit in order to be truly the Church, this witness to Jesus's lordship becomes manifest in its life, work, and words. Being this "people of God" means that the Church is being true to its calling to serve as a covenantal sign and instrument of God's ultimate intentions for the whole creation. It recognizes its rootedness in the original covenant with Abraham and Sarah, in which "all the families of the earth shall be blessed" (Gen. 12:3), as well as the in-grafting of the new covenant established in Christ until he comes again at the end of the age when the kingdom is finally realized.[18] The Church becomes, in effect, not just "the people of God," but "the people of God's *reign*," bearing witness in Christ through the Spirit to the world's original and ultimate reality, which the world of itself cannot see.

Yet for many contemporary Christians there seems to be a complete disjuncture between the Church and Jesus's preaching on the kingdom, or reign, of God. In fact, in 1902 the French biblical scholar Alfred Loisy famously observed that "Jesus foretold the kingdom and it was the church that came."[19] Many Christians hearing that quip today are apt to think it describes the all-too-familiar letdown of those frustrated by the gap between our spiritual yearnings and the mundane reality of actual Church life. Like many in Jesus's own lifetime, we long for something glorious, for true fulfillment and communion with God and others, while being disappointed that our everyday experiences so typically fall short. One hears a similar sentiment expressed in the cliché "I'm spiritual but not religious"—a distinction typically meant to dismiss the need for any institutional religion. The disjunction between the two seems unbridgeable.

In fact, the distance described between the supposed spiritual ideal and the disappointing reality seems to be not just a quantitative but a qualitative matter. Not only do we get so little of what we expected, but we get something entirely different. Perhaps too many Christians have set themselves up for such disappointment, by unconsciously assuming that God's in-breaking kingdom will be immediate and obvious, rather than mediated and veiled in secondary instruments—like leaven in the dough. Church history offers many examples of diverse groups working themselves into an apocalyptic frenzy

18. Mark 14:24–25; 1 Cor. 11:25–26.
19. Alfred Loisy, *The Gospel and the Church* (Philadelphia: Fortress, 1976), 166.

claiming that the "Last Days" have arrived, with Jesus soon to rule directly and obviously. Similarly, various small groups have sought to recapture the charismatic immediacy of the early Church as portrayed in Acts. This impulse seems akin to that desire for immediacy and glory displayed by the two disciples (or their mother) seeking to sit at Jesus's right and left hands when he will come into his kingdom. Jesus responds by turning their notions of glory upside down and saying that their greatness will come in their service.[20] His point was that Christians are not to define themselves according to their own private communion with, and proximity to, God. They are rather to see themselves as members of a concrete body, an eschatologically constituted "holy nation" serving and inviting the whole world to acknowledge God's sovereign intentions. Insofar as the outpouring of the Holy Spirit at Pentecost is the fulfillment of Jeremiah 31:31–34 and Joel 2, that reality is in fact still available to individual Christians and the Church as a whole.

The Value of the Church as Institution

It is a mistake, however, to assume that the charismatic, "noninstitutional" manner in which the Church *began* its life and mission must or even can remain the way the Church should *continue* its life and mission. Generically understood, an "institution" is merely a social arrangement created and wielded by a particular group to maintain some collective purpose, usually through explicit norms, procedures, and an inculcated ethos and identity, from one generation to the next. Institutions come in all shapes and sizes, can be more formal or less formal, and are as common to human existence as language and culture, and as all life's stages from birth to death.

This being the case, it would be out of character for the God who creates beings in his own image and likeness, endowing them with certain powers and responsibilities and entering into explicit covenant with them, *not* to employ some sort of human institution dedicated to the purposes of his kingdom. It is actually a kind of latter-day gnosticism to believe that a disembodied, noninstitutional church could or should somehow be the ideal. We are embodied, social, and historical beings, and our common life requires embodied, social, and historical structures.

Also, it would be just as out of character for God to commission such an institution and leave it to its own devices, that is, without also establishing and orienting its collective identity, ethos, character, and purpose. This it receives from the work of the Father's "right hand," namely, Jesus's teaching

---

20. Mark 10:35–45//Matt. 20:20–28. Cf. Luke 22:24–27.

and actions. Similarly, it would be out of character for God to commission such an institution without maintaining an ongoing and vital relation with it. This the Father accomplishes through the work of his other "hand," namely, the life-giving, sustaining, and guiding power of the Holy Spirit.

The People of God and the Kingdom of God

In other words, the Church cannot fully understand what it means to be "the people of God" without the Spirit's incorporating into its self-understanding the preaching, service, and miracles of Jesus heralding the "kingdom of God" and the "kingdom of heaven." The Church is indeed a "royal priesthood" and a "holy nation," but its sovereign is not simply another earthly ruler, and its nationhood not merely one among others. Indeed, through the powerful and universal movement of the Holy Spirit, the reign of God draws its members from across the nations and peoples of the earth and owes its allegiance to the ascended Lord, who rules over all the nations of the world.

The well-known admonition that Christians are to be "in the world, but not of the world" describes what the Church is meant to be as well. It is indeed embedded and involved in the everyday world, even while it exists as an embassy of a heavenly commonwealth. In this sense, the Church functions, through Christ and the Spirit, as a mediator or ambassador in the "vertical" dimension between earth and heaven. Similarly, the Church functions, through Christ and the Spirit, as a representative from God's eschatological future in the temporal, "horizontal" dimension between God's "already" and "not yet." The fact that Jesus often uses parables to describe God's kingdom, rather than straightforwardly presenting it in prosaic, political language, itself illuminates that the kingdom is not to be understood in simply human and worldly terms. This is one reason Jesus tells his disciples that his parables veil rather than reveal to those whose hearts are closed to God's purposes (Matt. 13:13–17). There is a dynamic tension between heaven and earth, between our present and God's future, which is amply illustrated in Jesus's diverse teachings and parables of the kingdom. The Church is called to live in and receive its identity from this dynamic, witnessing in word and deed to God's surprising accomplishment and expectation.

Consider how often Jesus's parables begin with some variation of the words "The kingdom of God is like . . ." or "To what shall I compare the kingdom of heaven . . .?"[21] Some parables speak to the small or inauspicious beginnings

---

21. E.g., Mark 4:26–29; Matt. 13:24–30; Matt. 13:31–32//Mark 4:30–32//Luke 13:18–19; Matt. 13:33//Luke 13:20–21; Matt. 13:44–52.

that attain an astonishing end.[22] Others describe the almost reckless abandon with which the blessing of the kingdom is offered.[23] Still others speak to the all-encompassing joy and dedication that come when one is encountered and embraced by this new reality breaking into our mundane and fallen world.[24] Together, these various images point to the hiddenness, the pervasiveness, and the unexpected power of God's grace. To those whose hearts are open to this grace, the images enable an entirely new and transformative way of seeing and understanding the world. Blinders are removed; scales fall from eyes; doors are opened; veils are lifted: what was previously assumed to be reality is now recognized as passing, and what was once yearned for as an unrealistic dream is now recognized as in fact the world's deep and true reality.

The Church's call is to proclaim and reflect this deep reality in its own corporate and institutional life, to be a community of grace, forgiveness, reconciliation, and new beginnings;[25] to be a community of blessing for the meek and the persecuted righteous;[26] to be a community of compassion and healing;[27] and to be a community of humility,[28] caring for the least and the outcast.[29] Will it always fulfill this calling? Of course not—at least, not this side of the last day. But the Church's collective orientation or "bent" should always lean this way and, when necessary, diligently be realigned this way, rather than modeling itself on the power structures, divisions, and dynamics of the world. The apostle Paul speaks to this same point, this new reality, this new ethos and way of being a people, when he states: "For as many of you as were baptized into Christ have put on Christ. There is neither Jew nor Greek, there is neither slave nor free, there is neither male nor female; for you are all one in Christ Jesus" (Gal. 3:27–28 RSV).

If one were to focus solely on the particular parables and similes to which I have alluded, one might be tempted to think that Jesus offers an idealized, even sentimental vision for our common life under God's rule. But Jesus was hardly naïve regarding our human situation. These teachings must be offset with those that Jesus gives when describing the various stumbling blocks to entry into the kingdom. He is quite clear that it is a narrow gate that leads to life, but a wide one that leads to destruction;[30] that lip service alone does

22. Matt. 13:8, 31–33.
23. Matt. 13:3–9, 18–23; 20:1–15.
24. Matt. 13:44–46.
25. Matt. 6:12–14; 18:21–35; Mark 11:25; Luke 17:3–4.
26. Matt. 5:5, 10.
27. Matt. 4:23; 9:35.
28. Matt. 18:1–5; 19:14.
29. Matt. 25:34–40.
30. Matt. 7:13–14//Luke 13:23–24.

not suffice, but one must do the will of the Father;[31] that one must not only hear Jesus's words but also act on them.[32] He warns people not to rely on their heritage to earn themselves a place at the table—indeed, one may need to renounce one's prior allegiances;[33] that one must fear not those who can kill the body but the One who can kill the soul;[34] and that loyalty to him will bring not peace but a sword of division, a son against father, and a daughter against mother.[35]

With comfort and realism, Jesus's words describe the wondrous works that God has done and will do, while also sketching the sort of "kingdom ethos" and "kingdom ethic" that derive from those divine acts. By making this distinction between, and conjunction of, "ethic" and "ethos," I am seeking to distinguish between a consistent set of behaviors (an ethic) and the way of being, or character (an ethos), that grounds and produces such behaviors. Now it could seem as if Jesus witnesses to two sides of the covenant: a "covenant of grace" describing God's initiative of blessing, and a "covenant of works" describing our human response. Some Christians have heard Jesus's teaching as an exhilarating call to action producing heroic deeds of faith. But for many it seems to establish an impossible ideal, which thereby becomes a counsel of despair. Consider the Sermon on the Mount (Matt. 5–7): it begins with Jesus's beatitudes on various groups, yet then presents a list of apparently ever more stringent demands. Presupposing the requirements of the Torah, Jesus makes true adherence a matter not merely of external behavior but of internal disposition. Yet who has complete mastery over his or her inner thoughts and desires? The culminating demand appears at the very heart of the sermon: "Be perfect, therefore, as your heavenly Father is perfect" (Matt. 5:48). Yet apart from Jesus himself, who could meet such a standard?

This last observation is, of course, precisely the point. No one can, relying on his or her own resources, achieve such a standard apart from Jesus. But when one is joined with Jesus, the risen Lord and Savior, through the power of the Holy Spirit, the seed is planted; the new life begins. Consider the concerned reaction of Jesus's disciples and others when Jesus states that it is easier for a camel to pass through the eye of a needle than for the wealthy to enter the kingdom of heaven: "Then who can be saved?" Jesus's response: "For mortals it is impossible, but for God all things are possible" (Matt.

---

31. Matt. 7:21–23//Luke 13:26–27.
32. Matt. 7:24–27//Luke 6:47–49.
33. Matt. 8:10–12//Luke 13:28–30; Matt. 10:34–39//Luke 12:51–53; 14:26–27.
34. Matt. 10:28//Luke 12:4–5.
35. Matt. 10:34–36//Luke 12:51–53.

19:23–26).[36] Everything that God requires *of* the faithful is based upon what he has already given *to* the faithful. In effect, God establishes the new ethos, the new cultural reality and character of his people, and it is only on this basis that the new ethic is also established. Specifically, God the Father's covenantal faithfulness in Christ the Son reaches its culmination with the bestowal of the Holy Spirit, first upon the disciples and then, with Pentecost, upon all who are baptized. The earliest instance of this new Spirit-effected "kingdom ethos" and "ethic" appears immediately following Peter's Pentecost sermon, as evidenced by Luke's account in Acts:

> And Peter said to them, "Repent, and be baptized every one of you in the name of Jesus Christ for the forgiveness of your sins; and you shall receive the gift of the Holy Spirit. For the promise is to you and to your children and to all that are far off, every one whom the Lord our God calls to him." And he testified with many other words and exhorted them, saying, "Save yourselves from this crooked generation." So those who received his word were baptized, and there were added that day about three thousand souls. And they devoted themselves to the apostles' teaching and fellowship, to the breaking of bread and the prayers.
>
> And fear came upon every soul; and many wonders and signs were done through the apostles. And all who believed were together and had all things in common; and they sold their possessions and goods and distributed them to all, as any had need. And day by day, attending the temple together and breaking bread in their homes, they partook of food with glad and generous hearts, praising God and having favor with all the people. And the Lord added to their number day by day those who were being saved. (Acts 2:38–47 RSV)

This passage paints a picture of a community in which Jesus's teaching given during his Sermon on the Mount has become a lived reality, a Spirit-produced image of an in-breaking heavenly and eschatological fulfillment that awaits us all. Of course, we know from Church history, indeed, from the New Testament itself, that this ideal did not endure. Several of Paul's letters reveal that various Church communities struggled to live up to the standard set before them. His letters to the congregation at Corinth indicate that that community was divided by religious, moral, business, and class issues,[37] while his letter to the Galatian churches implies divisions based on theological, ethnic, gender, and socioeconomic grounds.[38] Yet in all these letters Paul appeals to the Spirit as the basis for regaining communal unity and the virtues that sustain

---

36. Cf. Mark 10:24–27//Luke 18:24–27.
37. E.g., 1 Cor. 1:11–17; 3:1–8; 5:1–2, 9–13; 6:1–8, 12–20; 11:17–22.
38. E.g., Gal. 1:6–9; 3:28.

and reflect the kingdom ethos.[39] The realization of this new community, of a new culture that recognizes but also transcends the various ways we used to identify ourselves in our old cultures, takes time. It is no accident that so many of Jesus's parables use examples from agriculture or the domestic realm—stories of seeds or leaven growing—to illustrate the unfolding growth of God's reign. It is no accident that Paul describes some Christians new to the faith as "infants in Christ," not yet spiritually mature men and women. Thus, his teaching needed to feed them "milk, not solid food" (1 Cor. 3:1–2), until they became more fully established in the faith. God has been building up this new people ever since his first call of Abraham and Sarah. We should hardly be surprised when, even with Christ's coming and the outpouring of the Holy Spirit, God still determines to take time to gather and grow his new people. Of course, God's covenantal perspective extends not just back to Abraham and Sarah, or even to his covenant with Noah, his family, and the earth, but back to our first parents, to Adam and Eve, as another biblical comparison makes clear. For the time being, the "people of God" refers to those brought into, and made new by, the reality and purposes of God's kingdom. But ultimately, God intends for this to embrace all the peoples of his good creation.

The First Adam and the Last Adam

> Therefore, just as sin came into the world through one man, and death came through sin, and so death spread to all because all have sinned—sin was indeed in the world before the law, but sin is not reckoned when there is no law. Yet death exercised dominion from Adam to Moses, even over those whose sins were not like the transgression of Adam, who is a type of the one who was to come.
>
> But the free gift is not like the trespass. For if the many died through the one man's trespass, much more surely have the grace of God and the free gift in the grace of the one man, Jesus Christ, abounded for the many. And the free gift is not like the effect of the one man's sin. For the judgment following one trespass brought condemnation, but the free gift following many trespasses brings justification. If, because of the one man's trespass, death exercised dominion through that one, much more surely will those who receive the abundance of grace and the free gift of righteousness exercise dominion in life through the one man, Jesus Christ.
>
> Therefore just as one man's trespass led to condemnation for all, so one man's act of righteousness leads to justification and life for all. For just as by the one man's disobedience the many were made sinners, so by the one man's

39. E.g., 1 Cor. 2:10–16; 6:11–20; 12:3–13; 2 Cor. 3:3–6, 17–18; Gal 5:16–26.

obedience the many will be made righteous. But law came in, with the result that the trespass multiplied; but where sin increased, grace abounded all the more, so that, just as sin exercised dominion in death, so grace might also exercise dominion through justification leading to eternal life through Jesus Christ our Lord. (Rom. 5:12–21)

For since death came through a human being, the resurrection of the dead has also come through a human being; for as all die in Adam, so all will be made alive in Christ. But each in his own order: Christ the first fruits, then at his coming those who belong to Christ. Then comes the end, when he hands over the kingdom to God the Father, after he has destroyed every ruler and every authority and power. For he must reign until he has put all his enemies under his feet. The last enemy to be destroyed is death. For "God has put all things in subjection under his feet." But when it says, "All things are put in subjection," it is plain that this does not include the one who put all things in subjection under him. When all things are subjected to him, then the Son himself will also be subjected to the one who put all things in subjection under him, so that God may be all in all. (1 Cor. 15:21–28)

Thus it is written, "The first man, Adam, became a living being"; the last Adam became a life-giving spirit. But it is not the spiritual that is first, but the physical, and then the spiritual. The first man was from the earth, a man of dust; the second man is from heaven. As was the man of dust, so are those who are of the dust; and as is the man of heaven, so are those who are of heaven. Just as we have borne the image of the man of dust, we will also bear the image of the man of heaven. (1 Cor. 15:45–49)

When the apostle Paul employs the comparative image of the "first Adam" and the "last Adam," he makes clear that Jesus's life and work have universal significance, affecting not just members of the Church but the whole of humanity. His comparison offers more than just a timeless typology or generic human possibility, because he embeds it within the full sweep of God's creative and covenantal activity—an activity that precedes even creation itself, in the eternal purposes of the Triune God.[40] Just as Adam derailed for all the divine-human relation that God intended for humanity and ushered in death's reign, so now does Christ make possible for all the restoration of that relation and the final destruction of death. Just as Adam was the "universal man" in whom all humanity was represented, so too does Christ become the new "universal man" in whom all humanity is to be represented.

40. Recall my discussion of the *pactum salutis* and the *ordo salutis* in chap. 1 (pp. 3, 23).

Luke's Gospel echoes Paul's point in a manner that many modern readers might pass over, namely, in his listing of Jesus's genealogy and his editorial placement of that genealogy within his Gospel. Regarding the lineage of Jesus's ancestors, Luke—like Matthew—does trace his descent back through the generations to David and Abraham, the two key recipients of God's covenantal promises. But then, unlike Matthew, Luke continues tracing that lineage through Noah all the way back to Adam. Moreover, by placing this genealogy between his accounts of Jesus's baptism and his temptation in the wilderness, Luke signals that Jesus's anointing as Messiah and his initial "testing" as Messiah have a universal significance. This understanding is further supported in Luke's second book, the Acts of the Apostles. This work recounts the spread of the gospel, beginning with Peter's proclamation to the Jewish diaspora gathered for Pentecost in the Jewish capital of Jerusalem and concluding with Paul openly proclaiming the gospel in the capital of the gentile world, Rome. For Luke, the gospel message is certainly good news for the people of Israel, but that message is also meant to be good news for all people, Jew and gentile alike.

These things reiterate the point that the roots of the Church extend as far back as the creation of our first human parents, whom God made to live in communal harmony and love with him and with one another. As I discussed in chapter 1, human beings are intended to live not in isolation but in community—the most fundamental of which, as the biblical creation stories make clear, is that of man and woman, in all their common and complementary humanity.[41] Neither the man alone nor the woman alone fully defines "the human"; they must be considered together. More than that, neither do the woman and the man together in isolation fully define "the human"; only when taking them together *in proper relation to their Creator* does one truly define the human. To be sure, each one of us as a human being possesses an innate dignity and worth as a creature made "in the image and likeness of God." But we are likewise beings whose lives are irreducibly relational and communal, with the result that it is completely natural that we should also relate to our Creator *together*. We are meant not to have to "go it alone" but to have support and company for the journey.

From this recognition, several things should be unpacked further. First, as the point just made makes clear, the communion that God seeks with all human beings had its start at the very beginning—indeed, before the beginning. It is not something "added on" later. In this sense, the Church has existed from creation, because God has freely and graciously made a community

41. Gen. 1:26–27; 2:7, 18–25.

for himself from the very beginning. From this we should then recognize the perhaps less obvious second point that God's intention and purpose for the Church is not that it enable persons to be "religious," as if this were some particular trait or habit, feeling or attitude, adopted alongside various others of a nonreligious nature. Rather, God's intention and purpose for the Church from the very beginning has been that it help persons to become fully *human*. To paraphrase the famous quote from Blaise Pascal, "There is a God-shaped hole in us that only God can fill." We cannot be our truest and most full selves apart from God.

Third, becoming fully human means learning to live with others who are both like and unlike ourselves, in a relationship of mutual support and responsibility, of graciousness and accountability, in which others truly become "a part of you." The primordial expression of this ideal exists in the relation that God intended between Adam and Eve, between male and female, who are both like and unlike each other, in fulfilling complementarity. This is why the marriage of husband and wife so often serves in Scripture as an archetype for the deepest forms of human intimacy, but also as a parable of God's intimate relation with his people.

Fourth, as the scriptural narratives imply (both by the particular stories they relate and by the fact that they are *narratives*), realizing the full humanity with which we are endowed *takes time*, both for individuals and for peoples. We are bodily creatures, male and female, and we are also historical creatures, who through becoming one flesh of male and female reproduce the next generation, which is born, grows, reproduces, grows old, and passes on—generation upon generation. One of God's great gifts of grace is precisely the gift of time: time to grow, to mature, to learn, and to enjoy one another's company, both human companionship with one another and our companionship with God.

Affirming our common ancestry in Adam means we should understand this companionship in the broadest possible terms. Because we are all descended from him, we should recognize that all persons are, to a greater or lesser degree, "family." Persons from other nations and cultures are not strangers but "cousins"—and should be recognized and esteemed as such. This is meant by God to be the natural order of things. Yet sin has intervened, dividing us and raising suspicions and hostility toward those to whom we should be kindly disposed. Indeed, the biblical narrative of Cain and Abel illustrates our own experience that families can be, contrary to how they were intended, seedbeds of the most intense dysfunction, animosity, and violence. God does not want to leave us in this situation. Thus, with the coming of Christ, we are given a new common ancestor, one who takes away the sins that had previously divided us and who gives us a new basis for recognizing our familial relation.

Indeed, through the power of the Spirit joining us with Christ in baptism, we too are joined with him in his relation to our heavenly Father. This means we are no longer "cousins" but, more intimately, brothers and sisters with one another. We are given a new identity and family situation that are meant to supersede those identities and situations that used to divide us. This means the Church is called to recognize that those outside the Church are not finally aliens or even enemies but, potentially, new brothers and sisters.

Of course, Christ serves not just as our new beginning, our new common ancestor, but as our future as well. The passages cited from Paul's letters to the Romans and Corinthians at the outset of this section succinctly capture God's overarching plan for humanity, the purpose he had intended for us from the beginning—even in light of the fall. God will not abandon his beloved creatures to the consequences of their sin but will reclaim and restore them so that grace might abound all the more. This is why Paul calls the risen Christ the "first fruits" of the harvest, a surety of what is intended for us all (1 Cor. 15:20–24; cf. Jas. 1:17–18). Of course, this surety does not necessarily mean things will be easy. In Romans, Paul refers to believers as having the "first fruits of the Spirit"—that is, the first benefits of being joined with Christ—yet even they, along with creation, groan inwardly as they await their full redemption (Rom. 8:21–23). Making a similar point using a different image, the Letter to the Hebrews describes Jesus as "the pioneer and perfecter of our faith" (Heb. 12:2), to whom believers look to chart their future. That journey will continue to be a challenge and a struggle, requiring perseverance and discipline, just as it already has required of the "great cloud of witnesses" that preceded us in faithfulness (12:1–13). Even though the Church can witness to Christ's first coming in ways that the faithful in Old Testament times could only anticipate, it still shares with them the anticipation of Christ's second coming. We thus have in common with them the stance of looking toward, and yearning for, God's future. Until Christ returns, what was written of them will be true of us as well:

> These all died in faith, not having received what was promised, but having seen it and greeted it from afar, and having acknowledged that they were strangers and exiles on the earth. For people who speak thus make it clear that they are seeking a homeland. If they had been thinking of that land from which they had gone out, they would have had opportunity to return. But as it is, they desire a better country, that is, a heavenly one. Therefore God is not ashamed to be called their God, for he has prepared for them a city. (Heb. 11:13–16 RSV)

In joining together Paul's image of the first and the last Adam with these various images from the Letter to the Hebrews, I want to suggest that this yearning for a homeland, for a better country, is not just one that the faithful of many ages share. I believe those outside as well as those inside the community of faith experience such a pull because it is grounded in our very being as creatures made for communion with God. Does this mean that such yearning is in actual fact universal? Probably not—because there are those whose treasures are laid up too much in this world, whose present rewards and power have obscured any farther vision of, or desire for, a better country. Such persons live their lives as if the course set by the fallen "first Adam" were their only option, not recognizing that the risen "last Adam" offers the means to their fullest self-realization. To awaken persons such as these is one reason the Spirit lays upon the Church the task of embodying, in its proclamation and its communal living, the ethos of this better country, this heavenly city. The people of God are called to be the humanity of the "last Adam," Christ, rather than the "first Adam." Insofar as the Spirit enables this, the Church becomes a light to the nations illuminating lives lived out of God's glorious future, rather than out of humanity's own fallen and sinful past. If the Church remains largely indistinguishable from the surrounding culture, then it has obviously forsaken this task.

The Church's Relation to the World

This last statement raises important and perennial questions: What is the relation of the Church to the surrounding culture, and what should it be? Is there one more or less constant answer? Or does the Church need to be open to the Spirit's guidance, depending upon the providential circumstances it finds itself in? There is, of course, the saying that the faithful are called to be "in the world, but not of the world" (see John 17:14–18). But the line between "in" and "of" seems to be a constantly shifting target. Movements emerging to resist certain inroads of worldly temptation become structures incapable of recognizing or resisting new ones—which then gives rise to new movements of resistance. The history of various Catholic religious orders often follows this pattern, with new orders arising due to perceptions that the old religious orders have grown too accommodating to the world's norms. Similarly, many Protestant denominations are offshoots of older, established bodies that they perceived as being too lax or worldly in their structure and standards.

The matter is, of course, complicated by the example of the incarnation: God coming to humanity where we are, indeed, becoming one of us in order to redeem us. The apostle Paul imitates this example when he writes: "I have become all things to all people, that I might by all means save some. I do it all for the sake of the gospel, so that I may share in its blessings" (1 Cor.

9:22b–23). This impulse is why the Church, in its spread around the world, has so often adopted and adapted the trappings and customs of the cultures in which it finds itself. This is why Christian missionary groups have translated the whole Bible into over 500 languages and the New Testament into over 2,650 languages.[42] The true Church is indeed one, holy, catholic, and apostolic, but that does not mean that it must be a clone of some archetypal institution in every succeeding time and place. It is able to accommodate itself to a wide range of cultural and historical settings. Yet this observation brings us back to our initial question: When is accommodation too accommodating? Or not accommodating enough? That is, how should the Church relate to the world?

First, a little whirlwind Church history, to set the context: as students of Christianity's past know, for the first three centuries of its existence the Church held an uneasy place over against the Roman Empire. Sometimes it was left more or less alone and sometimes actively persecuted. The Church's self-understanding took seriously Jesus's words that his kingdom was not of this world (John 18:36). Christians instead saw themselves as a kind of "colony of heaven." That self-understanding changed in the fourth century when, in 313 under Emperor Constantine, Christianity first became legal, indeed favored, and then, by the end of the century under Emperor Theodosius, became the official religion of Rome. The Church went from being a culturally ostracized minority for whom membership was costly, even dangerous, to being a culturally favored majority for whom membership was the norm and thus easy. But this transition raised what has become a perennial question: Is the true character of the Church to be a more selective and thus usually small group of saints? Or to be a less selective and thus larger "mixed body" of saints and sinners? The tension came to a head in the Donatist controversy of the fourth century,[43] and the Church in effect chose to emphasize God's grace over human moral rigor. This is not to say that spiritual and moral standards were simply discarded, only that recognizing the continuing need for penance

42. United Bible Societies data. See http://www.unitedbiblesocieties.org/what-we-do/, accessed May 14, 2015.

43. The Donatists were North African Christians who asserted that those clergy who had surrendered the Scriptures (the *traditors*) to their Roman persecutors had by that act negated their ordained authority, so that any subsequent ecclesial acts on their part were invalid. This, of course, raised troubling questions for those whom such clergy might have baptized, offered absolution, or given the Eucharist. The response of the wider Church was to say that the authority for such ecclesial acts rests not on the personal piety and moral rigor of the priest but in the office of priesthood itself, so that the efficacy of these instruments of God's grace was not negated by any foibles of the priest. Keep in mind, the *traditors* were *not* unrepentant; they were *not* still engaging in their apostate behavior. Rather, they had repented their falling away, and were seeking forgiveness and a return to "good graces."

and forgiveness necessarily moderated perfectionistic impulses. Of course, the impulse toward spiritual rigor did not disappear; it simply shifted to the asceticism of the early desert fathers and mothers and the emerging monastic movement.

As the power of ancient imperial Rome waned, the influence of papal Rome filled the vacuum, as did later the emergence of the Holy Roman Empire, which historians typically signal as starting with Charlemagne, crowned by Pope Leo III on Christmas Day, AD 800. It was during these centuries that "Christendom" emerged, that is, the cultural arrangement in which the political and ecclesial powers were understood as distinct, yet complementary, institutions ordering society toward its God-given ends. In theory, the political power was more concerned with temporal ends, and the ecclesial with more eternal ones. Yet there were godly kings and worldly churchmen, so the practical reality was often blurred. When Church structures or mores became too enamored of worldly things, new religious orders and reform movements would arise, striving for more spiritual and moral rigor, while remaining under the umbrella of the Vatican.[44] This occurred throughout the medieval period and seemed to be occurring once more in the sixteenth century, when an Augustinian monk named Martin Luther sought to enact certain reforms. Of course, those reforms eventually led to a split in the Church: Lutherans over against Roman Catholics, and then also other "Protestant" groups. There were the Reformed, centered in Switzerland but eventually arising in Holland and Great Britain, and the "Anabaptists"—radical reformers seeking a return to a more "New Testament" church—appearing in various places around Europe. Reform movements continued to emerge within Catholicism, but they have also stayed within the Church. By contrast, the Protestant tendency had been set: movements seeking greater rigor and purity typically splintered from the older body and established a new denomination. This was true in the sixteenth century, and it has been repeated down the centuries ever since. To be sure, the twentieth-century ecumenical movement ameliorated some theological and moral divides, but institutional separation remains the norm for Protestantism.

So what conclusions should we draw from all this? Clearly, the Church is called to a certain standard of holiness; just as clearly, individuals and institutions all too often fall short of that standard. The Church is also called to witness, by word and example, to God's grace, forgiveness, and sanctifying power. So how does one reconcile these seemingly disparate calls? The Church

44. Obviously, this is a summary of the Church in the West. The divide between the Roman Church and Eastern Orthodoxy grew for several centuries, for a host of reasons, with the final split occurring in 1054.

affirms that God is holy *and* merciful, just as Christ is judge *and* savior, just as we are guilty of sin yet *also* forgiven, justified, and sanctified. These affirmations presuppose the context of the Church living in a still fallen world. So it seems both reasonable and not unfaithful to suppose that there will be no final reconciliation this side of the eschaton. This means that the Church remains a pilgrim people, living in the tension of the divine grace already given but not yet fulfilled in the world—or in the Church, for that matter. How the Church lives in this tension is, quite simply, something it can never settle once and for all but must constantly test. It must never cease from discerning the spirits of the age, to see whether they are of God or of the world, and to plot its course accordingly.

A brief consideration and critique of H. Richard Niebuhr's classic and influential book *Christ and Culture* might be illustrative here.[45] In it, he suggests five basic alternatives for the relation of the Church and the world: (1) Christ against culture; (2) Christ of culture; (3) Christ above culture; (4) Christ and culture in paradox; and (5) Christ the transformer of culture. The first includes those who insist that the Church, to maintain its critical purity, should reject any and all entanglements with the broader culture, due to the culture's corruption and continual enticements to sin. Niebuhr describes the theologian Tertullian (ca. 160–ca. 225), Mennonites, and Russian novelist Leo Tolstoy as representatives of this type. Niebuhr calls it a necessary but also inadequate position. It is the former because it bears rigorous witness to Christian ideals, but it is the latter because it naïvely believes that Christian individuals and communities actually can be separable from all cultural artifacts and assumptions—and that God in fact wills they should be. The second type goes to the opposite extreme, holding that the divine ideal can indeed be found in or undergirding the glories of human culture. Yes, there may be brokenness and sin, but surely the best of human society harmonizes with God's desires. Niebuhr lists the gnostics and the "culture Protestantism" of the nineteenth century as examples of this type. Niebuhr acknowledges that this second position avoids the problems of the first, but unfortunately the "Christ of culture becomes a chameleon," so that "the word 'Christ' in this connection is nothing but an honorific and emotional term by means of which each period attaches numinous quality to its personified ideals."[46] In sum, these two types resolve the tension between the Church and the world by simply severing the connection: either no accommodation between Christ and culture or complete accommodation. Neither is adequate according to Niebuhr.

45. H. Richard Niebuhr, *Christ and Culture* (New York: Harper & Row, 1951).
46. Ibid., 107.

This means that, to his mind, only the final three types remain responsible positions because they hold that a faithful Christian stance necessarily retains hope for redemptively influencing culture while also maintaining some critical distance from it. The third type, "Christ above culture," emphasizes that there will be some synthesis between the natural, social life and the life of faith because both are ordered by God. Revelation does not reject reason (which itself is God-given) but complements and completes it. According to Niebuhr, representatives of this position include early Church apologists Justin Martyr and Clement of Alexandria, the medieval Thomas Aquinas, and nineteenth-century Pope Leo XIII. The strength of this position is that it recognizes a divinely given role for culture, for human initiative and creativity, even while it reserves a higher standard and final authority to the transcendent law of revelation. The weakness of this type is that it tends to be politically hierarchical and culturally static.

The fourth type, "Christ and culture in paradox," is dualist, not synthetic: it recognizes that the Church bears a divinely given responsibility over against society as a whole, but there will be no easy harmony. The world is fallen, and even reason and well-intended institutions can be corrupted. The common good may require those holding social office to act in ways standing in stark contrast to the ideals of individual Christian faithfulness. Some key proponents of this view are, according to Niebuhr, the apostle Paul, the reformer Martin Luther, and nineteenth-century existentialist Søren Kierkegaard. The virtue of this type is that it acknowledges the true and dynamic tension between sin and grace existing in the time between Christ's first and second coming. The twin vices that this type can lead to are a kind of otherworldly antinomianism and a cultural conservatism: regarding heaven, one lives by grace, but in this world the law only has the negative role of restraining evil.

Thus Niebuhr arrives at his final type, "Christ the transformer of culture." As one might anticipate, he contends that the "transformer" or "conversionist" model shares the insights of the previous two types but avoids their more extreme tendencies. It has a more positive and hopeful attitude toward culture; it does not view the fall as a metaphysical cataclysm so great as to make human moral effort meaningless; to the contrary, it views the fall as the impetus for salvation history, that continuing interaction between God and humans that leads the faithful to focus on "the divine possibility of a present renewal."[47] Niebuhr sees this type represented in the Gospel of John and in the theologies of Augustine, Calvin, John Wesley, Jonathan Edwards, and, curiously, the rather obscure and idiosyncratic nineteenth-century Anglican

47. Ibid., 195.

divine F. D. Maurice. Maurice appeals to Niebuhr apparently due to the former's efforts to synthesize John's "realized eschatology" and universalism with Christian Socialism. That is, Maurice envisioned a progressive conversion of culture, grounded in the conversion of humankind from self-centeredness to Christ-centeredness, which necessarily also entails the transformation in very concrete ways of social customs, political structures, economic organizations, languages, and the self-understanding of persons.[48]

The vision is exhilarating, but Niebuhr omits details as to how it would actually be realized. Perhaps he neglected such details because he and his audience believed they were self-evident. This would not be surprising at a time when the mainline churches he represented were approaching the acme of their societal influence and prestige. Clearly, of the five models he considers, he preferred this final one. But as others have noted, having critiqued each of the first four categories, Niebuhr engages in no similar critique here. He does—borrowing a phrase and an existentialist approach from Kierkegaard—offer a "Concluding Unscientific Postscript" in which he acknowledges that the constant flux of our historical situation coupled with the fragmentary and frail nature of our faith prevents us from saying there is a "once and for all" correct choice of type. In spite of this, he affirms that Christ still summons us in each moment. Employing the revelation of Scripture and reason, we are called to choose, trusting that God will continue to be gracious and faithful.

In other words, Niebuhr qualified his own preference, yet he still failed to consider directly the implicit weakness of the "transformative" type. Specifically, he failed to recognize how much it presupposes certain Christian assumptions and sentiments established by more than a millennium of unselfconscious cultural habit in the Christian West. In effect, "Christ the transformer of culture" depends upon the "Christ of culture" type as a foundation. But once Christendom fractured within itself (between Catholicism and multiple forms of Protestantism) and then was challenged by self-consciously non-Christian or anti-Christian movements in modernity, these habits began at first to erode and then collapse. Deep-seated habits and entrenched cultural norms can, of course, be the most difficult to change. Yet their continuing sway also requires the existence of a principled and universally recognized ground. While not everyone need be capable of explaining that ground fully, the majority still needs to believe it exists and is explicable.

Once that ground is questioned, and plausible alternatives are offered—particularly ones that may be less demanding and serve new interests—then change may become irresistible. And that is what has happened with much of

48. Ibid., 224–29.

the Church in the Western European and North American contexts. Having sought to ground itself in its present moment and adapting itself to so many historically relative and modern ideas, the Church was no longer transforming culture but being co-opted and transformed by it. In sum, it seems that this type has an inherent weakness: its focus on historical relativity and the immediacy of decision means it is temporally unstable. As a consequence, it will always only be a matter of time before the transformative type as described by Niebuhr inevitably becomes a "Christ of culture"—or simply becomes irrelevant when the culture moves on and stops listening to it.

Recognizing this tendency in the "transformative" type and the reality of the Church's increasingly marginalized place in current Western culture, more recent Christian thinkers have reconsidered the "Christ against culture" type. By trying too hard to be relevant, they have observed, one often loses one's Christian identity. Moreover, one cannot maintain a Christian identity alone; to the contrary, it is irreducibly a communal undertaking because our identity is mediated and sustained by our social connections. We become "persons of God" because there is a "people of God" to nurture and shape us. This is why the Church must make a concerted and self-conscious effort to mediate and sustain its distinct identity in all times and places. There have been, and will continue to be, many variations of how the Church relates to the world and cultures around it, from establishment to persecution. And, of course, such cultures are not just external to the Church but are brought inside by its members. Sometimes these cultural imports are brought in by the laity, sometimes by the leadership; frequently they are what distinguish one denomination from another; sometimes such imports are benign, but too often they are not.

That is why the Church must constantly take care to avoid confusing its current life with its eschatological goal and fulfillment. The people of God should remain mindful that as the Church it is always a people in exile. Here the phrase coined by Stanley Hauerwas and William Willimon is useful: Christians must see themselves as "resident aliens."[49] Even in those places where Christianity still plays a vital, if diminishing, cultural role,[50] we do well to remember that as the "people of God" we are set apart, with our deepest identity derived from, and our ultimate allegiance oriented to, "another city."[51]

49. Stanley Hauerwas and William Willimon, *Resident Aliens: Life in the Christian Colony* (Nashville: Abingdon, 1989).

50. Consider the rise of the "Nones," that is, the increasing number of citizens who say they have no religious affiliation. See http://www.pewforum.org/2012/10/09/nones-on-the-rise/.

51. The phrase is borrowed from Barry A. Harvey's book *Another City: An Ecclesiological Primer for a Post-Christian World* (Harrisburg, PA: Trinity Press International, 1999), but of course, he himself is alluding to Augustine's distinction between the earthly city and the heavenly one in his great work *The City of God* (cf. Heb. 11:16).

On this matter we could learn some lessons from our Jewish cousins in the covenant. They have far more experience in being aliens in whatever culture they inhabit. That experience has run a gamut, from the Holocaust to exclusion in ghettos to neglect (sometimes indifferent, sometimes not). Even among assimilated Jews, the sense of being "other" lingers. As Christians, do we share a similar sense of otherness in our surrounding culture? If not, then we are likely too comfortable, and our identity and calling as Christians are at risk. While this is not the place to explore what further lessons we might learn, these observations do raise a prior question that we must address: theologically speaking, how should Christians, understanding themselves as "the people of God," relate to the Jewish community, whom we understand as the original "people of God"?

Israel and the Church

Now the Lord said to Abram, "Go from your country and your kindred and your father's house to the land that I will show you. I will make of you a great nation, and I will bless you, and make your name great, so that you will be a blessing. I will bless those who bless you, and the one who curses you I will curse; and in you all the families of the earth shall be blessed." (Gen. 12:1–3)

You worship what you do not know; we worship what we know, for salvation is from the Jews. (John 4:22)

And so all Israel will be saved; as it is written,

"Out of Zion will come the Deliverer;
    he will banish ungodliness from Jacob."
"And this is my covenant with them,
    when I take away their sins."

As regards the gospel they are enemies of God for your sake; but as regards election they are beloved, for the sake of their ancestors; for the gifts and the calling of God are irrevocable. Just as you were once disobedient to God but have now received mercy because of their disobedience, so they have now been disobedient in order that, by the mercy shown to you, they too may now receive mercy. For God has imprisoned all in disobedience so that he may be merciful to all. (Rom. 11:26–32)

How should the Church understand its relation to Israel? This is a question not of Christianity's relations to the modern political state of Israel but of how Christians should understand and relate to Jews, the Jewish community, the Jewish faith, and the Jewish people as a nation formed by God's call and covenant with them, regardless of where individual Jews may reside or their current citizenship.[52] The Church's first and proper theological impulse should be one of honor and gratitude, for "salvation is from the Jews" (John 4:22). Jesus was a Jew, "the son of David, the son of Abraham" (Matt. 1:1), raised by Jewish parents, and just as he honored his earthly parents, so too should we honor them. Moreover, it is through Jesus and the in-grafting work of the Holy Spirit that the Church participates in the covenant that God first made with Abram and Sarai. Israel is the original "people of God," to whom he shows "steadfast love to the thousandth generation" (Exod. 20:5–6; 34:6–7).

History of Christian Anti-Semitism

The second thing the Church must acknowledge is the historical reality that Christianity has in fact too often not honored or respected its Jewish ancestors or contemporary Jews. Indeed, it has too often been shameful in its treatment of the Jewish people, either through individual acts of prejudice or more collective attitudes or acts of discrimination or open persecution. Throughout Church history, both individual Christians and the Church by its policies have practiced anti-Semitism. Of this history all Christians must be mindful, and of this history the Church must repent.

But why has Christian anti-Semitism been so virulent, so pernicious over the centuries? For many intertwining reasons, of course, but a main factor has been its essential character of being a family feud or a bitter divorce. Christianity began as a sect of Judaism within Roman-occupied first-century Israel. Jesus was a Jew. The original twelve disciples were Jews, all the first believers were Jews, the community's sacred scriptures in its first centuries were the Jewish scriptures, the inherited traditions and mind-set of the community were Jewish, and Jesus's ministry challenged, and was challenged by, Jews of other perspectives. More specifically, the Church began as one way of being Jewish at a time when there was not one "Judaism" but several "Judaisms": the Sadducees, the Pharisees, the Essenes, the Zealots, and presumably eclectic combinations of these and others. Tensions and rivalries existed among these groups, and tensions and rivalries increased when another group of Jews emerged proclaiming the resurrected Jesus as Messiah—a claim not universally recognized. The first additions to this new group were converts from other branches of Judaism, although not all Jews recognized Christians' messianic claims. The Gospel accounts amply illustrate this situation and

---

52. How Christians should understand and relate to modern Israel is, of course, an important and complicated matter. But that is a discussion far beyond the purview of this book.

in their respective ways stake out a position for the emerging Church in this Jewish milieu. Paul's explanation of why not all Jews acknowledged Jesus as Messiah, which I will consider below, is the most involved and arguably the most interesting. In any case, this new group did not have any official standing and often disrupted the status quo within the Jewish world and in Judaism's relation to the imperial power of Rome. Fueled with the zeal of new converts, these Christians frequently provoked the concerns of various Jewish authorities who sought to dampen, channel, or undermine this new minority movement.

Sadly, as too often happens when the formerly powerless become the powerful, as the Church gained in (now predominantly gentile) numbers, influence, and, eventually, official status, it too often gave in to the temptation of acting on remembered grudges toward those Jews who had not converted to Christianity and those Jewish authorities who had sought to curb or control this new sect of Judaism. Various excuses or rationalizations could be mustered to justify the Church's anti-Semitism without recognizing the shameful and bitter irony that it was persecuting its own family, cousins stemming from a common ancestry. Of course, over the centuries, the waxing and waning of Christian anti-Semitism was often spurred as much by economic, ethnic, or political motivations as by strictly religious ones—if not more so. But baser motives could always be wrapped in ostensibly more noble theological ones. After all, it always sounds better to be acting on behalf of God than on behalf of one's own self-interest.

In our own era, the degree to which these patterns and habits of Christian anti-Semitism enabled, allowed, set the groundwork for, or undermined the prevention of the Holocaust remains a hotly debated topic. There were some "righteous gentiles," individual Christians who did what they could to save Jews from the Nazi death camps, from the Swedish diplomat Raoul Wallenberg, to the Dutch woman Corrie ten Boom, to the citizens of the French village of Le Chambon-sur-Lignon, to the German Oskar Schindler. There were other Christians, for instance, members of the "Confessing Church," who spoke out against the Nazi regime in more general ways. The theologian Karl Barth, expelled from his teaching post in Germany and returning to his native Switzerland, repeatedly urged his country to accept more Jewish refugees. Tragically, his pleas went mostly unheard. Pope Pius XII condemned Nazi anti-Semitism in the encyclical *Mit brennender Sorge* (With Burning Concern) and engaged in behind-the-scenes acts to rescue Jews, although a number of current scholars assert he did not do enough. Be all of this as it may, one indisputable fact remains: the Holocaust was carried out by a nation whose history and spiritual heritage were predominantly Christian. To regard the Nazi movement as itself a form of neo-paganism—for which a strong case can be made—is beside the point. How could the Holocaust have happened in a country so deeply rooted in the Christian faith? More pointedly, is the Christian faith inevitably and intrinsically anti-Semitic? Are there certain elements or strands of tradition that the later Church heard and fostered in anti-Semitic ways? Or is Christianity's anti-Semitism an aberration from and a perversion of its deepest and truest beliefs?

Theological Resources for Overcoming Christian Anti-Semitism

To begin addressing these questions, we need to recognize that, as posed, they intermingle the historical and the theological. As noted above, historically speaking, the Church has long engaged in anti-Semitic speech and activity. More recently, many branches of the Church have repented and sought forgiveness from and reconciliation with Jewish communities. But the record of the Church overall remains uneven. Moreover, the Church must acknowledge that it has frequently justified this sinful behavior on theological grounds. In that sense, it cannot be excused as simply an aberration. But theologically speaking, *must* this be the case? Must the Church understand itself as fundamentally at odds with Judaism, presuming that its "new" covenant supersedes God's covenant with Judaism? Or can an alternate theological case be made that a supersessionist view is actually a betrayal of the Church's truest identity and calling? If the latter seems possible, what biblical and theological resources must the Church recover to develop a more faithful understanding of its relationship to Judaism?

The Church can begin to address these questions theologically by understanding its history differently, particularly the history of its reading of Scripture. The modern mind-set often views history in evolutionary terms, with the more "primitive" past surpassed and outdated by the more "advanced." "Progress" becomes an ideology, such that old ways of doing things are replaced by new ways not just as a matter of fact but because they *ought* to be replaced: the new is more modern, is improved, is inevitably better. This mind-set was often used during the nineteenth century to justify colonialism by the Western industrial powers of more "backward" or "less civilized" cultures. It is still the basis of economic "planned obsolescence" and has certainly been taken advantage of by advertisers and marketers. And it remains a part of our moral and political landscape, as evidenced whenever anyone disparagingly says something like "That's so old-fashioned" or "Are you living in the dark ages?" When this mind-set is used to interpret Scripture (as became common in self-consciously "modern" Protestant circles during the nineteenth century), it almost inevitably views the faith of Israel as more primitive and the emergence of Christianity as an advance. In fact, the "father of liberal Protestantism," Friedrich Schleiermacher, stated that the continued use of the Old Testament in the Church was simply a habit, a carryover from its earliest years. Theologically speaking, only the New Testament was actually required to maintain the essentials of the faith.[53]

Evolutionary versus Typological Interpretation of the Bible

This evolutionary way of understanding history, however, is not the only way the Church may read and understand the Bible. In fact, as a number of scholars remind us, in the Church's long history of scriptural interpretation this progressive approach is actually only a rather recent development, supplanting the far more traditional narrative and figural method employed for centuries.[54] The typological or figural approach recognizes the movement of time from the past toward the future, but it does not necessarily see each successive age as "progressing" beyond or superseding the previous one. Instead, in this forward movement it recognizes certain recurring patterns and "types" that may differ in outward manifestations but fundamentally repeat or echo one another inwardly. Particular passages of Scripture certainly have a historical context and referent based on the time in which they were originally written, but one of the assumptions made in their being recognized as Scripture (rather than as just a historical text) is that they also have a fecundity of meaning that transcends their origin. They may simultaneously refer to something past and something contemporary and still foreshadow something yet to come—and continue to offer such richness through the Spirit's illumination, even with the unfolding years.

This typological approach is made possible by the assumption of the essential continuity between the Old and the New Covenants, because divine grace and divine law—"law and gospel"—exist in both and extend to a community that has an essential continuity in both. I have already cited an example of this assumption in chapter 2, namely, in John Calvin's understanding of God's covenants with Israel and the Church: "The covenant made with all the patriarchs is so much like ours in substance and reality that the two are

53. See Schleiermacher's argument for this claim in §§131–32 of his main theological work, *The Christian Faith*, ed. H. R. Mackintosh and J. S. Stewart (Edinburgh: T&T Clark, 1928).

54. See, for example, Hans Frei, *The Eclipse of Biblical Narrative* (New Haven: Yale University Press, 1974); Christopher R. Seitz, *Figured Out: Typology and Providence in Christian Scripture* (Louisville: Westminster John Knox, 2001); Ronald E. Heine, *Reading the Old Testament with the Ancient Church: Exploring the Formation of Early Christian Thought* (Grand Rapids: Baker Academic, 2007).

actually one and the same."[55] The outward forms differ, yet the inner reality is the same. Consider these additional words from Calvin, reflecting upon the division of the kingdom of Israel following the reign of Solomon:

> The true church existed among the Jews [i.e., the southern kingdom of Judah] and Israelites [i.e., the northern kingdom] when they kept the laws of the covenant. That is, by God's beneficence they obtained those things by which the church is held together. They had the doctrine of truth in the law; its ministry was in the hands of priests and prophets. They were initiated into religion by the sign of circumcision; for the strengthening of their faith they were exercised in the other sacraments. There is no doubt that the titles with which the Lord honored his church applied to their society.[56]

Practically speaking, this approach recognizes a certain back-and-forth fluidity between the ages. The ancient Jew or Israelite was found faithful or judged fallen on essentially the same basis as a latter-day Christian. Conversely, the faithful Christian might identify himself or herself with a pious figure from the Old Testament or be condemned as falling into idolatry like a faithless figure of old.

This point having been made, however, we must acknowledge that Judaism and Christianity do differ in their respective views on where God's grace is "located" and how the law is understood, both of which are influenced by differing understandings of human sin. In Judaism, God's graciousness is certainly demonstrated in his calling of the Israelites as the covenant people descended from Abraham, Isaac, and Jacob. It is demonstrated again in his deliverance of this people from its bondage in Egypt. And it is demonstrated yet again in his redemption of the remnant from its captivity in Babylon. But it is also made manifest in the giving of the law at Mount Sinai: the law itself is an embodiment of God's grace. The Torah is seen not as an imposition but as a wonderful gift, revealing God's ordering of creation and making clear how he expects the people to order their lives (see, e.g., Ps. 19:7–13). To be given such knowledge, as well as the legally prescribed cultic means for expiating sin and guilt when the people fall short, is understood as an unearned, gracious benefit of God's covenantal love and steadfastness.

Traditionally, Christianity agrees that the law comes from God but also insists that humans, due to their fallen nature and sin, can never fully attain the requirements of the law on their own. To overcome this reality, and to

---

55. John Calvin, *Institutes of the Christian Religion*, ed. John T. McNeill, trans. Ford Lewis Battles, Library of Christian Classics 20 and 21 (Philadelphia: Westminster, 1960), 2.10.2, p. 429.
56. *Institutes*, 4.2.7, p. 1048.

make expiation for sins once and for all, God the Father sent his Son to die and be raised for the people. Joined with Christ through the power of the Spirit, believers become a new creation, a people who with the continuing help of the Spirit are now able to follow those aspects of the law that are eternal. As this last point implies, not all aspects of the Old Covenant law are viewed as enduring: the ritual law, held to include laws pertaining to the temple cult and dietary regulations, is now understood to have only figural meaning and is not considered binding upon Christians. However, the moral law, that is, those laws pertaining to right relation to God and neighbor, remains in effect. But even that law is not the "location" of divine grace in the way it was considered to be previously; instead, that grace is located in a person, Jesus Christ, and made available through another, the Holy Spirit.

Practically speaking, this old/new historical framework does not necessarily mean that as moderns or as members of the Church, we are *by that fact alone* living in the "new." This old/new distinction is not so much a chronological as an existential differentiation. After all, Christian individuals and groups may be living as if Christ had not come. They may seek self-justification through their own efforts and implicitly or explicitly reject God's grace in Christ. Correspondingly, in a typological reading of Scripture, they are thereby recapitulating the attitudes and behavior of negative role models evident in both the Old and the New Testaments. Conversely, one's personal life may correlate to the new Christ-centered, Spirit-empowered reality now governing history; one has left the old ways behind. And intriguingly, here too one may be seen as recapitulating antecedent positive role models evident in both the Old and the New Testaments.

Such typological reading of Scripture is certainly evident between the Old Testament and the New Testament, but it was not an invention of the New Testament authors themselves. Rather, they were simply employing a technique for reading Scripture that was already well established within the Old Testament itself. That is, new behaviors or events are understood in light of, and in continuity with, old behaviors or events, while the old is understood to possess fuller and deeper significance in light of the new. Several classic examples of this may be found in Isaiah. In Isaiah 9:2–7 and 11:1–9, the prophet foretells the coming of a new David, a messianic king who will usher in true justice and righteousness. In 43:2, 16–21 and 48:20–21, announcing God's intention to redeem the exiles in Babylon, the prophet uses language that echoes the exodus of Israel from Egypt, of the Israelites passing through the waters of the Red Sea and Jordan River as well as through the wilderness. In Isaiah 51:3, the prophet comforts the exiles by saying that the Lord will make of Zion a new garden of Eden—a claim reinforced in 55:13. Indeed, in

60:19–22 and 65:17–25, the prophet proclaims an eschatological new creation that will far transcend the old.

Paul's Typology in Romans 9–11

It is this already well-established typological method that Paul draws on in writing Romans 9–11. There, to account for the self-evident fact that not all Jews have accepted Jesus as the Messiah, Paul offers a scripturally grounded explanation of God's providential purposes. Having been transformed from a persecutor of the Church into its leading missionary to the gentiles, in these chapters Paul addresses how Christians should understand and relate to Israel. Paul's thoughts on this matter are nuanced and thoughtful, drawing on his own experience as a Christian convert and as a former Pharisee. He considers Scripture and sees parallels between his situation and those experienced and spoken to by Israel's prophets. Indeed, over the course of these three chapters, Paul cites or alludes to more than fifty passages from the Torah, the Prophets, and the Writings, seeking to demonstrate such a "typological continuity." He also establishes several distinct, "nonnegotiable" theological givens on which he bases his reasoning, and it is essential to note certain inferences that he does not draw as well as those he does. And last but not least, it is crucial to recognize that Paul truly agonized over the matter: "For I could wish that I myself were accursed and cut off from Christ for the sake of my own people, my kindred according to the flesh" (Rom. 9:3).

Paul begins by recounting the many blessings that God has bestowed on Israel: adoption as God's children, God's glorious presence, the covenants, the law, the worship, the promises; "to them belong the patriarchs, and from them, according to the flesh, comes the Messiah" (Rom. 9:5). He then clarifies that inheriting these blessings is not automatic, merely as a consequence of being a lineal descendant of the patriarchs to whom the covenant was first made. Rather, as the scriptural story relates, it depends upon whom God chose: for example, Sarah, not Hagar; Isaac, not Ishmael; Jacob, not Esau. The true children of God are not merely "the children of the flesh" but "the children of the promise" (9:8). Paul concludes: "So it depends not on human will or exertion, but on God who shows mercy" (9:16). He then extends this logic, again echoing Scripture, saying that the same holds true when God demonstrates the ability to fulfill his purposes, even in the face of earthly opposition, such as when he hardened Pharaoh's heart. Paul anticipates the inevitable reply: "Well, if we can't earn it, and God can actually make us resist it, how can God find fault with us?" Paul indicates that such self-justification is misplaced, quoting the prophets declaring that the clay has no say in what the potter makes of it.[57] For indeed, God has greater plans in mind: extending the riches of his glory to show mercy on gentiles as well as Jews,[58] even using the resistance of some so that eventually righteousness might be available to all.[59] Paul then considers various Old Testament passages—including ones from Leviticus, Deuteronomy, Psalms, Isaiah, and Joel—to assert that this righteousness was all along intended to be attained not by means of the law but through faith in Christ (Rom. 10:1–21).

This bedrock assumption is, of course, the fundamental difference between Christians and Jews. Paul's dilemma is to make sense of the fact that not all Jews—whose very identity is grounded in their being called by God—who have heard the gospel proclamation have heeded *its* call. He knows that God has not rejected his people (Rom. 11:1). Yes, they have stumbled, a tendency they have demonstrated in the past, as Elijah, Isaiah, and David testify.[60] But they have not "stumbled so as to fall" (11:11). Indeed, God will ultimately deliver them and save all Israel (11:26–27), because Paul knows that God is faithful and therefore his original call is "irrevocable" (11:29). So the testimony of Scripture and his own reasoning led him to conclude that God must be using his people Israel—even unbeknownst to them—to accomplish some larger purpose.

We have witnessed this pattern of divine action before, throughout Scripture and in fact all the way back to the beginnings in Genesis. Recall the story of Joseph and his brothers, as I summarized it in chapter 1. Joseph's brothers originally intended to be rid of him, by one means or another—and given Joseph's obnoxious behavior at the time, this intent seemed understandable, if not excusable. Then there follows an apparently random series of events for both Joseph and his brothers, which finally leads to his having the power to preserve his now-increased family from famine and to reconcile with his brothers. This outcome, given how this whole chain of events began, leads Joseph to recognize that God can turn even acts of ill will to serve his larger purposes of salvation and reconciliation. And that larger purpose at the time of Paul's writing is the inclusion of the gentiles among the covenant people of God.

Now many modern-day Christians are leery of Paul's whole stance: his assumption that Jews ought to accept Jesus as Messiah, that Christians are called to proselytize Jews (cf. Rom. 10:14–17), that God intends to make Israel

57. Isa. 29:16; 45:9; 64:8; Jer. 18:6.
58. Paul cites Hos. 1:10 and 2:23 to support this claim.
59. Again, this is a pattern Paul saw already well established in the Old Testament, citing Isa. 10:22 and 1:9.
60. See Paul's citation of 1 Kings 19:10, 18; Isa. 29:10; and Ps. 69:22–23 in Rom. 11:2–10.

"jealous" by inviting the gentiles into the covenant (11:11, 14, 19), that "a hardening has come upon part of Israel" (11:25), that as "regards the gospel they are enemies" (11:28). We are concerned because we are mindful of the Church's complicity in anti-Semitic attitudes and acts over the centuries, and especially the Church's failings in preventing the Holocaust. Most branches of the Church have repented of these sins of commission and omission and sought forgiveness and reconciliation with the Jewish community. And we are reluctant, understandably and appropriately, to use language that might rekindle assumptions of Christian antagonism or supersessionism over against Judaism. But this does not mean that we can find no theological resources in Paul's thoughts here, even while recognizing that they are explicitly *Christian* (rather than, say, "Judeo-Christian" or somehow generic or universal) theological resources. The key takeaway from Paul's reasoning is that the Church's primary posture must be one of humility. We are in no position to boast: "For God has imprisoned all in disobedience so that he may be merciful to all" (11:32). Paul insists that we are all, Jew and gentile alike, on equal footing before God, in that we are alike dependent on God's mercy and faithfulness, not our own works. Just because it took a "special" effort on God's part to graft those of gentile heritage onto the olive tree that is Israel does not mean they gain a special status. To the contrary, if God can graft the branch of a "wild" (gentile) olive tree onto a "cultivated" (Jewish) one, he certainly has the power to graft the cultivated branches back on again—which Paul assumes God will eventually do (11:24).

Here Paul admonishes his hearers *not* to claim more knowledge than they have: it is a divine mystery that a "hardening" has come on part of Israel, "until the full number of Gentiles has come in" to the covenant people (Rom. 11:25). Once that number has been reached, then, as prophecy indicates,[61] all Israel will be saved (11:26–27). So again, our primary posture as Christians is to be one of humility: just as we are in no position to boast of our own righteousness, so too are we in no position to claim special insight into the detailed inner workings of God's unfolding covenantal plan. If there is a "hardening" in Israel, Paul says, we must ascribe it to God. This is noteworthy, because he thereby shifts the focus from what particular individuals have done to what God is doing through them. And if it is God's doing, then we need no longer worry about being privy to all its inner details. After all, our own experience bears witness to the fact that we cannot always know how God will use our actions to further his purposes, only that we are summoned to be faithful in pursuing his will as best we are able. So it should not be surprising if God's

---

61. Paul's scriptural quotation appears to be a paraphrase of Isa. 59:20–21 and 27:9.

continued work in and with Israel remains a mystery as well. In effect, Paul recognizes that for the foreseeable future, God has a different role for Israel to play, one that will work itself out alongside that of the Church—although ultimately, those roles will both serve the same divine end.

Respecting Jews as Our Forebears in Faith

So what implications does all this have for the Church's current relation to Israel, and for our recognition of mutually belonging to the "people of God"? For one, it requires our respect toward the covenant people to whom we have been engrafted. As noted above, our Savior was born of a Jewish mother and raised by a Jewish father, and just as he honored his earthly parents, so too should we honor them. Put another way, we do well to obey the fifth commandment with regard to our own Christian origins in Judaism, and on that basis we are also called to show respect for our modern-day Jewish cousins. This could involve learning from one another through mutual scriptural study and theological dialogue or simply social interactions between local churches and synagogues. Such respect also involves working together for those things that aid the cause of righteousness, justice, reconciliation, and shalom, while conversely standing in solidarity with the Jewish community against instances and attitudes of anti-Semitism. In other words, such respect recognizes and appreciates commonalities but is also mature and honest enough to acknowledge our distinct differences.

But more than this, God's irrevocable bond with the Jewish people helps expand the Church's own understanding of God's covenant by reminding us that God's covenantal work operates on a much broader scale than we might be inclined to realize. Yes, the Church is the unique creation of the Holy Spirit, and that Spirit has given us the image of the Church as "the body of Christ" to describe the Church's unique identity, its spiritual, even mystical grounding in the being and work of its risen Lord. But the Spirit also gives us the image of the Church as "the people of God" to help locate the Church in God's larger covenantal context, giving it a broader perspective on who it is and the task to which God has called it. Acknowledging the continuing role of the Jewish people in these covenantal purposes helps keep the Church from being too parochial in its self-understanding. Recognizing ourselves as this people, as citizens of God's "holy nation," is not a claim to judge ourselves superior. It is rather a claim put upon us to know ourselves set apart that we might with both joy and awe-filled humility participate in God's grand, redeeming purposes. Yet while not judging ourselves superior, we must not simply abandon the necessity of judging at all. For without

judgment—or perhaps less provocatively, without discernment—we open
the door to those influences and notions that would undermine our capacity
to remain a people at all. (Recall the end of the previous section regarding
the importance of maintaining a distinct identity in the face of a culture co-
opting and assimilating the Church.) We are a people not through anything
we are or possess on our own; we are a people because we are set apart for
God to be a "royal priesthood," a "holy nation." Being set apart is certainly
a gift of God's grace, but it also bears with it certain responsibilities due to
the reality that the Holy Spirit now tabernacles among and within us. To
consider this more fully, I turn next to a consideration of the Church as the
temple of the Holy Spirit.

5

The Temple of the Holy Spirit

The Spirit and God's Life-Giving, Life-Changing Presence

Then Jesus, filled with the power of the Spirit, returned to Galilee, and a report about him spread through all the surrounding country. He began to teach in their synagogues and was praised by everyone. When he came to Nazareth, where he had been brought up, he went to the synagogue on the sabbath day, as was his custom. He stood up to read, and the scroll of the prophet Isaiah was given to him. He unrolled the scroll and found the place where it was written:

> "The Spirit of the Lord is upon me,
> because he has anointed me
>   to bring good news to the poor.
> He has sent me to proclaim release to the captives
> and recovery of sight to the blind,
>   to let the oppressed go free,
> to proclaim the year of the Lord's favor."

And he rolled up the scroll, gave it back to the attendant, and sat down. The eyes of all in the synagogue were fixed on him. Then he began to say to them, "Today this scripture has been fulfilled in your hearing." (Luke 4:14–21)

And you show that you are a letter of Christ, prepared by us, written not with ink but with the Spirit of the living God, not on tablets of stone but on tablets of human hearts.

Such is the confidence that we have through Christ toward God. Not that we are competent of ourselves to claim anything as coming from us; our competence is from God, who has made us competent to be ministers of a new covenant, not of letter but of spirit; for the letter kills, but the Spirit gives life.

Now if the ministry of death, chiseled in letters on stone tablets, came in glory so that the people of Israel could not gaze at Moses' face because of the glory of his face, a glory now set aside, how much more will the ministry of the Spirit come in glory? For if there was glory in the ministry of condemnation, much more does the ministry of justification abound in glory! Indeed, what once had glory has lost its glory because of the greater glory; for if what was set aside came through glory, much more has the permanent come in glory!

Since, then, we have such a hope, we act with great boldness. . . .

Now the Lord is the Spirit, and where the Spirit of the Lord is, there is freedom. And all of us, with unveiled faces, seeing the glory of the Lord as though reflected in a mirror, are being transformed into the same image from one degree of glory to another; for this comes from the Lord, the Spirit. (2 Cor. 3:3–12, 17–18)

Jesus Christ is the incarnate Son and Word empowered by the Holy Spirit to be the prophet proclaiming and fulfilling the holy will of God the Father for his covenantal people and ultimately for all creation. Christ accomplishes this revelation in his office as the mediating Prophet, embodying in word and deed all that God intends for his creatures.[1] In this prophetic work announcing and enabling God's "still more excellent way" (1 Cor. 12:31), the words of Old Testament prophecy reverberate in Jesus's own: the calls to give God glory, the call to acknowledge God's sovereignty and tender mercy, the condemnations of false religion and hypocrisy, the call to care for the outcast and the oppressed, and the vision of a renewed covenant leading to a restored creation—in other words, the summons to true holiness and all that that entails. Jesus proclaims the reign of God and in so doing echoes Israel's prophets.

But of course such echoes are only natural, given that these earlier prophets of the covenant were themselves instruments of the divine Word and the Spirit. Just remember the recurring description of God's commissioning them: "The word of the Lord came to me . . ." or "Thus says the Lord . . ." or something similar,[2] coupled with some variation of "The Spirit of the Lord

---

1. For an extended treatment of Christ's prophetic work, see my *King, Priest, and Prophet: A Trinitarian Theology of Atonement* (New York: T&T Clark, 2004), chap. 6.

2. E.g., 1 Sam. 3:1–21; 15:10; 2 Sam. 7:4; 24:11; 1 Kings 6:11; Isa. 38:4; Jer. 1:2; 2:2; 13:3, 8; Ezek. 1:3; 3:16; 6:1; 7:1; 11:14; Hos. 1:1; Joel 1:1; Jon. 1:1; Mic. 1:1; Zeph. 1:1; Hag. 1:1; Zech. 1:1; Mal. 1:1.

is upon me. . . ."[3] Jesus's words and work did not replace the teachings and eschatological vision of the prophets but instead became their cornerstone, that they might finally have a grounding and orientation, that God the Father's purpose might be built up. Such edification has two parts: Christ's own prophetic ministry of teaching and miracles and the coming of the "Counselor, the Holy Spirit," whom the Father would send in Jesus's name (John 14:26 RSV). In other words, we once more see the Father's "two hands" work in concert to accomplish this aspect of his covenantal plan.

The Inspiring, Upbuilding Spirit

In chapter 3, I discussed some of the ways in which the Holy Spirit knits the Church together as "the body of Christ," called to be a witness in word, sacrament, and living to the new humanity available in Christ. In chapter 4, I discussed other ways in which the Holy Spirit may be understood as establishing the Church as "the people of God," a holy nation stemming from the divine covenant with Abraham and Sarah and from the resurrection victory of Christ as initiating God's in-breaking kingdom. With this chapter, we finally arrive at the last rubric I employ for describing the nature of Church, namely, "the temple of the Holy Spirit." Now some might wonder why I am connecting the image of "the temple of the Holy Spirit" with the rubric of "Christ the prophet" rather than "Christ the priest." Doesn't the latter rubric have a more natural association with temple imagery than the "prophet" rubric? In one sense, yes, of course it does. Having already developed the image of "the body of Christ" in association with his sacrificial offering of his body and blood to establish a new covenant, I could also develop the image of the "temple of the Holy Spirit" in ways that describe the implications of this sacrifice and new covenant for the Church. For example, as the "temple of the Holy Spirit," Christians become a "holy priesthood" called to imitate Christ by offering "spiritual sacrifices."[4]

Yet I want to draw the seemingly counterintuitive connection between "the temple of the Holy Spirit" and "Christ the prophet" to help illustrate several important points. First, the distinctions between various images and rubrics are not rigid but fluid; they should be understood not as in tension with one another but as complementary. Simply recall how often Jesus and the apostles used multiple, and often mixed, metaphors! Think of all the things to which Jesus compared the kingdom of God: a man sowing, a mustard seed, leaven, a hidden treasure, a pearl merchant, a fishing net, a householder, and

---

3. E.g., Judg. 6:34; 1 Sam. 16:13; 2 Sam. 23:1–2; Isa. 61:1; Ezek. 11:1, 4–5; Mic. 3:8.
4. 1 Pet. 2:5; cf. Rom. 12:1.

ten maidens, among others.[5] Consider how the phrase "royal priesthood" combines the kingly role with the sacerdotal,[6] and how Hebrews 10:12–16 seems to combine the priestly, royal, and prophetic functions into one act of the Triune God:

> But when Christ had offered for all time a single sacrifice for sins, he sat down at the right hand of God, then to wait until his enemies should be made a stool for his feet. For by a single offering he has perfected for all time those who are sanctified. And the Holy Spirit also bears witness to us; for after saying, "This is the covenant that I will make with them after those days, says the Lord: I will put my laws on their hearts, and write them on their minds."

The metaphorical language and images employed in Scripture often overlap and reinforce each other in ways that are not always strictly and literally logical. This only makes sense, because Scripture need not describe our everyday lives—what we know through our own experience. Rather, it seeks to evoke the deeper reality that undergirds and directs our life toward its transcendent and eternal goal.

Second, too often the prophetic office is understood in a constricted, exclusive sense. Some Christians emphasize prophets as advocates of social justice, railing against the oppressive powerful and rich, while condemning religious ceremonialism. Other Christians understand prophets primarily as predictors of the future, sometimes with moralistic overtones, and sometimes with apocalyptic ones. Each view is correct to focus on something indeed characteristic of biblical prophets, but wrong to exclude the other. And both views tend to downplay or ignore a fuller understanding of the prophet's role in relation to priests and kings, as well as to God's larger purposes. Prophets did indeed denounce the oppression of the weak and disenfranchised by the powerful, just as they condemned false religion. But the Spirit summoned them to this task, not contrary to Torah but on the basis of Torah. In effect, the prophets were calling the people back to their covenant obligations, not imposing new ones. And this is true in the religious realm of the people's common life as well as in the social and political. Torah was a gift of God's covenantal relation outlining how true communion, true *koinōnia*, could be established: the law prescribes how one maintains right relations with God and within the community, while also providing the means for forgiveness and reconciliation when there are breaches in that communion. Keep in mind that the whole cultic system of tabernacle, priesthood, and sacrifice was itself laid

---

5. Matt. 13:24, 31, 33, 44, 45, 47, 52; 25:1.
6. 1 Pet. 2:9.

out in the law given at Sinai, precisely to serve the purposes of communion and reconciliation. In this sense, God employed prophets and priests to serve the same ends of communion and holiness, although by means of different offices.

Yet the Spirit also intimated to the prophets that such communion and holiness are a work in progress. Yes, the law lets the people know what God expects of them in the covenantal relation, but the whole cultic system of sacrifice itself implies the people's repeated inability to live up to these divine expectations. After all, why would they need prescribed rituals for expressing repentance and removing their guilt if they could indeed live up to what the law requires of them? So while God's gift of Torah establishes the people in the here and now and provides them with what they need for the everyday living of life—including a recurring means for being reconciled to one another and to God—God also has grander plans. The covenantal relation is not static but has a trajectory into the future. Yes, the Spirit moved the prophets to denounce injustice and idolatry in the present, calling the people back to their covenant obligations. But the Spirit also moved them to proclaim God's eschatological purposes for his people, to give them a vision of what God has in store for them—and not just for them, but for the whole of creation. A new thing will happen, building on the old, fulfilling what had previously been only promised.

The Prophethood of All Believers: Called to Holiness

What is this new event in the unfolding of God's covenant that marks the beginning of the messianic age? One part, of course, is the sacrificial death and victorious resurrection of Jesus—the once-and-for-all sacrifice made by God's own High Priest. This is the death into which all Christians are baptized, "putting on" Christ and becoming themselves priests with him (1 Pet. 2:4–10). But another part is the outpouring of the Holy Spirit upon not just individual prophets but, in the words of Joel 2:28–32, "upon all flesh." In baptism, Christians are not only clothed with Christ but are sealed with the Holy Spirit.[7] Identifying a parallel with the well-established Protestant concept of the "priesthood of all believers," one could also say that the seal of the Holy Spirit establishes a comparable "prophethood of all believers." Christians are offered a living relation with God the Father, through their union with Christ and the empowering of the Holy Spirit. As a result, God's will for the people is no longer external to them, written on tablets of stone, but, as the prophet Jeremiah foresaw, written "upon their hearts," so that each person may know God intimately.[8]

7. Eph. 1:13; cf. Acts 2:38; 1 Cor. 12:13.
8. Jer. 31:31–34; cf. Heb. 10:15–16.

As Scripture makes clear (Gal. 3:15–4:7), it is not that the law is wrong, that God somehow "changes his mind" or "evolves" in his thinking. Remember, the Torah is recognized to be a gracious gift of God, so that the covenant people may know what God expects of them. The issue is that the law of itself is inert, unable of its own to help the people follow it. As such, it becomes a standard that cannot be met by human effort alone; as such, it becomes in fact "the killing letter." In the face of this reality, the outpouring of the Holy Spirit becomes the life-giving energy and power of God to restore and renew the divine holiness and will among the people, to make them in fact a "holy nation." The "finger of God" is the Holy Spirit, who previously wrote the law upon tablets of stone, but who now writes that law on human hearts.[9] The Holy Spirit is the agent who sanctifies the Church, as a body and as individual members, so that the Church becomes a living example and instrument of God's sanctifying work of guiding creation's various times and places to their eschatological goal. It is this body, these people, in whom the Holy Spirit chooses to "tabernacle," to be the presence of the living God in an intimate and glorifying manner.

And so we arrive at the last rubric I employ for describing the nature of Church, namely, "the temple of the Holy Spirit." Strictly speaking, the phrase has a limited usage in the New Testament, appearing only in Paul's first letter to the church at Corinth.[10] Yet Paul also employs a virtually synonymous image in 2 Corinthians, where he speaks of Christians collectively as "the temple of the living God," citing several Old Testament passages in support of this claim (2 Cor. 16–18). He uses another image associated with the temple when he urges Christians to become "living sacrifices" (Rom. 12:1). Similarly, Peter speaks of the Christian community as a "holy priesthood" (1 Pet. 2:5, 9), while much of the Letter to the Hebrews is an extended treatment of Christ as the High Priest, with his priestly sacrifice and the new temple now available. These and other apostolic references to a new understanding of the temple, its cultic practices, and the priesthood are, of course, rooted in the words and actions of Jesus himself.

Sanctification

When one recognizes how these and other images, descriptions, and allusions display a convergence with the theological heart of the specific phrase "temple of the Holy Spirit," it becomes quite natural to group them together

---

9. See Exod. 31:18, Deut. 9:10, and, tellingly, cf. Luke 11:20 with its parallel in Matt. 12:28, where the finger of God/Spirit equivalence becomes clear.

10. See 1 Cor. 3:9–17; 6:14–20.

and consider the ways they mutually reinforce and enrich one another. Generally put, these diverse images portray the Holy Spirit as filling believers, both individually and corporately, animating them and setting them apart for the eschatological fulfillment and perfection that the Son has enabled and the Father decreed. This animating power of the Holy Spirit has been considered in the previous chapters: it is the Holy Spirit who joins us to the body of Christ, enabling us to be born again with him in his resurrected life. It is the Holy Spirit who grafts the Church into the covenant people of God that has existed since Abraham and Sarah. In this chapter, I will address how that animating power of the Holy Spirit "sets us apart," enabling us to grow in faith and holiness. In traditional theological terms, my focus will be sanctification. More practically put, this chapter will deal with the covenantal accountability that God expects of his people, both individually and corporately.

So what does "sanctification" entail? Derived from the Latin word *sanctus*, it literally means "to be made holy," which in a broader sense means to be "set apart" for God. But this begs the question, what does "holy" mean? It describes the nature of the divine. In this regard, only God is intrinsically and fully holy. To ascribe holiness to God is to say that God alone is ineffably perfect: superlatively majestic, good, just, merciful, and almighty, transcending all that is profane or mundane. God alone is worthy of worship. In the words of the Danish theologian Søren Kierkegaard, an "infinite qualitative distinction" exists between God and creation, and the divine presence evokes in humans reverence, awe, and even terror. A classic biblical episode portrays Moses curiously approaching the divine presence in the burning bush (Exod. 3:1–6), at which God commands, "Come no closer! Remove the sandals from your feet, for the place on which you are standing is holy ground" (3:5). When the voice identifies itself, Moses hides his face in fear.

Fire represents energy and light; it is "disembodied" yet very real; it can be constructively used or it can destroy. Scripture often portrays God's presence in terms of fire or a flame: there is the burning bush just mentioned, but the Lord's encounters with the Israelites in the wilderness of Sinai are another recurring example.[11] Later in Israel's history, following Solomon's dedication, God is portrayed as occupying the new temple with these words:

> When Solomon had ended his prayer, fire came down from heaven and consumed the burnt offering and the sacrifices; and the glory of the LORD filled the temple. The priests could not enter the house of the LORD, because the glory of the LORD filled the LORD's house. When all the people of Israel saw the fire

11. E.g., Exod. 13:21; 19:18; 24:17.

come down and the glory of the Lord on the temple, they bowed down on the pavement with their faces to the ground, and worshiped and gave thanks to the Lord, saying,

> "For he is good,
> for his steadfast love endures forever."

Then the king and all the people offered sacrifice before the Lord. (2 Chron. 7:1–4)

Isaiah prophesies that the restoration of the temple on Mount Zion will occur in a similar manner (Isa. 4:5), and Zechariah envisions God as a "wall of fire" protecting the restored city of Jerusalem (Zech. 2:5). And, of course, the account of Pentecost in Acts describes the Holy Spirit descending upon the apostles like "tongues of fire" (Acts 2:1–4).[12]

This last example, among others, also illustrates how holiness may be communicated to creatures, which, of course, are not intrinsically divine or holy. In some instances, this transfer occurs as a result of proximity. In keeping with the fire imagery, holiness is depicted as a power or energy field, and persons or things coming within its sphere "catch fire" or are "irradiated" with holiness. After Moses descended Mount Sinai, "the skin of his face shone because he had been talking with God" (Exod. 34:29), which frightened the Israelites (vv. 30–35). In another mountaintop theophany, Jesus was transfigured (Matt. 17:1–8) so that "his face shone like the sun, and his clothes became dazzling white" (v. 2), while the witnessing disciples, like the Israelites seeing Moses, were overcome by fear. And John's apocalyptic vision (Rev. 1:13–17) saw one "like the Son of Man" (v. 13) whose eyes were "like a flame of fire" (v. 14) and whose face was "like the sun shining with full force" (v. 16), causing John to fall down in fear. Individuals encountering the divine holiness have reason to fear, because its power can indeed be dangerous, just as fire can be dangerous. The careless, disobedient, or sinful experience holiness as wrath,[13] and it can prove deadly.[14]

Of course, the Bible also portrays God communicating holiness through specific designation, through the consecration, dedication, or hallowing of all manner of creaturely things. Indeed, the Church affirms that the writings of Scripture themselves are a continuing object of God's sanctifying power and designation. To affirm the Scriptures as "inspired" means that the human authors were sanctified—"set apart"—for the writing and collection of these

---

12. Cf. Matt. 3:11//Luke 3:16.
13. Deut. 8–21; Ps. 78; Isa. 4:4; Ezek. 22:23–31; Rom. 2:1–16; Heb. 12:28–29.
14. Exod. 19:21–24; Lev. 10:1–3; cf. Luke 9:52–55.

scriptures by the Holy Spirit, just as the Church prays that in its continued hearing of these scriptures it might be "illuminated" by the same Holy Spirit. In both cases the Holy Spirit is understood to make them instruments employed by God the Father to communicate his Word.[15] Scripture then also describes various places, times, convocations, buildings, garments, and instruments of the cult being sanctified and set apart for divine purposes. Most significantly, both individuals and peoples may be so claimed by God. God calls Israel to be a holy nation, a royal priesthood (Exod. 19:6). The "Holiness Code" has as its recurring refrain God's declaration "You shall be holy, for I the LORD your God am holy" (Lev. 19:2; cf. 11:45; 20:26). Jesus echoes this call in his Sermon on the Mount ("You, therefore, must be perfect, as your heavenly Father is perfect" [Matt. 5:48]), and the Church understands itself as set apart and called to holiness, grafted onto Israel's earlier call.[16] The conversion of Saul of Tarsus combines elements of earlier theophanies with such a specific call: he is struck to the ground by a blinding light and a voice from heaven, in order to become Paul, the "chosen instrument" to carry the Lord's name "before the Gentiles and kings and the sons of Israel" (Acts 9:1–19).

This communicable character of holiness is, of course, the presupposition of the Holy Spirit's sanctifying work in the Church's communion and the lives of individual believers. In such sanctification, the faithful experience regeneration and strengthening in Christ and receive a foretaste of that eschatological holiness promised for the end of the age. But that holiness also exercises a cleansing or, to use a traditional term, "mortifying" power. Again, the image of holiness as fire highlights these tempering and purging qualities. Confronted by holiness, believers cannot help but be humbled, knowing how far they fall short. The writings of mystics and those having undergone intense conversions often describe in heartfelt terms the feelings of inadequacy and unworthiness that the experience evokes.

This feeling certainly has moral implications, yet the Christian understanding of holiness does not limit it to merely ethical categories. Catherine of Genoa's writings on purgatory offer an interesting commentary on this point. Catherine understood purgatory's cleansing fire not as a punishment but as a benefit, giving individuals the means to strip away everything base or disgraceful, allowing them to face God without guilt or shame.[17] One need not

15. John Webster has written two clear and helpful books on these topics: *Holiness* (Grand Rapids: Eerdmans, 2003) and *Holy Scripture: A Dogmatic Sketch*, Current Issues in Theology (Cambridge: Cambridge University Press, 2003).

16. Matt. 5:1–7:29, esp. 5:48; 1 Cor. 3:16–17; 1 Pet. 1:15–16; 2:9.

17. See Catherine of Genoa, *Purgation and Purgatory/The Spiritual Dialogue*, trans. Serge Hughes, Classics of Western Spirituality (Mahwah, NJ: Paulist Press, 1979), 71–72, 75–78, 83.

affirm the notion of purgatory to say that confronting divine holiness stirs up the desire to bring only one's purest and best when entering God's presence. To describe this in primarily or exclusively moral terms is to miss how holiness enkindles not just the desire to correct one's behavior but the overwhelming yearning to transform one's very being. Liturgically, this point is expressed by the tradition of having confession before participating in the Lord's Supper. To properly participate in this holy ritual, one should be cleansed from the taint of sin. As one theologian observes, baptism has typically been this "washing before supper,"[18] but part of the liturgical act of repentance, confession, and absolution is that it "returns" one to the moment of one's baptism.

The biblical portrayal of God's holiness indicates that while the "qualitative distinction" between the holy and the mundane is indeed "infinite," it is not meant to be eternal. The covenantal arc presented in Scripture's narrative demonstrates God's desire to overcome the chasm separating the holy and the mundane. True, the hallowing of creation on the first Sabbath (Gen. 2:2–3) and the divine-creaturely communion of the garden are disrupted by the fall. Yet the biblical story concludes with the final sanctification of the new heaven and the new earth, when God's original intention will be fulfilled and all will see God face-to-face (Rev. 22:3–4; 1 Cor. 13:12). This holy project to bless all the nations of the earth begins with the covenantal promise to Abraham and Sarah (Gen. 12:1–3). God's purpose advances through the covenant established with Israel at Sinai (the description of which begins in Exod. 19), an encounter that includes God's instructions for the construction of the ark of the covenant, with its "mercy seat," and of the tabernacle, the "tent of meeting" where the ark is to be housed. The Lord tells Moses to ask of the people an offering of various raw materials and then says: "And let them make me a sanctuary, *that I may dwell in their midst*" (Exod. 25:8 RSV, emphasis added). In this command we see reiterated God's desire to be among his people, just as he had walked with Adam and Eve in the garden. To be sure, this divine presence remains a mostly mediated one: it is Moses, or Moses and Aaron, who have immediate contact with the Lord, while the people remain at a greater or lesser distance.[19]

---

18. Martha Moore-Keish, "Washing before Supper?," *Reformed Liturgy & Music* 34, no. 4 (2000): 15–21.

19. See, e.g., Exod. 33:7–11 (RSV):

Now Moses used to take the tent and pitch it outside the camp, far off from the camp; and he called it the tent of meeting. And every one who sought the LORD would go out to the tent of meeting, which was outside the camp. Whenever Moses went out to the tent, all the people rose up, and every man stood at his tent door, and looked after Moses, until he had gone into the tent. When Moses entered the tent, the pillar of cloud would descend and stand at the door of the tent, and the LORD would speak with Moses. And when all the people saw the pillar of cloud standing at the door of the tent, all the people

The same pattern is followed when the tabernacle is replaced by the temple during the reign of King Solomon and the divine glory descends from heaven as fire, as related in the 2 Chronicles passage already cited above. As temple worship became regularized, God's presence among the people continued to be mediated through the priesthood, and especially the high priest, who alone was allowed to enter the inmost Holy of Holies in the temple, and that only on the annual Day of Atonement.

The Exile and the Rise of Synagogues

We can thus only imagine what an unmitigated shock it was for the Jewish community when the empire of Babylon conquered Judah, overwhelmed Jerusalem, and destroyed the temple in the sixth century BC. With this defeat and many political and religious leaders of the nation carried off into captivity, questions inevitably arose: Where is God? Has the Lord abandoned us? How are we to worship if we no longer have access to the temple and its appointed priests? It was during the exile that a new thing arose in the history of God's covenant people: the emergence of the synagogue as a place of worship, study, and prayer—and "rabbinical Judaism." Through the study of the Scriptures and the words of the prophets, the captives came to recognize that God was indeed still present but had used the conquest to chastise a nation that had abandoned him. Yes, there was a yearning to return to the promised land, but in the meantime, one could worship God by gathering the community together and meditating on the covenant. Faithfulness and sacrifice could be measured as a practice of the heart, and not just by the ritual acts of the temple cult. Prompted by the Spirit, the prophets reinforced this recognition that Torah is not simply something external but is meant to be something internal:

> Behold, the days are coming, says the LORD, when I will make a new covenant with the house of Israel and the house of Judah, not like the covenant which I made with their fathers when I took them by the hand to bring them out of the land of Egypt, my covenant which they broke, though I was their husband,

---

would rise up and worship, every man at his tent door. Thus the LORD used to speak to Moses face to face, as a man speaks to his friend. When Moses turned again into the camp, his servant Joshua the son of Nun, a young man, did not depart from the tent. See also Lev. 9:22–24 (RSV):

Then Aaron lifted up his hands toward the people and blessed them; and he came down from offering the sin offering and the burnt offering and the peace offerings. And Moses and Aaron went into the tent of meeting; and when they came out they blessed the people, and the glory of the LORD appeared to all the people. And fire came forth from before the LORD and consumed the burnt offering and the fat upon the altar; and when all the people saw it, they shouted, and fell on their faces.

says the LORD. But this is the covenant which I will make with the house of Israel after those days, says the LORD: I will put my law within them, and I will write it upon their hearts; and I will be their God, and they shall be my people. And no longer shall each man teach his neighbor and each his brother, saying, "Know the LORD," for they shall all know me, from the least of them to the greatest, says the LORD; for I will forgive their iniquity, and I will remember their sin no more. (Jer. 31:31–34 RSV)

Just as intriguing are the writings of the prophet Ezekiel, who, it should be remembered, was a priest before being taken into exile. His entire book is an account of the visions he had when overcome by the word of God, visions of what the Lord would be doing to and for his people:

Therefore say to the house of Israel, Thus says the Lord GOD: It is not for your sake, O house of Israel, that I am about to act, but for the sake of my holy name, which you have profaned among the nations to which you came. And I will vindicate the holiness of my great name, which has been profaned among the nations, and which you have profaned among them; and the nations will know that I am the LORD, says the Lord GOD, when through you I vindicate my holiness before their eyes. For I will take you from the nations, and gather you from all the countries, and bring you into your own land. I will sprinkle clean water upon you, and you shall be clean from all your uncleannesses, and from all your idols I will cleanse you. A new heart I will give you, and a new spirit I will put within you; and I will take out of your flesh the heart of stone and give you a heart of flesh. And I will put my spirit within you, and cause you to walk in my statutes and be careful to observe my ordinances. You shall dwell in the land which I gave to your fathers; and you shall be my people, and I will be your God. (Ezek. 36:22–28 RSV)

Of course, the Jews did eventually return from exile and did eventually rebuild both Jerusalem and the temple. The Second Temple again became the heart of Jewish faith, yet synagogues had become places where the lifeblood of that faith also circulated. Journeying to Jerusalem to celebrate festivals such as Passover remained a high point of Jewish spirituality. But true pilgrimage was now as much a matter of the heart as the feet and could be accomplished through an interior journey of prayerful meditation upon the Torah and the local practice of one's covenantal obligations.

Christ Brings Holiness in a New Way

With the incarnation of the eternal Son, God's holiness enters the world in a new and unique way (Luke 1:26–35). God came into the world and, in effect, took the world into himself. This is not to say that God "divinized" the world, for it remains a creature. However, a new—or rather, renewed—intimacy between the divine and the human has come into God's covenantal relation. And Jesus's promise to send the "Counselor" (John 14:15–17, 26; 15:26; 16:7 RSV), realized in the manifestation of the Holy Spirit at Pentecost (Acts 2) and to the gentiles (Acts 10:44–48), enlarges the "royal priesthood and holy nation." This advances God's holiness project one stage further. The Church presently exists in this time between Pentecost and the *eschaton*, the time of "last things." As his public ministry came to a conclusion and the events of his passion approached, Jesus prophesied about the end of the old age and the in-breaking of the new age. Scholars often label these sections of the Synoptic Gospels Jesus's "apocalypse," that is, his revelation regarding the end times.[20] It includes his descriptions of the coming trials and troubles (the destruction of the temple, the desolating sacrilege, the afflictions besetting the peoples, the emergence of false prophets), his predictions of the coming of the Son of Man, and his admonitions to take heed and be watchful.

A key part of this apocalyptic vision revolves around the place and role of the temple, a focus evident at other times in Jesus's life and teaching. In the childhood story recounted by Luke (Luke 2:46–50), Jesus tells his searching parents, "I must be in my Father's house" (v. 49). During the temptation following his baptism, the devil brings Jesus to the pinnacle of the temple seeking to seduce him with overreaching divine power.[21] At one point Jesus cryptically announces, "Something greater than the temple is here" (Matt. 12:6), yet he also shows a zeal for the temple's true purpose that makes it clear he is not simply rejecting its role in Israel's faith but rather purifying it.[22] Indeed, that he cures the blind and the lame there (Matt. 21:14) serves as an eschatological sign that he is broadening and fulfilling its role in the life of the people, and doing so on divine authority.[23] Jesus also cites Psalm 118:22–23 ("The stone that the builders rejected has become the chief cornerstone. This is the LORD's doing; it is marvelous in our eyes"; see Matt. 21:42//Mark 12:10–11//Luke 20:17) as a litmus test regarding his teaching over against that of his opponents.[24] Among other things, he asserts that the kingdom of God will come to those who produce fruits of the kingdom and will be taken from those who do not (Matt. 21:43). Yet he had also taught that the temple will be torn down[25]—and been

20. Matt. 24:1–44//Mark 13:1–37//Luke 21:5–36.
21. Matt. 4:5–6//Luke 4:9–11.
22. Matt. 21:12–13//Mark 11:15–17//Luke 19:45–48//John 2:14–17.
23. Matt. 21:23–27//Luke 20:1–8. Cf. John 7:14–18.
24. Matt. 21:42–46//Mark 12:10–12//Luke 20:17–19.
25. Matt. 24:1–2//Mark 13:1–2//Luke 21:5–6.

accused and mocked for saying that he would rebuild it in three days.[26] Finally, at the moment of his death on the cross, the curtain separating the holy of holies from the rest of the temple is torn from top to bottom.[27]

The Holy Spirit Now Tabernacles in Believers

What do all these episodes mean? How did the Church come to understand all these things, given the centrality of the temple to its inherited faith from Israel and in light of Jesus's resurrection and ascension to sit at the right hand of God? Following the crucifixion and resurrection, the apostles recognized that the scriptural citation about the rejected stone becoming the cornerstone referred not just to Jesus's teaching but to Jesus himself as the sole basis of God's salvation (Acts 4:10–12). No longer is direct access to God the Father's glory limited to the high priest alone; rather, Christ opens it for all as our forerunner (Heb. 6:19–20). In the Son's resurrection after three days in the grave, a new temple *has* been constructed, one built not with human hands but rather one that is his body (John 2:21; Heb. 9:11).

These events manifest the in-breaking of a new age and a new order, one in which the role of the Holy Spirit becomes the incorporation of Christ's followers into these new and saving realities. Through the power of the Holy Spirit, Christians are joined with Christ the High Priest, making a priesthood of all believers (1 Pet. 2:5, 9) and granting them new access to God. Through the power of the Holy Spirit, Christians themselves become a temple of the Holy Spirit, having within and among them the glory and holiness of God. Consider how Jesus says not that he *knows* the truth but that he *is* the truth: "I am the way, and the truth, and the life" (John 14:6). In other words, the truth of God is located not in a set of teachings or a body of knowledge but in a person. In the Word's incarnation, God's truth has become embodied. In a similar manner, the presence and glory of God is "located" no longer in a place (the temple) but in *persons*, the assembly or *ekklēsia* of Christ. Christians individually—and collectively as the Church—become the temple of God's presence. This is so not because it is a generic human possibility ("the divine spark within") or because we become lesser deities, but because in our baptisms we are joined with Christ through the life-giving work of the Holy Spirit.

Let me explore this notion more closely by considering the two passages where Paul speaks of Christians as "temples of the Holy Spirit" (1 Cor. 3:9–17 and 1 Cor. 6:14–20). Both passages exhibit Paul's concern that this new temple

26. Matt. 26:61; 27:40//Mark 14:58; 15:29//John 2:18–20.
27. Matt. 27:51//Mark 15:38.

not be desecrated. In the first passage he describes how the community is God's "building," erected on the foundation of Jesus Christ. He depicts his own apostolic preaching as laying that foundation, even as he knows that others have followed him and built upon his original efforts. Aware that factions have emerged within the congregation as a result, he seeks to diffuse the partisanship by saying that God will be the final judge: if the work is good, it will endure, but if not it will perish. Paul is far less concerned with the builders (cf. 1 Cor. 1:10–17) than he is with what has, in fact, been built. In effect, he tells the Corinthians to look not to their additional teachers but to themselves and what they have become in the eyes of God: "Do you not know that you are God's temple and that God's Spirit dwells in you? If anyone destroys God's temple, God will destroy that person. For God's temple is holy, and you are that temple" (1 Cor. 3:16–17).

How could God's temple be open to destruction? In the next passage, Paul indicates one way in which a person's own actions would serve to desecrate this temple.

> Do you not know that your bodies are members of Christ? Should I therefore take the members of Christ and make them members of a prostitute? Never! Do you not know that whoever is united to a prostitute becomes one body with her? For it is said, "The two shall be one flesh." But anyone united to the Lord becomes one spirit with him. Shun fornication! Every sin that a person commits is outside the body; but the fornicator sins against the body itself. Or do you not know that your body is a temple of the Holy Spirit within you, which you have from God, and that you are not your own? For you were bought with a price; therefore glorify God in your body. (1 Cor. 6:15–20)

While the wording varies, a similar dynamic appears in a passage from 2 Corinthians, where the "partner" is not a prostitute but unbelief and idolatry. The violation, in other words, is against not the second tablet of the law but the first tablet: a breach of the great commandment concerning the love of the Lord God, rather than a failing in love of neighbor.

> Do not be mismatched with unbelievers. For what partnership is there between righteousness and lawlessness? Or what fellowship is there between light and darkness? What agreement does Christ have with Beliar [i.e., Satan]? Or what does a believer share with an unbeliever? What agreement has the temple of God with idols? For we are the temple of the living God; as God said,
>
>> "I will live in them and walk among them,
>>   and I will be their God,
>>   and they shall be my people.

Therefore come out from them,
and be separate from them, says the Lord,
and touch nothing unclean;
then I will welcome you,
and I will be your father,
and you shall be my sons and daughters,
says the Lord Almighty." (2 Cor. 6:14–18)

The temple is holy—and God expects it to remain such, which means some ways of being or actions are excluded. Significantly, Paul supports his claim by appealing to several different passages of Old Testament scripture,[28] weaving them together in a manner that bookends an admonition to holiness between two statements of the covenantal promise. Grace is the major theme, but the necessary minor theme is the call to be separate—or "set apart," which, as noted above, is a root meaning of the Hebrew and Greek words translated "holiness"—and to avoid the unclean.[29] Concerning this minor theme, consider 2 Timothy 1:13–14, which admonishes: "Follow the pattern of the sound words which you have heard from me, in the faith and love which are in Christ Jesus; guard the truth that has been entrusted to you by the Holy Spirit who dwells within us" (RSV).

Other New Testament writers echo this complex of scriptural connections to the temple, its cultic practices and history, and its broader spiritual evocations and associations. First Peter in particular links the Psalms passage mentioned above (that is, the rejected stone becoming the cornerstone) with passages from Isaiah 8:14–15 and 28:16, reinforcing and broadening the psalm's meaning in reference to Jesus as the basis for the people's new covenant relation with God. The Church has become "a chosen race, a royal priesthood, a holy nation, God's own people" (1 Pet. 2:9). And as with Paul's understanding, Peter states that with this new status and nature in God come certain responsibilities. On the one hand, his listeners are to proclaim the mighty acts of God. On the other, he also urges them "to abstain from the desires of the flesh that wage war against the soul" (1 Pet. 2:11).

In sum, an intimacy and communion with God has become the new reality for the Church, a living temple made not with human hands but through the Holy Spirit's work in building it up upon Christ. But this new reality carries responsibilities as well, regarding how one behaves and what one believes.

28. In the order that Paul alludes to them, they are Lev. 26:12; Ezek. 37:27; Isa. 52:11; and 2 Sam. 7:14.

29. Paul's use of the term "unclean" no longer has the ritual or dietary connotations it once had under the law. Cf. Rom. 14:14–15 and 1 Cor. 7:14.

The Holy Spirit's work always displays this twofold transformation: a new and glorious life awaits, rich in deep and unexpected ways. But its counterpart is always that the old life and its inclinations will and must be left behind.[30]

Fruit of the Spirit, Gifts of the Spirit

For you were called to freedom, brethren; only do not use your freedom as an opportunity for the flesh, but through love be servants of one another. For the whole law is fulfilled in one word, "You shall love your neighbor as yourself." But if you bite and devour one another take heed that you are not consumed by one another.

But I say, walk by the Spirit, and do not gratify the desires of the flesh. For the desires of the flesh are against the Spirit, and the desires of the Spirit are against the flesh; for these are opposed to each other, to prevent you from doing what you would. But if you are led by the Spirit you are not under the law. Now the works of the flesh are plain: fornication, impurity, licentiousness, idolatry, sorcery, enmity, strife, jealousy, anger, selfishness, dissension, party spirit, envy, drunkenness, carousing, and the like. I warn you, as I warned you before, that those who do such things shall not inherit the kingdom of God. But the fruit of the Spirit is love, joy, peace, patience, kindness, goodness, faithfulness, gentleness, self-control; against such there is no law. And those who belong to Christ Jesus have crucified the flesh with its passions and desires.

If we live by the Spirit, let us also walk by the Spirit. (Gal. 5:13–25 RSV)

Now there are varieties of gifts, but the same Spirit; and there are varieties of services, but the same Lord; and there are varieties of activities, but it is the same God who activates all of them in everyone. To each is given the manifestation of the Spirit for the common good. To one is given through the Spirit the utterance of wisdom, and to another the utterance of knowledge according to the same Spirit, to another faith by the same Spirit, to another gifts of healing by the one Spirit, to another the working of miracles, to another prophecy, to another the discernment of spirits, to another various kinds of tongues, to another the interpretation of tongues. All these are activated by one and the same Spirit, who allots to each one individually just as the Spirit chooses. (1 Cor. 12:4–11)

30. For two more Pauline citations noting this twofold distinction, consider 2 Cor. 3:18 ("And all of us, with unveiled faces, seeing the glory of the Lord as though reflected in a mirror, are being transformed into the same image from one degree of glory to another; for this comes from the Lord, the Spirit") and Rom. 12:1–2 ("I appeal to you therefore, brothers and sisters, by the mercies of God, to present your bodies as a living sacrifice, holy and acceptable to God, which is your spiritual worship. Do not be conformed to this world, but be transformed by the renewing of your minds, so that you may discern what is the will of God—what is good and acceptable and perfect").

And God has appointed in the church first apostles, second prophets, third teachers, then workers of miracles, then healers, helpers, administrators, speakers in
various kinds of tongues. Are all apostles? Are all prophets? Are all teachers? Do
all work miracles? Do all possess gifts of healing? Do all speak with tongues?
Do all interpret? But earnestly desire the higher gifts. (1 Cor. 12:28–31 RSV)

For all the associations and evocative power of Christians being "the temple
of the Holy Spirit," the image does have the limitation of being based on an
inanimate and static object. Christians both individually and collectively know
that they are built up as such a temple by the work of the Holy Spirit. Christians both individually and collectively know that they are to open themselves
to be filled with the Holy Spirit. As such a temple, they know that they will
encounter God and his holiness. But what is the impact and effect of all this
on Christian living? How does this encounter with God's Holy Spirit animate
and enhance the Church and its members in their life and mission? A passage
from Ephesians employs the temple imagery but also blends it with civic, familial, and organic images to give a richer picture of the theological dynamic.

So then you are no longer strangers and aliens, but you are citizens with the
saints and also members of the household of God, built upon the foundation
of the apostles and prophets, with Christ Jesus himself as the cornerstone. In
him the whole structure is joined together and grows into a holy temple in the
Lord; in whom you also are built together spiritually into a dwelling place for
God. (Eph. 2:19–22)

This excerpt clearly mixes metaphors in a rather haphazard way, but in so
doing it demonstrates that the key concern is not literary precision but evoking the new reality made possible in Christ through the Spirit.

Fruit of the Spirit

Hence, the organic image of the "fruit of the Spirit" can be seen to complement and expand upon the temple imagery, while also reinforcing the primacy
of the divine initiative. The phrase "fruit of the Spirit" appears in Paul's Letter
to the Galatians. Taken individually, each fruit is a well-known marker of the
faithful Christian life: love, joy, peace, patience, kindness, goodness, faithfulness, gentleness, and self-control (Gal. 5:22–23). Now one could be inclined to
think of them as simply a list of admirable virtues, the sort of ethical habits
that would serve anyone well. But if one understands virtues to be defined
as those good character traits and habits that individuals themselves develop
through their own willpower and effort, then Paul's list is not one of virtues.

The key is the image itself: these are not something we accomplish; they are rather the natural outcome of allowing the Holy Spirit to act within us. Fruit does not produce itself through its own decision and effort but is the effect of interactions going on between the plant and its environment and how those interactions are brought to life within the plant. Again mixing metaphors, Paul writes, "If we live by the Spirit, let us also walk by the Spirit" (5:25 RSV). That is, having become a new creation as the Holy Spirit implants the life of Jesus within us, we should also be open to the Holy Spirit's tending of that new life, that it might grow, blossom, and come to fruition in us. It is no accident that the antithesis Paul draws between "works of the flesh" and "fruit of the Spirit" is asymmetrical: the former are acts our "old self" undertakes, but the latter are products of the Spirit acting within us. As I have noted previously, Christian discipleship is in the first instance better understood not as our effort or assertion but as our surrender, in order to allow the Spirit to work in and through us.

This fruit of the Spirit consists of that set of virtues that enable a community to attain true communion, authentic *koinōnia*. That is, they are not so much civic or political virtues as they are the habits of the heart needed to knit together a family, a community of love. They are interpersonal virtues that put others before self so that the relationship might thrive. This contrasts starkly with the works of the flesh, which consistently put self before others and exemplify diverse attempts to manipulate and control various relationships. In other words, the *works* of the flesh fragment, but the *fruit* of the Spirit unifies. Note that Paul's antithesis is not merely a body-spirit dualism that sees these vices as simply the product of our physical existence. For him, the flesh-Spirit antithesis is a matter of the *whole* person: either one's whole being—body, mind, and spirit—is oriented toward God and open to the Holy Spirit's activity, or one's whole being—body, mind, and spirit—is oriented away from God and a prisoner to one's various disordered appetites. That is why some of the works Paul lists certainly are grounded in a bodily appetite (for example, fornication, licentiousness, and drunkenness), but others seem more appropriately understood as a disordered appetite of the mind or of the spirit (enmity, strife, dissension, party spirit, jealousy, idolatry, and sorcery). And while some of these "works of the flesh" might seem to be an individual matter (e.g., drunkenness), anyone who has experienced them firsthand knows how they nevertheless undermine communion. Other works of the flesh are by definition disruptive of communion (e.g., enmity, strife, and dissension), while still others may promote a false comradeship (e.g., party spirit) that is nevertheless finally destructive of a larger communion.

Paul's image of the "fruit of the Spirit" gains a richer resonance when it is heard together with Jesus's use of a similar metaphor employing images of a vine grower, a vine, and its fruit. Consider the words recorded in the Gospel of John.

> I am the true vine, and my Father is the vinegrower. He removes every branch in me that bears no fruit. Every branch that bears fruit he prunes [*kathairei*] to make it bear more fruit. You have already been cleansed [or "pruned," *katharoi*] by the word that I have spoken to you. Abide in me as I abide in you. Just as the branch cannot bear fruit by itself unless it abides in the vine, neither can you unless you abide in me. I am the vine, you are the branches. Those who abide in me and I in them bear much fruit, because apart from me you can do nothing. Whoever does not abide in me is thrown away like a branch and withers; such branches are gathered, thrown into the fire, and burned. If you abide in me, and my words abide in you, ask for whatever you wish, and it will be done for you. My Father is glorified by this, that you bear much fruit and become my disciples. (John 15:1–8)

Here the divine initiative becomes a triune occurrence: the fruit of the Spirit grows on the branch connected to Jesus the vine, which is tended by the Father for the Father's purposes and glory. The Father tends, or "prunes," by means of the word that Jesus has spoken, and one's fruitfulness stems from abiding in Jesus and his words. Indeed, in an echo of Jesus's parables of the mustard seed, where the smallest seed becomes the greatest of shrubs and even the smallest faith moves mountains (Matt. 13:31; 17:20), abiding in Christ will bring unexpected and extraordinary results. The upshot of the full flourishing of such fruit in each member of the community is true *koinōnia* for the whole community. The fruit of the Spirit is available to each Christian and is the Spirit's both causing and effecting that person's individual sanctification. But while growing in each person, this fruit also benefits the whole body of believers.

Gifts of the Spirit

The situation with the gifts of the Spirit differs somewhat from this, in that individuals typically have gifts that are unique to them. Yet while unique, they all come from the same source and are intended for the benefit of the whole:

> Now there are varieties of gifts, but the same Spirit; and there are varieties of services, but the same Lord; and there are varieties of activities, but it is the same God who activates all of them in everyone. To each is given the manifestation of the Spirit for the common good. To one is given through the Spirit the utterance of wisdom, and to another the utterance of knowledge according to the same Spirit, to another faith by the same Spirit, to another gifts of healing by the one Spirit, to another the working of miracles, to another prophecy, to another the discernment of spirits, to another various kinds of tongues, to another the

interpretation of tongues. All these are activated by one and the same Spirit, who allots to each one individually just as the Spirit chooses. (1 Cor. 12:4–11)

As with the fruit of the Spirit, these gifts from the Spirit are not to be thought of as personal virtues or accomplishments. They are endowments to be received with gratitude and to be employed as the Spirit intends. They should neither be hidden under a bushel basket nor be a cause for personal boasting, but dedicated to the upbuilding of the whole. While we might distinguish them from each other (in part because Paul explicitly describes the "fruit" in his letter to the Galatians and the "gifts" in his letter to the Christians at Corinth), they are meant to be mutually reinforcing, to the benefit of the community. Consider this passage from Romans, where Paul explicitly mentions a number of "gifts," while interweaving them with several of the Spirit's fruit (which I have italicized):

For as in one body we have many members, and not all the members have the same function, so we, who are many, are one body in Christ, and individually we are members one of another. We have gifts that differ according to the grace given to us: prophecy, in proportion to faith; ministry, in ministering; the teacher, in teaching; the exhorter, in exhortation; the giver, in generosity; the leader, in diligence; the compassionate, in cheerfulness.

Let *love* be genuine; hate what is evil, hold fast to what is *good*; love one another with mutual affection; outdo one another in showing honor. Do not lag in zeal, be ardent in spirit, serve the Lord. *Rejoice* in hope, be *patient* in suffering, persevere in prayer. Contribute to the needs of the saints; extend hospitality to strangers.

Bless those who persecute you; bless and do not curse them. Rejoice with those who rejoice, weep with those who weep. Live in harmony with one another; do not be haughty, but associate with the lowly; do not claim to be wiser than you are. Do not repay anyone evil for evil, but take thought for what is noble in the sight of all. If it is possible, so far as it depends on you, live *peaceably* with all. Beloved, never avenge yourselves, but leave room for the wrath of God; for it is written, "Vengeance is mine, I will repay, says the Lord." No, "if your enemies are hungry, feed them; if they are thirsty, give them something to drink; for by doing this you will heap burning coals on their heads." Do not be overcome by evil, but overcome evil with good. (Rom. 12:4–21)

While Paul does not explicitly list the other fruit of kindness, faithfulness, gentleness, and self-control, these are certainly implied in the picture he paints of the lives the Roman Christians are called to lead. In this regard, the "organic" metaphor of fruit, the "interrelational" metaphor of gifts given and received, and the "construction" metaphor of being built up into a temple all make the same point about the Church: they emphasize the unique importance of each individual involved, while also showing how together the whole is far more than simply the sum of its parts. All three metaphors encourage and strengthen each part, while also directing them to a larger common calling and purpose beyond themselves.

Pentecost as the New Sinai

> When the day of Pentecost had come, they were all together in one place. And suddenly from heaven there came a sound like the rush of a violent wind, and it filled the entire house where they were sitting. Divided tongues, as of fire, appeared among them, and a tongue rested on each of them. All of them were filled with the Holy Spirit and began to speak in other languages, as the Spirit gave them ability.
>
> Now there were devout Jews from every nation under heaven living in Jerusalem. And at this sound the crowd gathered and was bewildered, because each one heard them speaking in the native language of each. Amazed and astonished, they asked, "Are not all these who are speaking Galileans? And how is it that we hear, each of us, in our own native language? . . . All were amazed and perplexed, saying to one another, "What does this mean?" But others sneered and said, "They are filled with new wine."
>
> But Peter, standing with the eleven, raised his voice and addressed them, "Men of Judea and all who live in Jerusalem, let this be known to you, and listen to what I say. Indeed, these are not drunk, as you suppose, for it is only nine o'clock in the morning. No, this is what was spoken through the prophet Joel:
>
> > 'In the last days it will be, God declares,
> >   that I will pour out my Spirit upon all flesh,
> >   and your sons and your daughters shall prophesy,
> >   and your young men shall see visions,
> >   and your old men shall dream dreams.
> > Even upon my slaves, both men and women,
> >   in those days I will pour out my Spirit;
> >   and they shall prophesy.
> > And I will show portents in the heaven above
> >   and signs on the earth below,
> >   blood, and fire, and smoky mist.
> > The sun shall be turned to darkness
> >   and the moon to blood,
> >   before the coming of the Lord's great and glorious day.
> > Then everyone who calls on the name of the Lord shall be saved.'"
> >   (Acts 2:1–8, 12–21)

Imagine playing with matches while oblivious to the pool of gasoline right behind you: this is the situation of too many Christians when it comes to the fearful reality and awesome responsibility of being filled with the Holy Spirit. How many Christians even know that God intends for the Holy Spirit to dwell within us? Certainly the growing numbers of Pentecostal Christians have recognized and embraced this divine power and reality. But the faith of countless other Christians seems closer to sleepwalking than a life of power and charisma. Being filled with the Spirit remains a remote and strange idea—and certainly not a lived reality. Yet the scriptural portraits of the early Church show time and again that life in the community is by definition life in the Holy Spirit.

The classic and defining episode is the Father's pouring out of the Holy Spirit on the disciples at Pentecost (Acts 2). This outpouring of the Spirit fulfills not only a promise made by Jesus[31] but the words of the prophets.[32] To fully understand the meaning and resonances of Pentecost as a cardinal event for the Church, one needs to recognize its layered meanings in the Jewish context and its resonances with the Old Testament. Pentecost was originally a festival celebrating God's blessings at the end of the harvest season (the "Festival of Weeks"), but it came to have various covenantal associations. In the Jewish book of *Jubilees*, written sometime in the second century BC, it was presented as the anniversary day of God's covenant with Noah.[33] At a later date it also came to be understood as that festival following fifty days (hence the name, "Pentecost") after Passover commemorating the giving of the law at Mount Sinai.[34] That is, following God's redemption of the people from their bondage in Egypt, it was the festival honoring the basis upon which those people were now to live in covenant relation with God and one another. Next, recall the various messianic hopes that yearned for the day when God's law would no longer need to be written on tablets of stone because it would be written on the people's hearts (e.g., Jer. 31:31–34).[35] And alternately, recall the messianic hopes that longed for a day when the Spirit

31. Luke 24:49; John 14:16–17, 26; 15:26; 16:7.

32. Jer. 31:31–34; Joel 2:28–32.

33. See James C. VanderKam, "Weeks, Feast of," in *The New Interpreter's Dictionary of the Bible*, ed. Katharine Doob Sakenfeld (Nashville: Abingdon, 2009), 5:829–31.

34. There is scholarly debate as to when this Jewish association of Pentecost with the giving of the Torah at Sinai began—specifically, whether it already existed at the time of the apostles or if it only emerged in later centuries. A passage making the connection explicit does appear in the Talmud (*Pesahim* 68b) but apparently dates from a period several centuries after the events described in Acts. Of course, this does not preclude the possibility that the tradition existed earlier but means only that concrete evidence confirming it does not exist.

35. Cf. Ezek. 36:22–28.

would be poured out not just on isolated prophets but on *all* the people (e.g., Joel 2:28–29).

Now, in this context, consider the outpouring of the Holy Spirit upon the disciples gathered in Jerusalem on that festival day. It becomes easy to recognize that Pentecost does not merely represent the founding of some new religious organization, nor was it—in the modern parlance of the sociology of religion—a "voluntaristic association of like-minded individuals." Rather, it represents the coming to fruition of a covenantal seed planted long before, it represents the realization of messianic hopes, it represents the establishing of a new covenant with a new "constitution" for relating to God and one's neighbors—and it is all accomplished by the direct activity of the Holy Spirit.[36] To hammer the point home, Pentecost means that it is the Holy Spirit who creates, equips, directs, and sustains the Church. The Church is not in the first instance a primarily human institution. True, from a theological perspective it is a human institution in secondary ways—but this distinction just reinforces my point. Note that even in the later, "Pastoral" epistles of the Pauline school (1–2 Timothy and Titus) and the "Catholic" epistles (1–2 Peter, 1 John, and Jude), which scholars recognize as concerned with consolidating the Church for the long haul, the language used continues to describe the true Church in spiritual terms. A similar approach holds true even in Acts, when it describes the choice of the first deacons (Acts 6:3, 5)[37] and gives an account of the Jerusalem Council (Acts 15).

But just because the Church is understood in primarily spiritual terms does not mean it is without structure. After all, the prophetic hope was not that the order of the law would be negated but that its ordering principles would no longer be external, being rather written on human hearts, that its precepts would become second nature to the faithful. And the "temple of the Holy Spirit" image with which we began this chapter itself presupposes a structure, even if that structure is no longer a building but rather the community of believers grounded upon the cornerstone of Christ. We also considered how the "fruit of the Spirit" and the "gifts of the Spirit" help serve the upbuilding and life of this community. Still, because of what God has done in Christ, the place and purpose of the law have changed for Christians. What is the nature and extent of that role, given Christ's fulfillment of the law and the coming of the Holy Spirit?

---

36. Recognition of a typological parallel between Passover (exodus)/Sinai and Passover (Good Friday–Easter)/Pentecost and their covenantal implications appeared in the Christian theological tradition at least as early as Augustine. See his "Letter to Januarius," chap. 16, in *The Nicene and Post-Nicene Fathers*, series 1, ed. Philip Schaff (Grand Rapids: Eerdmans, 1983), 1:313.

37. Cf. Acts 11:24; 20:28.

The "Third Use of the Law"

> As God's chosen ones, holy and beloved, clothe yourselves with compassion, kindness, humility, meekness, and patience. Bear with one another and, if anyone has a complaint against another, forgive each other; just as the Lord has forgiven you, so you also must forgive. Above all, clothe yourselves with love, which binds everything together in perfect harmony. And let the peace of Christ rule in your hearts, to which indeed you were called in the one body. And be thankful. Let the word of Christ dwell in you richly; teach and admonish one another in all wisdom; and with gratitude in your hearts sing psalms, hymns, and spiritual songs to God. And whatever you do, in word or deed, do everything in the name of the Lord Jesus, giving thanks to God the Father through him. (Col. 3:12–17)

> So then let us not fall asleep as others do, but let us keep awake and be sober; for those who sleep sleep at night, and those who are drunk get drunk at night. But since we belong to the day, let us be sober, and put on the breastplate of faith and love, and for a helmet the hope of salvation. For God has destined us not for wrath but for obtaining salvation through our Lord Jesus Christ, who died for us, so that whether we are awake or asleep we may live with him. Therefore encourage one another and build up each other, as indeed you are doing.
>
> But we appeal to you, brothers and sisters, to respect those who labor among you, and have charge of you in the Lord and admonish you; esteem them very highly in love because of their work. Be at peace among yourselves. And we urge you, beloved, to admonish the idlers, encourage the fainthearted, help the weak, be patient with all of them. See that none of you repays evil for evil, but always seek to do good to one another and to all. Rejoice always, pray without ceasing, give thanks in all circumstances; for this is the will of God in Christ Jesus for you. Do not quench the Spirit. Do not despise the words of prophets, but test everything; hold fast to what is good; abstain from every form of evil.
>
> May the God of peace himself sanctify you entirely; and may your spirit and soul and body be kept sound and blameless at the coming of our Lord Jesus Christ. The one who calls you is faithful, and he will do this. (1 Thess. 5:6–24)

> Remind them to be subject to rulers and authorities, to be obedient, to be ready for every good work, to speak evil of no one, to avoid quarreling, to be gentle, and to show every courtesy to everyone. For we ourselves were once foolish, disobedient, led astray, slaves to various passions and pleasures, passing our days in malice and envy, despicable, hating one another. But when the goodness and loving kindness of God our Savior appeared, he saved us, not because of any works of righteousness that we had done, but according to his mercy, through the water of rebirth and renewal by the Holy Spirit. This Spirit he poured out on us richly through Jesus Christ our Savior, so that, having been

justified by his grace, we might become heirs according to the hope of eternal life. The saying is sure.

I desire that you insist on these things, so that those who have come to believe in God may be careful to devote themselves to good works; these things are excellent and profitable to everyone. But avoid stupid controversies, genealogies, dissensions, and quarrels about the law, for they are unprofitable and worthless. After a first and second admonition, have nothing more to do with anyone who causes divisions, since you know that such a person is perverted and sinful, being self-condemned. (Titus 3:1–11)

One key distinction between Christianity and Judaism is their respective understandings of the place and role of the law. To be sure, attitudes toward the law differ within Judaism itself, as they do among the various branches of Christianity. But the law remains the central focus in Jewish faith, while for Christianity that central place belongs to Christ himself.

The Role of the Law in the Unfolding Covenant

Jesus said that he came not to abolish the law but to fulfill it (Matt. 5:17). But his other words and actions, both prior to his crucifixion and in his postresurrection appearances, indicate that this fulfillment requires a fundamentally new understanding of the law. For example, his association with "tax collectors and sinners"[38] violated accepted understandings of the law's purity requirements. In addressing the human needs of hunger and healing, Jesus violated accepted understandings of the law's Sabbath obligations (Matt. 12:1–14). Jesus also stated that it is not what goes into a person's mouth that defiles him or her but what comes out of it, thereby, as Mark notes, declaring all foods clean (Mark 7:19; cf. Matt. 15:10–20).

Following his resurrection, Jesus explained the ways in which he had fulfilled the things written about him in the Law and the Prophets (Luke 24:27, 44–45). It is this new understanding of Scripture that becomes the backdrop for Peter's subsequent heavenly vision indicating that he should no longer distinguish between clean and unclean food—a vision he later realizes is not solely about dietary restrictions, but about taking the gospel not just to the Jews but also the gentiles (Acts 10:9–11:18). In a similar manner, aspects of the cultic laws are also no longer necessary because what they were pointing to has been realized with the coming of Christ.[39] Reflecting on the logic undergirding these apparent changes, Paul writes that the law was a form of

38. See, e.g., Matt. 9:10–11; 11:19.
39. Heb. 7–10, but see specifically Heb. 7:12, 23–28; 8:6–7, 13; 9:1–10 in comparison to 9:11–15, 23–26; 10:8–10.

guardian or custodian, under whose tutelage the covenant had been carried out until the appropriate time when the people had "come of age," so to speak, receiving their inheritance rights through their union with Christ in faith, to be adopted sons and daughters of God (Gal. 3:23–26).

One common way of summarizing this change is to claim that Christianity holds the dietary and cultic requirements of the law to be no longer binding, while adherence to the moral aspects of the law is. John Calvin, for example, distinguished between the moral law—by which he meant primarily the Ten Commandments—and the ceremonial law.[40] But this formulation can be used inappropriately to reduce Christian faithfulness to mere ethics and to abstract Christian behavior from God's broader covenantal purposes. We do well to keep in mind Acts 15, which recounts the Jerusalem Council deliberating the inclusion of the gentiles into the up-until-that-time predominantly Jewish Christian church. One faction insisted that gentile converts be circumcised and charged to keep "the law of Moses" (Acts 15:5). But through their openness to the Holy Spirit's promptings, their consideration of Scripture, and the thoughtful conclusions they derived from that consideration, the council determined that converts need not be circumcised or follow the whole of Torah. Their decision instead was summarized thus: "For it has seemed good to the Holy Spirit and to us to lay upon you no greater burden than these necessary things: that you abstain from what has been sacrificed to idols and from blood and from what is strangled and from unchastity. If you keep yourselves from these, you will do well" (Acts 15:28–29).

Now this list may seem to exclude all but a handful of prohibitions from "the law of Moses," representing a watering down of the law's commands. But in fact these proscriptions hearken back to an earlier, broader covenant, namely, the one that God made with Noah following the flood (Gen. 9:1–17). This covenant was traditionally understood as one that God made with all humanity (indeed, all creatures)—because, of course, all humanity was understood as descending from Noah and his family, the sole survivors of the flood. So far from being a loosening of God's covenantal obligations, the Spirit-guided decision described in Acts 15 should be understood as a reengagement with another, older covenant. In other words, bringing the gentiles into the Church in this manner demonstrates that God's covenantal purposes are coming together and aligning themselves more fully toward his ultimate plan.

40. John Calvin, *Institutes of the Christian Religion*, ed. John T. McNeill, trans. Ford Lewis Battles, Library of Christian Classics 20 and 21 (Philadelphia: Westminster, 1960), 2.7.1–16, pp. 348–65.

We can look at this alignment in another way. If Pentecost is to Easter in the new covenant as the theophany at Mount Sinai is to the exodus in the old covenant, then the law of God is not abrogated but instead becomes a continuing work of the Holy Spirit in the hearts of believers. Christians do not put faith in their own works to attain salvation; they know that faith's object is Christ and what he has already accomplished for them. But having been redeemed in Christ, Christians also look forward to their continuing transformation in Christ, which follows the pattern of Christ's fulfillment of the law, in a very concrete sense the "still more excellent way" evocatively portrayed in Paul's famous hymn to love in 1 Corinthians 13. The law does not "save" us, and Christians no longer need fear the law's power to condemn us, because Christ has taken any such condemnation upon himself. But the law does continue to be a guide and touchstone for Christian living. This comes through the sanctifying and glorifying work of the Holy Spirit, who writes God's law on believers' hearts. Our human openness to such inscription and active participation is itself a work of the Holy Spirit joining with our spirits. In the Reformed theological tradition, such participation is understood to be based on "the third use of the law"—a phrase that obviously begs the question, "What are the first two uses?"

Law Keeping as Joyful Gratitude and Becoming Fully Human

For Calvin, the first use of the law is to make sinners aware of their fallen state and absolute need for God's grace.[41] The second use of the law has a more civic focus, namely, to restrain evildoers through fear of punishment to protect society at large.[42] But its third and, to Calvin's mind, principal use consists in the law's ability to clarify God's will for believers and to exhort them to follow that will.[43] In other words, it serves our understanding and our motivation, our knowledge of God's goal for our living and the encouragement to align ourselves with it, relying on the Spirit's sanctifying power working within us. This is certainly true of the moral law, the Ten Commandments in particular. Consider Jesus's Sermon on the Mount: taken at face value, Jesus seems to increase the law's demand to such an extent that no one could possibly meet its standard. Yet what Jesus portrays is not mere outward obedience but inward transformation—and he soon announces how that begins:

Ask, and it will be given you; seek, and you will find; knock, and it will be opened to you. For every one who asks receives, and he who seeks finds, and to

41. Ibid., 2.7.6–9, pp. 354–58.
42. Ibid., 2.7.10–11, pp. 358–60.
43. Ibid., 2.7.12–13, pp. 360–62.

him who knocks it will be opened. Or what man of you, if his son asks him for bread, will give him a stone? Or if he asks for a fish, will give him a serpent? If you then, who are evil, know how to give good gifts to your children, how much more will your Father who is in heaven give good things to those who ask him! (Matt. 7:7–11)

We accomplish this inward transformation not on our own but only in the power of God's life-giving Spirit, whom Jesus sends.

One of the most evocative explanations of the continuing role of the law in Christian life may be found in the Heidelberg Catechism of 1562. To my mind, what is most telling in this catechism's exposition of the law—that is, the Ten Commandments—is not so much the particular details it imparts but its placement in the catechism's structure. The catechism is divided into three main parts. The first, rather brief section describes the misery of the human situation, given sin and the fall. The second and longest section addresses how God graciously redeems humanity from its miserable condition. And the final section, entitled "Thankfulness," describes the manner in which we should respond to this gracious gift: by doing "good works," to express our gratitude, thereby glorifying God, assuring our faith by producing its fruits, and winning our neighbor to Christ through our "reverent behavior."[44] The catechism then goes on to say that the clearest norm for determining true "good works" resides in the Ten Commandments, which it then briefly expounds. In other words, obeying the law is not something we do to earn God's favor. To the contrary, it really becomes possible only as a *result* of God's favor, that is, Christ's redemptive death and resurrection, which becomes ours through the transforming work of the Holy Spirit within us to conform us to Christ's image. Aligning ourselves with God's will is not a drudging prerequisite for his mercy but a joyous and enthusiastic effect of, and Spirit-generated response to, his mercy.

Our gratitude should also help us recognize that the divine law is not some external, alien imposition upon us but is rather the ordering that allows us to become fully ourselves. True, the very term "Ten Commandments" can seem imposing, especially for flawed and fallible human beings earnestly trying to live up to the commandments' standards—or willfully trying to ignore them! But what if we thought of the law less as a set of constraints limiting us and more as our human "owner's manual," something like a set of instructions enabling us to get the most out of life over the long run? After all, if God is our maker, why should we be surprised that he also supplies us with specific

44. Heidelberg Catechism, Q. 86, found in Office of the General Assembly, Presbyterian Church (U.S.A.), *Book of Catechisms—Reference Edition* (Louisville: Geneva Press, 2001), 43.

guidance and a maintenance schedule for "best results"? Yes, we can ignore these instructions—and perhaps suffer no apparent ill effects in the short term. But eventually, our disregard of them will lead to breakdown and failure. God created us to be in true communion with him and with our fellow human beings, and it is precisely this intention that the two tablets of the Ten Commandments are designed to serve. God's law corresponds exactly to what we are and what we are meant to be. It is not foreign to our nature—even though in our sinfulness we typically perceive it that way—but is, in fact, a set of directions leading to our truest selves.

So what, then, should Christians think of the "ceremonial law," that is, all the requirements involved in the temple and the sacrificial system centered there? Calvin writes that "they have been abrogated not in effect but only in use."[45] In making this distinction, he is simply echoing the logic of the New Testament:[46] as the final High Priest and ultimate sacrifice, Christ has fulfilled that which the ceremonial law had always prefigured, the redemption of humanity. All the rituals of tabernacle and temple were grounded in, and served as a divine pledge for, this singular atoning event. What Christ accomplished, he accomplished "once and for all"—and therefore the particular requirements of the ceremonial law, while truly foreshadowing and participating in this accomplishment, need no longer be implemented. Indeed, continuing them would actually diminish if not implicitly deny the finality of Christ's life, death, and resurrection. But this does not mean that we should forget them, because in crucial ways the temple and ceremonial law give Christians the grammar and vocabulary for understanding what Christ has done and our appropriate response to that accomplishment.

The most obvious example of this is the rubric we are considering in this very chapter, namely, Paul's calling Christians the "temple of the Holy Spirit." Yes, Paul has been inspired to change his understanding of God's true temple in light of Christ's work—but his change is comprehensible only if one also knows the previous definition. The same holds true for his admonition that Christians present their bodies as a "living sacrifice" (Rom. 12:1). Strictly speaking, this is a contradiction in terms, but the image is an arresting and effective one precisely because his audience was fully versed in the vocabulary and "logic" of the sacrificial system. Yes, Paul "spiritualizes" the ceremonial requirements of the law, yet those requirements still call for concrete acts on the believer's part, namely, the daily "dying to self," that the Spirit might create

45. *Institutes*, 2.7.16, p. 364.
46. Calvin alludes to diverse NT passages, including Col. 2:17; Matt. 27:51; Heb. 10:1; Luke 16:16; and John 1:17.

a new self, one patterned after Christ's example and teaching. In effect, the fundamental orientation of the ceremonial law toward the mercy and holiness of God still orients Christians toward the mercy and holiness of God. As a result, our adherence to the moral law does not happen in a vacuum. It happens only—indeed, it is *possible* only—when it is grounded in our praise and gratitude toward God and all that he has done for us. In that sense, Christian ethics are the fruit of our worship, which itself is the work of the Holy Spirit joined with our spirits, united with Christ, in adoration of the Father.

These observations need to be kept in mind as we turn to our next topic, namely, Christian accountability within the community.

"The Power of the Keys": Church Discipline

> He said to them, "But who do you say that I am?" Simon Peter answered, "You are the Messiah, the Son of the living God." And Jesus answered him, "Blessed are you, Simon son of Jonah! For flesh and blood has not revealed this to you, but my Father in heaven. And I tell you, you are Peter, and on this rock I will build my church, and the gates of Hades will not prevail against it. I will give you the keys of the kingdom of heaven, and whatever you bind on earth will be bound in heaven, and whatever you loose on earth will be loosed in heaven." (Matt. 16:15–19)

In an age when being "nonjudgmental" seems to be the cardinal virtue, are we even allowed to discern among differing worldviews and moralities anymore? Within the Church, can individual Christians be held accountable for what they believe and how they act? Can the Church itself be held accountable?

Complicated Questions

In the current mind-set of American culture, these questions are more complicated than they might first appear. The attitude of secular modernity—which many Christians share—is that religious belief and personal behavior are a private matter, largely grounded in individual experience and not open to public assessment. If there is accountability, it is between the individual and God. The attitude of postmodernity—which influences many younger Christians—is more open to "spirituality." Yet in terms of accountability, the outcome is not all that different. Individual faith and behavior may grow out of a particular narrative shared by others, so a certain peer pressure toward conformity can exist. But cultural relativism is assumed: among narratives, who is to judge? Selecting one over the other seems more a matter of emotional or aesthetic preference, and individuals are free to move between narratives simply based on feeling or taste. In either context, whether modern or postmodern, the conviction that an objective truth and goodness exist that should stand as criteria for holding individuals accountable for faith and behavior is marginalized or rejected. Thus, for all practical purposes, the general assumption seems to be that Christians are really accountable only to themselves. If they are called to task on some matter and disagree with the reproach, it is not uncommon for them to move to another church or stop attending altogether.

Is the Church as an institution accountable for what it believes and how it acts? Here current attitudes appear more clear-cut, given public dismay and calls for justice whenever a new ecclesiastical scandal erupts. Such reactions presuppose that the Church should be held accountable whenever it crosses certain lines. Yet even here the answer may not be as obvious as it first appears. What is meant by "the Church"? Individual congregations, particular institutional structures or officials, specific denominations, or "the Church universal"? And accountable on what basis? Only for a violation of local, state, or federal law? For overstepping a generic set of professional ethics? Or for bending or breaking specifically Christian norms of belief and behavior?

In addition to these questions, another complicates matters further: to what or to whom is the Church accountable? Certainly, individual denominations have structures and policies in place that maintain certain norms, particularly in matters of professional standards and ethics. Yet to what extent are these only norms derived from general cultural criteria, and to what extent are they derived from specifically Christian ones? And to what extent are various churches and denominations accountable to one another, or the Church universal, with regard to their Christian witness?

Addressing all these questions adequately would take us far beyond the intentions and scope of this book, but I do need to affirm several key principles raised by them. The first is that our starting point must be based not on generic but on explicitly theological—even trinitarian—foundations. Thus, we must first affirm that God is good and God is gracious, and our salvation depends upon our trusting in what he accomplishes for us, rather than on what we do on our own for ourselves. God loves us, indeed "proves his love for us in that while we were still sinners Christ died for us" (Rom. 5:8). Yet God also loves us too much to leave us in that sinful state, but rather intends our sanctification and ultimately our glorification. As Paul admonishes us: "Do not be conformed to this world, but be transformed by the renewing of your minds, so that you may discern what is the will of God—what is good and acceptable and perfect" (Rom. 12:2). We are not left to our own devices in accomplishing this transformation. On this point Paul also notes that Christ "will transform the body of our humiliation that it may be conformed to the body of his glory, by the power that also enables him to make all things subject to himself" (Phil. 3:21). Paul's assumptions and admonitions are echoed by Peter: "Therefore prepare your minds for action; discipline yourselves; set all your hope on the grace that Jesus Christ will bring you when he is revealed. Like obedient children, do not be conformed to the desires that you formerly had in ignorance. Instead, as he who called you is holy, be holy yourselves in all your conduct; for it is written, 'You shall be holy, for I am holy'" (1 Pet. 1:13–16).

The crux of this admonition is that holiness is not an external norm to which we conform ourselves, nor is it ultimately alien to us. (Recall my discussion of the "third use of the law" in the preceding section.) It is rather an internal possibility and our truest self-realization made available to us through the outpouring of the Holy Spirit upon all flesh and the indwelling of the Holy Spirit within each heart. To be sure, this possibility and realization have been, and continue to be, derailed due to human sinfulness. But they are grounded in God's original creation and intention for us, and they have become available once more in Christ and through the Spirit. In that light, Paul's admonitions to holiness exemplify the Church's view, which may be summarized: become what you already are in Christ; live into this new reality made available to you through the Holy Spirit's uniting you to Christ.

That is the first principle. The second complements it: just as God does not leave you to your own personal devices in attaining this transformation, neither does he leave you to attain it alone. As noted, the true agent of this transformation is the Holy Spirit, who is available to each believer. But the Spirit does not come to each believer individually in order to keep her or him in isolation. Rather, the Spirit comes in order to draw each into communion, into God's continuing body on earth, the Church. Indeed, we in the North American context need to be more open to the fact that in actual practice the nurture and guidance of the Spirit *working through the Church* has the greater impact in helping individuals avoid conformity to the disorders and evil of this world, while shaping and transforming them to the norms of God's reign. In this, I am simply building on a premise given at the outset of this book, namely, that we are irreducibly social beings. And we are stronger together than we are alone.

Correction and Discipline: Guided by the Spirit through Scripture and the Church

All of the above must be taken into consideration as the context for a discussion of Church discipline, traditionally known as "the power of the keys." The term stems from Jesus's words to Peter, following the latter's confession of Jesus as the Messiah. In particular, Jesus's words "whatever you bind on earth will be bound in heaven, and whatever you loose on earth will be loosed in heaven" (Matt. 16:17–19) have traditionally been understood as granting the Church a corrective and disciplinary power in matters of faith and behavior. If the Church is to be "one, holy, catholic, and apostolic," there must be some structural means for ensuring that this remains, in fact, the case.

Roman Catholicism, of course, has understood Jesus's words as vesting that power in the apostle Peter and thereby in his direct successors as bishops of Rome, namely, in the papal office. This is why a pair of crossed keys appear on the papal coat of arms. The Eastern Orthodox Church holds that such authority is not restricted to Peter's direct successors alone but passes on to all those elevated to episcopal office. In other words, the historic succession is not a single line but a branching tree. Some Protestant denominations who include bishops in their institutional structure echo this Orthodox view, such as Episcopalians, some Lutherans, and Methodists. Other Protestants are of a Presbyterian or "free church" tradition that does not maintain the office of bishop as historically understood, but that assigns this traditional role of "overseer" or "superintendent" (the literal meaning of the Greek word *episkopos*) to some other body or officer in the Church. On this point, when Matthew 18:15–20 repeats Jesus's language of "binding and loosing," it appears to be directed toward all the disciples, and by extension toward "wherever two or three are gathered" in Christ's name.[47]

A common justification for this more diffused understanding of ecclesial authority is the claim that many corruptions have entered the Church in spite of—and in some cases, actually due to—particular bishops and popes. If this is the case, then mere historic succession is insufficient to maintain true apostolicity. In effect, this kind of succession runs the risk of becoming just another worldly bureaucracy and subject to worldly failings, self-interest, and sin. What counts more is openness to the guidance of the Spirit. As John Calvin writes,

> So true is it that Christian faith must not be founded on human testimony, not propped up by doubtful opinion, not based on human authority, but engraved on our hearts by the finger of the living God, so as not to be obliterated by any deceitful error. There is then nothing of Christ in him who does not hold the elemental principle, that it is God alone who enlightens our minds, to perceive his truth, who by his Spirit seals it on our hearts, and by his sure testimony of it confirms our conscience.[48]

47. I will address this passage further below, pp. 206–7.
48. "Reply to Sadolet," in *Calvin: Theological Treatises*, trans. J. K. S. Reid, Library of Christian Classics (Philadelphia: Westminster, 1954), 244.

Of course, this divine enlightening of God sealed on our hearts by the Holy Spirit derives its content from the Bible, the Word. Calvin's concern was to emphasize a closer adherence to scriptural norms (understood, we must recognize, through the assumptions of a creedal orthodoxy) as the basis for the Church's belief and life.[49] Yet history suggests that such forms of ecclesial discipline, especially in its free-church manifestations, are subject to their own forms of ossification and corruption. For one thing, the more minimal the explicit power structures are, the more likely they are to be shadowed by "behind the scenes" networks where the real power is exercised by insiders. For another, without explicit structures to maintain them, clear and rigorous norms tend to be more susceptible to fading over time and to accommodation to the influences of external cultural norms.

So denominational disagreements over who has the prerogatives and responsibility for exercising "the power of the keys" continue, as do the particular shortcomings and blind spots associated with each type. These are practical problems and questions of polity that this book will not seek to address in detail. It is not just that I want to avoid getting bogged down in debates over polity—which is no small concern, to be sure! It is rather that I understand Scripture to be open to a variety of ecclesial structures precisely so that the Church may be adaptable to the needs of the diverse concrete contexts it finds itself in and to the constantly mutating challenges to, and corruptions of, whatever structures a church employs. Obviously, this understanding is not a neutral one but rather shapes and reflects my own Protestant assumptions, in particular my free-church heritage in the Congregationalist tradition. Whether more bureaucratic and hierarchical, charismatically unstructured and egalitarian, or somewhere in between, the Church has demonstrated throughout its history that no one institutional form is perfect or foolproof. Each has its strengths and weaknesses. The crucial matter is that some form does exist[50] and that it is exercised with openness to the guidance of Spirit and

---

49. This is why *sola scriptura* was such a watchword for the original Protestant Reformation. And it is hardly coincidental that so many of those early Reformers were Bible scholars. As John Calvin writes in his reply to Cardinal Sadolet, "Let your pontiff, then, boast as he may of the succession of Peter; even should he make good his title to it, it only follows that obedience is due to him from Christian people so long as he himself maintains his fidelity to Christ and does not deviate from the purity of the gospel" (ibid., 243).

50. For example, the Scots Confession of 1560 lists three "notes" or essential characteristics of the "true Kirk": (1) "the true preaching of the Word of God," (2) "the right administration of the sacraments of Christ Jesus," and (3) "ecclesiastical discipline uprightly ministered." See Office of the General Assembly, Presbyterian Church (U.S.A.). *The Constitution of the Presbyterian Church (U.S.A.)*, part 1: *Book of Confessions* (Louisville: Office of the General Assembly, 2002), 19.

Scripture and discernment toward the ways it may be abused. On this general principle, there is still a basic consensus that the very *being*—and not just the *well*-being—of the Church requires some institutional form.

Purpose of Discipline: Sanctification and Glorification

What, then, is the meaning and purpose of "the power of the keys," understood theologically? First, it is a responsibility given to the Church to be exercised under the lordship of Christ and the endowing of the Holy Spirit to advance their work on behalf of the Father. On this understanding, the power of the keys is not primarily punitive or merely an exercise in power. Rather, the power of the keys is meant to serve as an instrument in realizing the telos God has intended since before our creation and reaffirmed in our redemption, namely, our gradual sanctification and ultimate glorification. The power of the keys is not an end in itself but a means in bringing us to the perfection that enables our full communion with God, with one another, and with all of creation. To be sure, the benefits of such accountability come not just at the end of the age but may be experienced along the way in our earthly pilgrimage. The fruit of the Spirit is its own reward, as well as a divine instrument in growing us toward glory. Still, we recognize that the full realization of these benefits remains something to be brought about by God only at the end of the age. In the meantime, we acknowledge that we are on a journey and that our spiritual warfare continues. Therefore, we must maintain appropriate humility. Perfection is not the prerequisite for reaching the goal; it is rather the goal to which we are being brought.

While all this might sound rather idealized and vague, Scripture actually presents a very practical description of how to exercise this mutual accountability of the power of the keys. It is to operate on what could be called a grace-oriented "sliding scale," starting with quiet encouragement and admonition and moving toward a more public and formal application only when absolutely necessary. The classic example of this comes from Jesus himself:

> "If another member of the church sins against you, go and point out the fault when the two of you are alone. If the member listens to you, you have regained that one. But if you are not listened to, take one or two others along with you, so that every word may be confirmed by the evidence of two or three witnesses. If the member refuses to listen to them, tell it to the church; and if the offender refuses to listen even to the church, let such a one be to you as a Gentile and a tax collector. Truly I tell you, whatever you bind on earth will be bound in heaven, and whatever you loose on earth will be loosed in heaven. Again, truly I tell you, if two of you agree on earth about anything you ask, it will be done

for you by my Father in heaven. For where two or three are gathered in my name, I am there among them."

Then Peter came and said to him, "Lord, if another member of the church sins against me, how often should I forgive? As many as seven times?" Jesus said to him, "Not seven times, but, I tell you, seventy-seven times." (Matt. 18:15–22)

One thing to keep in mind from this passage: by his own behavior, the wayward person has effectively made himself an outsider. When Jesus says to treat that person as "a Gentile and tax collector," he likely means not to disdain him but rather to treat him as someone who (again) needs conversion, in order to be brought back within the fold. Moreover, Jesus's response to Peter's follow-up question makes clear that the Church should always maintain a bias toward forgiveness and reconciliation.

The scenario just described reflects a more obvious and egregious breach of appropriate behavior, with the matter escalating to a formal hearing. But we should not confine our understanding of the power of the keys solely to a disciplinary structure. There are other passages that speak to the mutual encouragement, admonition, and accountability that should characterize the Church's life together. And it seems clear that this mutuality is not just negative, that is, a corrective for when things go wrong. Rather, it is more akin to the mutuality of a team effort, of "training" together. Yes, there is a need for individual discipline, as Paul's metaphor of the boxer affirms.[51] But several other passages from the Pauline letters clearly indicate that Christians need not and should not go it alone. In Colossians 3:12–17 (RSV), we find these words:

Put on then, as God's chosen ones, holy and beloved, compassion, kindness, lowliness, meekness, and patience, forbearing one another and, if one has a complaint against another, forgiving each other; as the Lord has forgiven you, so you also must forgive. And above all these put on love, which binds everything together in perfect harmony. And let the peace of Christ rule in your hearts, to which indeed you were called in the one body. And be thankful. Let the word of Christ dwell in you richly, teach and admonish one another in all wisdom, and sing psalms and hymns and spiritual songs with thankfulness in your hearts to God. And whatever you do, in word or deed, do everything in the name of the Lord Jesus, giving thanks to God the Father through him.

In a similar vein, Paul writes in 1 Thessalonians 5:12–22 (RSV):

---

51. "Every athlete exercises self-control in all things. They do it to receive a perishable wreath, but we an imperishable. Well, I do not run aimlessly, I do not box as one beating the air; but I pommel my body and subdue it, lest after preaching to others I myself should be disqualified" (1 Cor. 9:25–27 RSV).

But we beseech you, brethren, to respect those who labor among you and are over you in the Lord and admonish you, and to esteem them very highly in love because of their work. Be at peace among yourselves. And we exhort you, brethren, admonish the idlers, encourage the fainthearted, help the weak, be patient with them all. See that none of you repays evil for evil, but always seek to do good to one another and to all. Rejoice always, pray constantly, give thanks in all circumstances; for this is the will of God in Christ Jesus for you. Do not quench the Spirit, do not despise prophesying, but test everything; hold fast what is good, abstain from every form of evil.

Note the gracious tone, but also realism, the awareness of human fallibility and the various means of overcoming it. Yes, Paul relied on his own apostolic authority in prescribing these various behaviors (and no doubt hoped his hearers would respect that authority and act accordingly). But what these passages describe is less a disciplinary structure and more a culture of mutual support and accountability, one that is maintained in part through admonition, but also through cultivating the habits of encouragement, forbearance, instruction, prayer, song, gratitude, and the like.

In our day, the Church would do well to be mindful and creative in fostering various informal structures and methods serving this sort of cultural formation. Our own everyday experience tells us how much easier it is to attain certain goals (losing weight, stopping smoking, getting exercise) if our effort is done with other people rather than alone. Effective partners give support, challenge us to keep going, remind us of what happens if we give up—and are perceptive enough to know when we need to be pushed with a more forceful word or encouraged with a more sympathetic one. We should more intentionally adapt this recognition to our life together as Christians and our growth in the Spirit.

The reclamation of ancient Church spiritual disciplines by Christians and congregations more accustomed to contemporary approaches can serve this purpose in refreshing and challenging ways. For example, a serious reclaiming of Lenten disciplines by traditionally nonliturgical churches could be very fruitful for those participating. Likewise, undertaking a small group spiritual retreat with an appropriate mix of prayer, biblical contemplation, spiritual reflection, hymns, and recreation might prove a short-term exercise that encourages some new longer-term habits. Creating a labyrinth and being immersed in the pilgrimage spirituality associated with such structures can help reorient Christians floundering in the secular world. Similarly, the common practice of Bible study could be undertaken with a clearer sense that it is not just "informational" but "formational." Small groups of Christians who already have a personal respect for one another could be brought together to form teams committed to deeper mutual support and accountability, coaching, and friendship.

Undergirding all these ideas should be a rededication on the Church's part to catechesis as a recurrent part of the community's life together. Particularly given the impact of an increasingly post-Christian culture on our assumptions and attitudes, instruction in the faith should be ongoing, in multiple forms and for all ages. I have already considered the nature and purpose of catechesis earlier, so I need not repeat those things here.[52] The one point I would emphasize now is that, under the rubric of the power of the keys, catechesis is not optional for the Church but obligatory. That is, one aspect of our accountability to one another, as individuals and as a community, is to know our faith, its basic beliefs and practices, in order to serve one another and to bring it to those outside the Church. Essentially, the power of the keys comes into play whenever we reflect on our life together: does this belief or that behavior build up and strengthen the community's *koinōnia*, or does it undermine it? Does it reflect the fruit of the Spirit and serve God's coming reign, or is it a "work of the flesh" that detracts from or denies God's gospel and reign? Knowing the faith gives the community common and open criteria for making such determinations. In effect, it helps the Church "remember who we are" as the temple of the Holy Spirit in order to encourage and strengthen our common efforts in the sanctifying journey to which God calls us.

52. See above, chap. 3, especially pp. 109–12.

6

A Pilgrim Community of the New Heaven and the New Earth

For we know that if the earthly tent we live in is destroyed, we have a building from God, a house not made with hands, eternal in the heavens. Here indeed we groan, and long to put on our heavenly dwelling, so that by putting it on we may not be found naked. For while we are still in this tent, we sigh with anxiety; not that we would be unclothed, but that we would be further clothed, so that what is mortal may be swallowed up by life. He who has prepared us for this very thing is God, who has given us the Spirit as a guarantee. So we are always of good courage; we know that while we are at home in the body we are away from the Lord, for we walk by faith, not by sight. (2 Cor. 5:1–7 RSV)

But as it is, they desire a better country, that is, a heavenly one. Therefore God is not ashamed to be called their God; indeed, he has prepared a city for them. (Heb. 11:16)

Therefore, since we are surrounded by so great a cloud of witnesses, let us also lay aside every weight and the sin that clings so closely, and let us run with perseverance the race that is set before us, looking to Jesus the pioneer and perfecter of our faith, who for the sake of the joy that was set before him endured the cross, disregarding its shame, and has taken his seat at the right hand of the throne of God. Consider him who endured such hostility against himself from sinners, so that you may not grow weary or lose heart. (Heb. 12:1–3)

Then I saw a new heaven and a new earth; for the first heaven and the first earth had passed away, and the sea was no more. And I saw the holy city, the new Jerusalem, coming down out of heaven from God, prepared as a bride adorned for her husband. And I heard a loud voice from the throne saying,

> "See, the home of God is among mortals.
> He will dwell with them;
> they will be his peoples,
> and God himself will be with them;
> he will wipe every tear from their eyes.
> Death will be no more;
> mourning and crying and pain will be no more,
> for the first things have passed away." (Rev. 21:1–4)

We are people who yearn. We yearn for love; we yearn for beauty; we yearn for purpose and meaning. We long for happiness. In the midst of deprivation, we hunger for sustenance. In the midst of plenty, we thirst for something greater. Our desire, it appears, is insatiable; our hearts are always restless. Even when we have all that we might dream of, we long for some greater fulfillment that ever and again eludes us, like a feather that stirs past our hand just as we try to grasp it.

The Communion We Long For and Travel Toward

This yearning is not alien or wrong. In fact, it is fully natural, because we were created for something beyond ourselves, indeed, beyond the reaches of time and space. We were created to be in communion with God. We are finite beings meant for relation with the infinite—which is why, as Augustine recognized, our hearts are restless until they rest in God. We long for happiness because it echoes the profound happiness and contentment we have in communion with the divine. We were *designed* for this joy and fulfillment. Yes, we remain creatures; yet God intended this divine end for us even before he made us. This was his eternal purpose and the eternal decree of his covenantal love. It is why the Father enfolds us into his arms of Son and Spirit, first to create us and then to reclaim us, relating to us by making us one with Christ and breathing into us the breath of life through his Spirit.

Of course, from the moment of that creation, the story of our lives—both individually and collectively, down the eons of our past to this very moment—is our consistent habit of focusing this deep-seated yearning on those things that cannot finally fulfill it. The ultimate object of our desire was meant to be our communion with God. Had we oriented our desire in that way, everything else would have fallen into place. Our desire for God would bring to fruition all our other relations: our human communion with one another, and our communion with the whole created order. But directing our desire toward lesser things, we inevitably became disoriented. And such disorientation—our fall into self-centeredness, our fall into sin—became habitual, a "second nature" to us passed from one generation to the next. That second nature became so embedded in our thoughts, our attitudes, our feelings, and our behaviors that on our own we could no longer escape it. Yet God chose not to let us remain "curved in upon ourselves" (one common definition of sin). Rather, God chose to call us out of ourselves to look beyond ourselves in order to regain and discover ourselves for the first time—the true selves that God, granting us at creation a place and time to grow, originally meant us to become. God made us to become more than we were at the beginning. God made us to grow, to mature, to set out on a journey for life and fulfillment. And God meant us to undertake that journey and transformation in the company of others. God intended this with our creation, and God reiterated this intention in undertaking his saving covenant, always holding before our eyes a vision of the fulfillment he has in store for us.

The first chapter of this book described that journey's start: with God's call of Abram and Sarai, promising that through them all the nations of the world would be blessed (Gen. 12:1–3); with his "cutting" a covenant with Abram regarding his descendants' homeland (15:1–21); and with his changing Abram's and Sarai's names and reaffirming his everlasting covenant with their offspring through the sign of circumcision (17:1–21). Of course, the biblical narrative of Abraham and Sarah describes far more than just these and other milestone encounters with God. It also includes accounts of entirely mundane events and occasional references to the passing years. The same holds true with accounts of Abraham and Sarah's offspring: from Isaac and Rebekah, to Jacob and Esau, to Jacob, Leah, and Rachel and their twelve sons. All together these stories establish the apparent pattern of God being intermittently involved and then either leaving his covenant partners to their own devices or, as Joseph's later statement clarifies, working "behind the scene" to accomplish his purposes—even when we humans are unaware and may actually have other intentions in mind (50:19–20). I recall this pattern here because even with the coming of Christ and the outpouring of the Holy Spirit establishing the Church as Christ's body, as God's people, and as the Spirit's own temple, we remain a community "under way." We may be blessed with ecstatic moments of immediate divine presence, but we should also expect moments, even seasons, in which we experience God's presence more peripherally—or perhaps not at all. At times such as these, we recall the gift of past encounters and rely upon the presence of God's Spirit mediated through our companions in faith. As the Church, we have a calling to live up to, day in and day out—and the shared worship, prayers, encouragement, correction, and support of our sisters and brothers in Christ are the ordinary means by which we realize that call.

The Church Is a Blessing and an Instrument of Blessing

Is the Church therefore a means to an end, or an end in itself? It is both. On the one hand, it serves as the covenantal instrument God has chosen to proclaim the gospel of mercy, healing, righteousness, and reconciliation and summoned to be as well a living exemplar of this gospel. As such an instrument, the Church should be preoccupied not with institutional self-preservation or self-aggrandizement but only with faithfulness. In another sense, however, many of the Church's activities are indeed ends in themselves, precisely because these activities do not just proclaim but realize God's purposes. Worship is an end in itself, done for its own sake, because when undertaken with true openness to God's moving Spirit, it enacts the proper relationship that the Father would have with us in Christ, and we with one another as the family of God. Similarly, acts of mercy and kindness and reconciliation and justice are ends in themselves, done for their own sakes, because they realize the way God would have us relate to one another in the world. So the Church is necessary—not that anything compelled God to institute it, but that since he has freely chosen this means, it becomes necessary for us. That is, it has been ordained by God from before creation as that ordinary means by which the purposes and benefits of his reign are made available to humanity. This is not to say that God's grace cannot make use of other, extraordinary means. To say the Church is necessary does not limit God. Rather, it says that God would have us immerse ourselves within this assembly in order to be incorporated into his unfolding covenantal work.

In the midst of this ordinary, day-to-day journey, we need to keep before us the vision and the privileged tasks that first set us on our way. The Christian Church is created, sustained, and perfected through the work of the Holy Spirit on behalf of the Son to serve with joy and gratitude the eternal purpose of the Father. Essentially, this divine purpose is the Church's witness to *koinōnia*—the full communion of peace and righteousness, of joy and love—that God originally intended and ultimately intends that *all* creatures should enjoy with one another and their Creator. The Church knows it has been given a unique vision and vocation in this regard. It knows its utter dependence upon the life-giving power of the Holy Spirit to animate, sustain, and perfect its witness to this communion through its words and its way of life. It knows that this communion is ever and again disrupted and corrupted by human sin. But it also knows that the redeeming and reconciling power of the Father in Christ and the Spirit restores and perfects this communion, and that its call is to witness to this gracious and continuing act of salvation.

On the one hand, this witness necessarily includes the Church's acknowledgment of its own continuing human fallibility. As the Church, we know that our human spirit, whether understood collectively or individually, is still subject to the vicissitudes of the fall. We know that we are prone to sin. We know that our spirit, both collectively and individually, tends to resist or seek to control God's Holy Spirit toward our own ends, not God's. So in spite of the great treasures with which it has been entrusted, the Church remains a creature, an earthen vessel (2 Cor. 4:6–7). Part of the Church's witness is therefore to embody the humility proper to such self-knowledge, to be a community of forgiveness, reconciliation, mutual support, and encouragement. It is to make clear that we continue to be as much in need of God's grace and transforming power as the world "outside" the Church.

On the other hand, the Church also knows that it has already received new life: it has experienced liberation from bondage; it has experienced restored communion; it has felt the joy of being made new; it has received a vision and a taste of future glory. It knows itself to be an instrument made and commissioned by God to be a herald of this new reality, of God's gracious and perfecting will toward creation. As the Church, we are called to proclaim the good news of God's reconciling and redeeming work in Jesus Christ made available through the Holy Spirit. As the Church, we are called to entrust ourselves in joyful obedience to the Spirit's transforming discipline. And as the Church, we are called to look forward in hope and courage to our future glory, living lives of such gratitude and wonder that the world sees and cannot help but want to join us in moving toward that divinely appointed end.

Images of the Church That Form Us

Scripture uses a number of recurring and complementary motifs to emphasize this transformative movement running through the biblical story: journeying from the land of one's birth to a new home, bondage and liberation, wilderness testing and arrival, exile and restoration, what might be called "witnessing pilgrimage," and, of course, the fact that the whole story starts in a garden and ends with the new Jerusalem and the new heaven and earth.

This movement toward God's goal, this "teleological momentum," pervades the Bible. I am not suggesting that these motifs replace or are to be added to the three I have considered in the preceding chapters. Instead, I suggest we understand the images of "the body of Christ," "the people of God," and "the temple of the Holy Spirit" as essentially dynamic ones, as having embedded within themselves this teleological momentum toward God's glorious future. The God who made us, who accompanies us as a covenantal companion along our way, also has a final destination in mind for us.

The Church naturally recapitulates this movement in large and small ways. As one practical example, consider how the Church as "the body of Christ" has sought to live into his lead, to imitate his behavior. After Jesus's baptism, the Spirit drove him into the wilderness for a forty-day period of prayer and testing before the start of his ministry, in which he would fulfill the purposes of his Father. Liturgically, the Church recapitulates this time of prayer and testing during the forty days of Lent, when Christians undertake a season of mindful openness to the Spirit, in order to align themselves more fully and deeply with their Lord and his will for their lives. As Jesus's teaching and healing came to a close, "he set his face to go to Jerusalem" (Luke 9:51) to offer himself on the cross. With the coming of Holy Week, the Church meditates on Christ's passion but also recognizes itself as joined with him, both in the new covenant of his body and blood and in his call that Christians take up their own cross and follow him (Matt. 16:24). Individually, we ponder Christ's suffering, and wonder: would we imitate Peter and deny our Lord? Would we echo the crowd calling, "Crucify!"? Would we taunt him at Golgotha? Or would we, having died to ourselves in baptism, joining him in his suffering and death, be courageous and faithful in our witness to his sacrifice? With his resurrection and ascension, are we courageous and faithful in our witness to the hope and new life that his lordship and the gift of the Holy Spirit offer? The rhythms of the Church year and liturgy help Christians recognize that living into what we already are as the body of Christ is a recurring discipline. With each new day, the Holy Spirit offers individual members and the body as a whole the opportunity to advance along the path the Father sets before us, knowing that the Lord has gone ahead to prepare a place for us (John 14:1–4).

Of course, the image of spiritual journey and pilgrimage also highlights the teleological momentum of the next image considered, "the people of God." The Old Testament in particular provides several ways in which we can understand the Church's present circumstance and its call. One is the wilderness wanderings of the Hebrew people. To be sure, understanding the Church's life as akin to that of the Hebrews' wandering in the wilderness is not an entirely reassuring one. Scripture relates many episodes of the peoples' grumbling, misbehavior, sloth, and the like, behavior that eventually leads God to punish them by excluding that generation from reaching the promised land. If we are honest with ourselves, we can see our own attitudes and behaviors recapitulating those of our ancestors. In our own ways we yearn for the "fleshpots of Egypt"—the easy life that in reality enslaves us—rather than boldly trusting in God's liberating summons to follow him. Yet examples drawn from the wilderness years are not entirely negative. In its better moments, the assembly knows itself to be utterly dependent upon God and rejoices in this fact and God's abundant goodness.[1] Given the exigencies of the wilderness, the people have no other choice but to travel light and trust God's providence. Correspondingly, God's home among the Israelites is no grand temple or cathedral, but a tent wherein the glory of the Lord "tabernacles" with his people (Exod. 40:34–38) when not leading them onward in a pillar of cloud by day and a pillar of fire by night (13:21–22).

We should also recognize that not all journeys are voluntary or filled with expectation. Another Old Testament example that can help the Church understand its present circumstance and its future hope derives from accounts of the Jewish people's exile from their homeland to the distant and foreign land of Babylon. Jerusalem had been taken and the temple destroyed, just as the prophets Isaiah and Jeremiah had warned. Many of the city's inhabitants were made captive and transplanted to the capital of their conqueror. They found themselves surrounded by an alien and dominating culture, facing temptations of syncretism and accommodation—which threatened their very identity as the covenant people of God. The lament of the psalmist still evokes their anguish:

> By the waters of Babylon,
> there we sat down and wept,
>   when we remembered Zion.
> On the willows there
>   we hung up our lyres.
> For there our captors
>   required of us songs,
> and our tormentors, mirth, saying,
>   "Sing us one of the songs of Zion!"
> How shall we sing the Lord's song
>   in a foreign land? (Ps. 137:1–4 RSV)

Yet even as strangers in a strange land, the people were encouraged by the prophets to take comfort: in a new exodus, God would again free them from

---

1. See Exod. 15:1–21; 24:3–8; 35:20–29; 36:2–7.

their captivity, preparing a highway to bring them home (see Isa. 40:1–5; 45:1–3; 48:20). Of course, for millennia the faithful have recognized these encouragements of comfort and hope as speaking not just to the restoration of the Babylonian captives in that time and place but to the eventual restoration of all creation. After all, one can feel a sense of exile and alienation even in the midst of worldly peace and comfort, so the yearning for a greater, universal restoration remains. These and other ancient words still have the power to give voice to the hope that lies before us.

The Church knows that with the life, death, resurrection, and ascension of Christ, the Father has accomplished the key milestone of his covenantal purposes. Hence, the Church knows with clarity the gifts of Christ that its ancestors in covenant faithfulness viewed only dimly from afar (Heb. 11:13). Still, it shares with them a status as sojourners yet under way in the movement toward God's final consummation of creation. The Church knows that this work of the Spirit in growing and expanding the covenant and its promise remains incomplete. Acknowledging this, the Church knows it remains on a journey, recognizing that, even as it looks back with joy and gratitude on all it has received, it persists as a pilgrim people. It is no accident that the image of pilgrimage has played such a central and influential role in Christian history, particularly with regard to Christian spirituality and piety. Pilgrimage has been understood both literally and symbolically. From the earliest centuries, faithful Christians have traveled from their homes to seek out places or people of special holiness, both as a means of penance and as a path to spiritual insight and blessing. And the spiritual benefit comes not just at the destination but in the ardors of the journey along the way.

The final image, the Church as "the temple of the Holy Spirit," also has a distinct teleological momentum. At first blush, this may seem a rather odd claim. After all, temples are buildings, and buildings by definition are stationary. Yet when Paul calls the Church as a whole and its individual members the "temple of the Holy Spirit," he intentionally uses this seemingly paradoxical image to make his claim all the more pointed. God's glorious presence is no longer located within the precincts of a sacred building, nor does his holy commission extend only to those designated for special duties within those precincts. The temple curtain has been torn in two (Mark 15:38), and God's Spirit comes to all those who repent of their sins and accept Christ (Acts 2:38). "Sacred spaces" are no longer confined to particular locations but may be found wherever the faithful are—and as the faithful increase and spread the gospel, so too does the world itself become touched by the spread of God's holiness.

In a way, it is a return to the model of the exodus, when God tabernacled with his people as they moved toward the promised land. And yet it also broadens and deepens that model: on the one hand, there is no longer only one "tent of meeting" but many. Wherever two or three are gathered in Christ's name, indeed, wherever any Christian is open to the Spirit's presence and guidance, there is God. On the other hand, this expanded presence is not just external but internal. The "sacred space" created by the holy presence is found within and among Christians and brings with it certain norms of attitude and behavior. To put it another way, having been joined with Christ the High Priest in baptism, each Christian now shares in his priesthood, an office that requires certain standards of rigor, discipline, and holiness wherever individual Christians or the Church may go. In traditional theological language, it requires the mortification of the old person and the sanctification of the new, as we die to the flesh and are made alive in the Spirit. It requires us to resist temptations in our diverse wildernesses so that we may become in our everyday lives what we already are in Christ. Thus, the heart of pilgrimage is more the inner journey than the actual outer one—although real pilgrimages or spiritual retreats may still serve a useful role by lifting us out of our daily ruts and offering openings for the Spirit. Whatever practices help inculcate the mind and habits of holiness are a good thing.

A Perilous Pilgrimage

All of this taken together indicates why the notion of "pilgrimage" is a much more apt and helpful metaphor for describing the role of the Church in God's economy of salvation than other concepts might be, especially more modern ones such as "process" or "development" or "evolution." The first term has overtones of something too controlled, even mechanistic, like an assembly line or utterly predictable routine. The latter two terms allow for the new and different, but often while implying that the past is left behind because it is now obsolete. Pilgrimages by definition entail a break from the routine, and while they are purposefully open to new insights and realizations, they also never discard lessons from the past.

To be sure, the term "pilgrimage"—and nowadays the perhaps more commonly used phrase "spiritual journey"—can become rather clichéd in certain contexts and usages. The greatest danger lies in its almost infinite malleability: the term can mean almost anything, with the consequence being that it finally means almost nothing. A pilgrimage is not something superficial, nor is it merely a "trip," as if the whole thing were planned by a well-connected travel agent who has set out the itinerary to be as safe and predictable as possible. Real pilgrimage, a true spiritual journey, does not have such assurances that things will unfold smoothly. Rather, unexpected interruptions, delays, and challenges are often the norm, as are unintended consequences even when matters may seem to be unfolding as they ought.

Christian tradition also affirms that it is not just the natural limitations, accidents, and intransigence of life that disrupt the journey's progression; it is the active opposition of human sin and Satan causing setbacks and failures. A much-beloved and influential description of such challenges may be found in John Bunyan's classic eighteenth-century allegory *The Pilgrim's Progress*.[2] The challenges Bunyan's protagonist, Christian, faces illustrate why the Church as a pilgrim people needs to be not just prepared but on guard. It is no hyperbole when Christian scripture and tradition insist that we are engaged in spiritual warfare. There are, of course, ample instances of this from the Old Testament. But in the New Testament as well, we are urged—by Jesus, by Paul, and by John of Patmos in his vision of the end—to recognize and prepare for the on-slaughts we will face.[3] Indeed, one key lesson the Church can draw from John's revelation is that the closer we draw to our God-appointed end, the fiercer the resistance grows to our attaining it. We need to be adequately prepared.

This may be one reason for the renewed interest in the spiritual teachings and disciplines of the early Church's "desert fathers" and "desert mothers." These were individuals who sought out the desert as a place to escape the easy comforts of a society in which the Church was now accepted in culture. To be sure, they did not escape temptation simply by escaping society: tempta-tions followed them into the desert. Yet the desert brought a reduction of life to its essentials, such that those temptations stood out in greater relief and clarity. Given the fact that most Christians in contemporary Western culture are hardly likely to be understimulated, might the Church recognize as part of its calling the provision of a more "desertlike" environment? Ancient prac-tices of fasting could now include abstaining not just from food but from the overload of information, social media, and electronic entertainment that so inundate us 24/7.

Similarly, there is renewed interest in Celtic spirituality, especially the daily liturgies and prayers that help discipline Christians to reconnect with God's presence in the beauty and vitality of creation and the rhythm of the seasons. I believe examples of these prayers and liturgies are all the more powerful because they are so often explicitly and concretely trinitarian, exemplifying how Father, Son, and Spirit intertwine one's own life with the biblical story,

2. The work was originally published in two parts, in 1678 and 1684, and first published as a single volume in 1728. Since then it has been published in multiple editions and translated into numerous languages.

3. See Matt. 10:34; Luke 22:36–38; Eph. 6:14–17; 1 Thess. 5:8; Rev. 2:12–17; 19:11–16.

the Church's past, present, and future, and the whole of creation as it moves toward God's new heaven and earth. Perhaps the best known example, recognizing the commitment, the struggle, the power, and the awe in store, is Saint Patrick's "Breastplate":

> I bind unto myself today
> the strong Name of the Trinity,
> by invocation of the same,
> the Three in One and One in Three.
>
> I bind this day to me for ever,
> by power of faith, Christ's incarnation;
> his baptism in the Jordan river;
> his death on cross for my salvation;
> his bursting from the spicèd tomb;
> his riding up the heavenly way;
> his coming at the day of doom;
> I bind unto myself today.
>
> I bind unto myself the power
> of the great love of the cherubim;
> the sweet "Well done" in judgment hour;
> the service of the seraphim;
> confessors' faith, apostles' word;
> the patriarchs' prayers, the prophets' scrolls;
> all good deeds done unto the Lord;
> and purity of virgin souls.
>
> I bind unto myself today
> the virtues of the starlit heaven;
> the glorious sun's life-giving ray;
> the whiteness of the moon at even;
> the flashing of the lightning free;
> the whirling wind's tempestuous shocks;
> the stable earth, the deep salt sea;
> around the old eternal rocks.
>
> I bind unto myself today
> the power of God to hold and lead;
> his eye to watch, his might to stay;
> his ear to hearken to my need;
> the wisdom of my God to teach;
> his hand to guide, his shield to ward;
> the word of God to give me speech;
> his heavenly host to be my guard.

Against the demon snares of sin,
the vice that gives temptation force,
the natural lusts that war within,
the hostile men that mar my course;
or few or many, far or nigh,
in every place and in all hours,
against their fierce hostility,
I bind to me these holy powers.

Against all Satan's spells and wiles,
against false words of heresy,
against the knowledge that defiles,
against the heart's idolatry,
against the wizard's evil craft,
against the death wound and the burning,
the choking wave and the poisoned shaft,
protect me, Christ, till Thy returning.

Christ be with me, Christ within me,
Christ behind me, Christ before me,
Christ beside me, Christ to win me,
Christ to comfort and restore me.
Christ beneath me, Christ above me,
Christ in quiet, Christ in danger,
Christ in hearts of all that love me,
Christ in mouth of friend and stranger.

I bind unto myself the Name,
the strong Name of the Trinity,
by invocation of the same,
the Three in One and One in Three,
of Whom all nature hath creation,
eternal Father, Spirit, Word:
Praise to the Lord of my salvation,
salvation is of Christ the Lord.[4]

Binding ourselves to a faith such as this helps reorient and strengthen us: away from the superficial and fleeting and back toward our divinely rooted desire to leave behind all that distracts, afflicts, and corrupts us and to attain true communion with creation, one another, and God. Even just a moment's self-reflection tells us that our lives are a journey. To conclude that they are

4. This prayer is available from many sources, but this rendition was found at the following internet address: http://www.prayerfoundation.org/st_patricks_breastplate_prayer.htm. I have made minor alterations in punctuation.

just aimless wandering is debilitating, even deadly. But to realize that they have a God-given purpose and destination truly transforms them into pilgrimages. More than that, knowing that the Spirit, the Lord and Giver of Life, has made us one body in Christ, has joined us inseparably as one people of God, and has come to us so intimately as to make us his own living temple means that the diverse pilgrimages of the faithful in many times and lands merge into one pilgrimage. We are not alone. We have the "great cloud of witnesses" preceding us, the sisters and brothers in Christ accompanying us, and the sons and daughters who will follow us. These are the companions along the way who inspire us, support us, encourage us, defend us, challenge us, laugh with us, cry with us, forgive us, and bless us. Together we are called to that promised land which God has prepared for us since before the beginning. Through his Spirit, he offers new life to the whole of creation. By his Spirit, he calls us home.

Bibliography

Anselm of Canterbury. "Why God Became Man." In *A Scholastic Miscellany: Anselm to Ockham*, edited and translated by Eugene R. Fairweather, 100–183. Library of Christian Classics 10. Louisville: Westminster John Knox, 1956.

Augustine. "Letter to Januarius." In *The Nicene and Post-Nicene Fathers*, series 1, edited by Philip Schaff, 1:303–16. 1886–89. Reprint, Grand Rapids: Eerdmans, 1983.

Aulén, Gustaf. *Christus Victor*. New York: Macmillan, 1969.

Barth, Karl. *Church Dogmatics* I/1. Edinburgh: T&T Clark, 1975.

———. *Church Dogmatics* III/1. Edinburgh: T&T Clark, 1958.

Bavinck, Herman. *Reformed Dogmatics*. Edited by John Bolt. Translated by John Vriend. 4 vols. Grand Rapids: Baker Academic, 2006.

Bellafante, Ginia. "Jodi Picoult and the Anxious Parent." *New York Times Magazine*, June 17, 2009.

Boff, Leonardo. *Holy Trinity, Perfect Community*. Maryknoll, NY: Orbis, 2000.

Bonhoeffer, Dietrich. *Life Together*. Translated by John Doberstein. New York: Harper & Row, 1954.

Brown, Michael. "Mitochondrial Eve." Molecular History Research Center website. http://www.mhrc.net/mitochondrialeve.htm.

Butin, Philip W. *Reformed Ecclesiology: Trinitarian Grace according to Calvin*. Studies in Reformed Theology and History 2.1. Edited by David Willis-Watkins. Princeton: Princeton Theological Seminary, 1994.

Calvin, John. *Commentaries on the First Book of Moses Called Genesis*. Translated by John King. Grand Rapids: Eerdmans, 1948.

———. *Institutes of the Christian Religion*. Edited by John T. McNeill. Translated by Ford Lewis Battles. Library of Christian Classics 20 and 21. Philadelphia: Westminster, 1960.

———. "Reply to Sadolet." In *Calvin: Theological Treatises*, translated by J. K. S. Reid, 221–56. Library of Christian Classics. Philadelphia: Westminster, 1954.

Catherine of Genoa. *Purgation and Purgatory/The Spiritual Dialogue.* Translated by Serge Hughes. Classics of Western Spirituality. Mahwah, NJ: Paulist Press, 1979.

Cyprian of Carthage. *On the Church: Select Treatises.* Translated by Allen Brent. Popular Patristics Series 33. Crestwood, NY: St. Vladimir's Seminary Press, 2006.

DeYoung, Rebecca Konyndyk. *Glittering Vices: A New Look at the Seven Deadly Sins and Their Remedies.* Grand Rapids: Brazos, 2009.

Erickson, Millard. *Making Sense of the Trinity: Three Crucial Questions.* Grand Rapids: Baker Academic, 2000.

Frei, Hans. *The Eclipse of Biblical Narrative.* New Haven: Yale University Press, 1974.

Gunton, Colin. *The Christian Faith: An Introduction to Christian Doctrine.* Oxford: Blackwell, 2002.

Harvey, Barry A. *Another City: An Ecclesiological Primer for a Post-Christian World.* Christian Mission and Modern Culture. Harrisburg, PA: Trinity Press International, 1999.

Hauerwas, Stanley, and William Willimon. *Resident Aliens: Life in the Christian Colony.* Nashville: Abingdon, 1989.

Heine, Ronald E. *Reading the Old Testament with the Ancient Church: Exploring the Formation of Early Christian Thought.* Grand Rapids: Baker Academic, 2007.

Hick, John. *Evil and the God of Love.* New York: Macmillan, 1966.

Hickman, Hoyt L., Don E. Saliers, Laurence Hull Stookey, and James F. White. *The New Handbook of the Christian Year.* Nashville: Abingdon, 1992.

Hippolytus: A Text for Students. Introduction, translation, commentary, and notes by Geoffrey J. Cuming. Nottingham: Grove Books, 1987.

Horton, Michael S. *Covenant and Salvation: Union with Christ.* Louisville: Westminster John Knox, 2007.

Irenaeus of Lyons. *Against Heresies.* Translated by A. Cleveland Coxe. In *The Ante-Nicene Fathers,* edited by Alexander Roberts and James Donaldson, 1:309–567. 1885–87. Reprint, Grand Rapids: Eerdmans, 1973.

———. *On the Apostolic Preaching.* Translated by John Behr. Crestwood, NY: St. Vladimir's Seminary Press, 1997.

Jenson, Robert. *Canon and Creed.* Interpretation: Resources for the Use of Scripture in the Church. Louisville: Westminster John Knox, 2010.

Johnson, William Stacy, and John H. Leith, eds. *Reformed Reader: A Sourcebook in Christian Theology.* Vol. 1, *Classical Beginnings, 1519–1799.* Louisville: Westminster John Knox, 1993.

Leith, John H. ed. *Creeds of the Church.* Rev. ed. Richmond: John Knox Press, 1973.

Loisy, Alfred. *The Gospel and the Church.* Philadelphia: Fortress, 1976.

Luther, Martin. *Luther's Works.* Vol. 41, *Church and Ministry III.* Edited by Helmut T. Lehman. Philadelphia: Fortress, 1961.

McFadyen, Alistair. *Bound to Sin: Abuse, Holocaust and the Christian Doctrine of Sin.* Cambridge Studies in Christian Doctrine. Cambridge: Cambridge University Press, 2000.

Minear, Paul S. *Images of the Church in the New Testament.* Philadelphia: Westminster, 1960.

Moore-Keish, Martha. "Washing before Supper?" *Reformed Liturgy & Music* 34, no. 4 (2000): 15–21.

Niebuhr, H. Richard. *Christ and Culture*. New York: Harper & Row, 1951.

Niebuhr, Reinhold. *Moral Man and Immoral Society: A Study in Ethics and Politics*. New York: Scribner's Sons, 1932.

———. *The Nature and Destiny of Man: A Christian Interpretation*. New York: Scribner's Sons, 1941.

Office of the General Assembly, Presbyterian Church (U.S.A.). *Book of Catechisms—Reference Edition*. Louisville: Geneva Press, 2001.

———. *The Book of Confessions*. Louisville: Office of the General Assembly, 2002.

Richter, Sandra L. *The Epic of Eden: A Christian Entry into the Old Testament*. Downers Grove, IL: IVP Academic, 2008.

Saliers, Don E., Laurence Hull Stookey, and James F. White. *The New Handbook of the Christian Year*. Nashville: Abingdon, 1992.

Schleiermacher, Friedrich. *The Christian Faith*. Edited by H. R. MacKintosh and J. S. Stewart. Edinburgh: T&T Clark; Philadelphia: Fortress, 1928.

Seitz, Christopher R. *Figured Out: Typology and Providence in Christian Scripture*. Louisville: Westminster John Knox, 2001.

Sherman, Robert. *King, Priest, and Prophet: A Trinitarian Theology of Atonement*. New York: T&T Clark, 2004.

Smith, James K. A. *Desiring the Kingdom: Worship, Worldview, and Cultural Formation*. Cultural Liturgies 1. Grand Rapids: Baker Academic, 2009.

VanderKam, James C. "Weeks, Feast of." In *The New Interpreter's Dictionary of the Bible*, ed. Katharine Doob Sakenfeld, 5:829–31. Nashville: Abingdon, 2009.

Volf, Miroslav. *After Our Likeness: The Church as the Image of the Trinity*. Grand Rapids: Eerdmans, 1998.

Webster, John. *Holiness*. Grand Rapids: Eerdmans, 2003.

———. *Holy Scripture: A Dogmatic Sketch*. Current Issues in Theology. Cambridge: Cambridge University Press, 2003.

Wilson, Jonathan R. *Living Faithfully in a Fragmented World: Lessons for the Church from MacIntyre's After Virtue*. Christian Mission and Modern Culture. Harrisburg, PA: Trinity Press International, 1997.

World Council of Churches. *Baptism, Eucharist and Ministry*. Faith and Order Paper No. 111. Geneva: World Council of Churches, 1982.

Additional Resources

Alston, Wallace M., Jr. *The Church of the Living God: A Reformed Perspective*. Louisville: Westminster John Knox, 2002.

Anderson, Ray S. *An Emergent Theology for Emerging Churches*. Downers Grove, IL: InterVarsity, 2006.

Bockmuehl, Markus, and Michael B. Thompson, eds. *A Vision for the Church: Studies in Early Christian Ecclesiology*. Edinburgh: T&T Clark, 1997.

Boff, Leonardo. *Ecclesiogenesis: The Base Communities Reinvent the Church*. Translated by Robert R. Barr. Maryknoll, NY: Orbis, 1986.

Bonhoeffer, Dietrich. *The Communion of Saints: A Dogmatic Inquiry into the Sociology of the Church*. New York: Harper & Row, 1963.

Buckley, James J., and David S. Yeago, eds. *Knowing the Triune God: The Work of the Spirit in the Practices of the Church*. Grand Rapids: Eerdmans, 2001.

Farrow, Douglas. *Ascension and Ecclesia: On the Significance of the Doctrine of the Ascension for Ecclesiology and Christian Cosmology*. Grand Rapids: Eerdmans, 1999.

Haight, Roger, SJ. *Christian Community in History*. Vol. 3, *Ecclesial Existence*. New York: Continuum, 2008.

Hauerwas, Stanley. *A Community of Character: Toward a Constructive Christian Social Ethic*. Notre Dame, IN: University of Notre Dame Press, 1981.

Healy, Nicholas M. *Church, World, and the Christian Life: Practical-Prophetic Ecclesiology*. Edited by Colin Gunton and Daniel Hardy. Cambridge Studies in Christian Doctrine. Cambridge: Cambridge University Press, 2000.

Hodgson, Peter C. *Revisioning the Church: Ecclesial Freedom in the New Paradigm*. Minneapolis: Fortress, 1988.

Horton, Michael S. *Lord and Servant: A Covenant Christology*. Louisville: Westminster John Knox, 2005.

———. *People and Place: A Covenant Ecclesiology*. Louisville: Westminster John Knox, 2008.

Kärkkäinen, Veli-Matti. *An Introduction to Ecclesiology: Ecumenical, Historical, and Global Perspectives*. Downers Grove, IL: InterVarsity, 2002.

Lohfink, Gerhard. *Does God Need the Church? Toward a Theology of the People of God*. Translated by Linda M. Mahoney. Collegeville, MN: Liturgical Press, 1999.

McKim, Donald K., ed. *Encyclopedia of the Reformed Faith*. Louisville: Westminster John Knox, 1992.

McKnight, Scot. *A Community Called Atonement*. Nashville: Abingdon, 2007.

Moltmann, Jürgen. *The Church in the Power of the Spirit*. Minneapolis: Fortress, 1993.

Reno, R. R. *In the Ruins of the Church: Sustaining Faith in an Age of Diminished Christianity*. Grand Rapids: Brazos, 2002.

Seitz, Christopher R., ed. *Nicene Christianity: The Future for a New Ecumenism*. Grand Rapids: Brazos, 2001.

Stevenson, Tyler Wigg. *Brand Jesus: Christianity in a Consumer Age*. New York: Seabury, 2007.

Stroup, George, ed. *Reformed Reader: A Sourcebook in Christian Theology*. Vol. 2, *Contemporary Trajectories, 1799–Present*. Louisville: Westminster John Knox, 1993.

Tillard, J.-M. R. *Flesh of the Church, Flesh of Christ: At the Source of the Ecclesiology of Communion*. Translated by Madeleine Beaumont. Collegeville, MN: Liturgical Press, 2001.

Webster, John. *Confessing God: Essays in Christian Doctrine II*. London: T&T Clark, 2005.

Wilson, Jonathan R. *Why Church Matters: Worship, Ministry, and Mission in Practice.* Grand Rapids: Brazos, 2006.

Yoder, John Howard. *The Royal Priesthood: Essays Ecclesiastical and Ecumenical.* Edited by Michael G. Cartwright. Scottdale, PA: Herald Press, 1998.

Zizioulas, John D. *Being as Communion: Studies in Personhood and the Church.* Crestwood, NY: St. Vladimir's Seminary Press, 2002.

Subject Index

Abraham and Sarah
  God's covenant with, 26–30,
    50–51, 130, 137–38, 180
  and Isaac, binding of, 28–30
  See also covenant: transgen-
    erational nature of
Advocate. *See* Holy Spirit: as
  Advocate
anti-Semitism, 160–70
Apostles' Creed. *See* creeds:
  Apostles' Creed
ascension, Jesus's
  and prophecy, 52–53, 109,
    117, 129, 184
  and return, 125, 127
  and the Trinity, 40, 143,
    216, 218
Augsburg Confession. *See*
  confessions: Augsburg
  Confession

baptism
  and confirmation, xv
  and eschatology, 79
  infant, 67–68, 96, 107, 110
  Jesus's, 71n5, 88, 92–94, 221
  and the Lord's Supper, xiv–
    xv, 74, 89–92, 101–4, 180
  meaning of Christian, 94–
    96, 101–4, 175, 180, 184
  and the old covenant, xiv,
    95–96, 102
  ritual of, 42, 67n34, 113

the Trinity and, 41–42,
  93–94, 151, 175, 184
Barth, Karl. *See* Reformed
  theologians: Barth, Karl
bishop, office of, 119, 204
bride of Christ. *See* Church:
  as bride of Christ

Cain and Abel, 24, 25n20,
  136, 150
Calvin, John. *See* Reformed
  theologians: Calvin, John
catechesis, 67n34, 108n50,
  109–13, 120, 209
catechisms
  Catechism of the Catholic
    Church, 108n50
  Heidelberg Catechism,
    47n13, 199, 199n44
  Westminster Shorter Cate-
    chism, 38
Church
  as bride of Christ, xiv–xv,
    79–80, 212
  as counterculture, 135,
    138–39
  as institution, 117–20, 126–
    27, 142–43, 194, 202–6
  and institutional archetypes,
    44, 153
  marks/notes of the, 64,
    114–16
  as mother, 107–9

in relation to culture, 10,
  14–30, 66–67, 72, 85,
  132–39, 152–59
visible, 108
Communion. *See* Lord's
  Supper
communion of saints, 67n34,
  131,188
confessions
  Augsburg Confession, 67n34
  Scots Confession, 55, 67n34,
    205n50
  Westminster Confession,
    56, 59
Counselor. *See* Holy Spirit
covenant
  and Abraham. *See* Abraham
    and Sarah: God's covenant
    with
  with Abraham, Isaac, and
    Jacob, 51, 54, 164
  berit, 51
  and David, 52, 127, 130,
    149, 165
  and Jacob, 30–31, 138, 164,
    213
  and Moses, 51, 76–77, 90,
    130–31
  and Noah, 26, 51, 137, 147,
    193, 197
  old and new, 52–53, 69–70,
    90, 96–99, 138, 141, 162–
    63, 194, 198

Author Index

Scripture Index